T0246053

THE
COLD CASE
FOUNDATION

How a Team of Experts Solves Murders
and Missing Persons Cases

GREGORY M. COOPER
AND THOMAS McHOES

Prometheus Books

Essex, Connecticut

Ⓟ Prometheus Books

An imprint of The Globe Pequot Publishing Group, Inc.
64 South Main Street
Essex, CT 06426
www.globepequot.com

Distributed by NATIONAL BOOK NETWORK

Copyright © 2024 by Gregory M. Cooper and Thomas McHoes

All rights reserved. No part of this book may be reproduced in any form or by any electronic or mechanical means, including information storage and retrieval systems, without written permission from the publisher, except by a reviewer who may quote passages in a review.

British Library Cataloguing in Publication Information Available

Library of Congress Cataloging-in-Publication Data

Names: Cooper, Gregory M., 1954– author. | McHoes, Thomas, author.
Title: The cold case foundation : how a team of experts solves murders and missing persons cases / Gregory M. Cooper and Thomas McHoes.
Description: Lanham, MD : Prometheus Books, 2024. | Summary: "What started with just a half-dozen or so retired FBI and homicide detectives has now ballooned to more than 150 women and men who volunteer their time in an effort to help families of deceased or missing loved ones bring closure to cases that have gone 'cold.' The Cold Case Foundation shares the most riveting and rewarding cases that the foundation has helped to solve, from high-profile missing persons cases to decades-old murders"—Provided by publisher.
Identifiers: LCCN 2024016043 (print) | LCCN 2024016044 (ebook) | ISBN 9781493084647 (cloth ; alk. paper) | ISBN 9781493084654 (epub)
Subjects: LCSH: Cold cases (Criminal investigation) | Murder—Investigation. Missing persons—Investigation.
Classification: LCC HV8073 .C6345 2024 (print) | LCC HV8073 (ebook) | DDC 363.25/9523—dc23/eng/20240618
LC record available at https://lccn.loc.gov/2024016043
LC ebook record available at https://lccn.loc.gov/2024016044

♾️™ The paper used in this publication meets the minimum requirements of American National Standard for Information Sciences—Permanence of Paper for Printed Library Materials, ANSI/NISO Z39.48-1992

CONTENTS

Foreword   *John E. Douglas*   v

Introduction: The Four Keys to Cold Case Resolution   xi

1   Five Thousand Dollars and a Credit Card   1

2   The Cases That Haunt   29

3   A Timeless Process   53

4   The Four Cs   81

5   Coordination: The More People Looking, the Better   119

6   Cooperation: The Team Approach   145

7   Communication and Our Most Important Customers   165

8   Collaboration   185

9   The Evolution of Cold Case Investigation   201

10 What Can You Do?   219

Acknowledgments   225

FOREWORD

John E. Douglas

The concept for the Cold Case Foundation germinated thirty-five years ago in the basement of the FBI Academy, when Greg and I worked together in the Investigative Support Unit (ISU). The ISU was the FBI's first official unit designated to house their famed criminal profilers who were exclusively assigned to provide specialized investigative support services to law enforcement agencies confronted with especially challenging cases. Due to our successes, the increase in case submissions, and the respective demands for our unique services, ISU was approved for three additional criminal profiler positions to augment our exclusive team of experts. As the Unit Chief, I selected Greg from a competitive field of FBI Special Agent applicants to join our elite serial crime unit.

As it turned out, the timing of bringing the additional profilers on board couldn't have been better. Later that year, our work in the ISU was showcased in the motion picture *Silence of the Lambs*. It was a blockbuster that won Academy Awards in all five major categories. As to be expected, ISU received an onslaught of notoriety because of the film's success, adding to an already high demand for our services. Consequently, the amount and nature of the work required our newly appointed profilers to adapt quickly to a heavy caseload, while also attending a twelve-month comprehensive training curriculum. Greg liked to describe the experience as "taking a long and deep drink from a fire hydrant!"

As the FBI's chief profiler and Unit Chief of the ISU, I personally selected and trained all the profilers and enjoyed a close and cooperative relationship with them. Greg accepted the challenge with enthusiasm and adapted quickly while excelling in his responsibilities. In fact, in my *New York Times* bestseller, *Mindhunter: Inside the FBI's Elite Serial Crime*

Unit, I referred to Greg as a "true disciple," due to his commitment to the craft of criminal profiling, application of his skillset, and outstanding performance.

The ISU consisted of three specialized programs: the Criminal Investigative Analysis Program (CIAP), where the criminal profilers were assigned; the Arson and Bombing Investigative Services (ABIS), which included arson/bombing specialists; and the Violent Criminal Apprehension Program (ViCAP) allocated with major case specialists and crime analysts.

ViCAP is the FBI's national database that serves as a repository for unsolved homicides, missing persons, unidentified remains, and sexual assaults with serial characteristics. Its function is to compare and analyze unsolved cases that have been submitted by police departments from across the United States and to determine if a common serial offender may be responsible for a select number of cases. Once determined, ViCAP advises the respective police departments and offers to coordinate a Multi-Investigative Agency Team (MIAT) to initiate a collaborative investigative effort.

Greg had been a Police Chief and criminal investigator before joining the ranks of the FBI. Because of his unique professional background and distinguished FBI service, I promoted him as the ViCAP Program Manager. I tasked him with restructuring the personnel assigned to each of the programs to effectively interface their exceptional abilities into investigative teams aligned with geographical regions across the United States. This reorganization created specialized teams composed of criminal profilers, major case specialists, and crime analysts from all three programs. It fostered a cohesive and interdependent working environment better equipped to support the effective delivery of our services to law enforcement. Furthermore, it enhanced *communication* between program personnel; improved *coordination* of their specialized resources; instilled an attitude of *collaboration* between the specialized program tasks; and instilled *cooperation* between all three programs. Moreover, it proved to be an excellent model that facilitated successful delivery of ISU services to the many law enforcement agencies across the United States.

While working closely with Greg, we often strategized over the ISU's administrative challenges and how to adequately provide our specialized services to law enforcement agencies on a national scale. Keeping up with the demand and upholding the quality of key personnel was a constant issue. The FBI is a large organization with many responsibilities in an ever-changing world. Over the last several years, the ISU has undergone several changes and reorganizations to adapt accordingly. Naturally, the dynamics related to the evolution of organizational demands often result in the displacement of resources with unfavorable consequences, including the inability to provide services in an effective and timely manner. Naturally, this high velocity environment causes stress and frustration for both the service provider and its customers while also impeding the primary objective, which is to solve cases.

This is especially difficult when confronted with the compounding effects and rising tide of unsolved cold cases. Depending on the staffing levels of experienced and trained personnel, these cases often remain open for years and sometimes indefinitely. Such cases are often very difficult and present unique challenges to law enforcement agencies hard pressed for personnel who are familiar with investigating the unfamiliar territory of uncommon and bizarre types of crimes and criminals (i.e., serial killers, serial rapists, etc.). For example, the manner of approaching a domestic homicide can be very different from tackling a sexual homicide or auto-erotic death investigation. The method, motive, and manner of the offender's behavior and personality type often require a tailored investigative approach designed to address the unique challenges associated with those crimes.

While assigned to the ISU, we had the privilege of working with police departments and dedicated investigators from across the country who were chronically challenged by these issues. It was clear to us that these obstacles would only multiply over time and at a rapid pace. We also became keenly aware that law enforcement's resources, particularly within the budgetary and operational constraints of small and medium-sized police departments, may be stretched beyond their expectations. As expected, over the last several decades, the number of unsolved cold cases has grown exponentially along with the inherent troubles for law enforcement, victims, and their families.

It's also important to be reminded that for every unsolved violent crime there is also a criminal who is at liberty to continue their predatory pursuit of victims until they are identified, apprehended, and convicted. We must never forget that victims and their families should be considered as our principal clients. The investigator's primary role is to seek justice on their behalf by providing a successful investigation that delivers an appropriate level of accountability to the offender who violated the rights of the victims. Solving crimes equates to preventing further victimization. When it comes to public safety and crime prevention, both police and civilians must work together.

Motivated by our experience in the ISU and our desire to relieve some of the burdens shouldered by law enforcement and victims' families, Greg and I established the Cold Case Foundation (CCF). The CCF is a 501c3, nonprofit organization capable of supplementing both the operational, and when appropriate, financial resources to those agencies that request assistance to solve cold cases. To that end, it was important to us that all services be provided to law enforcement, victims, and their families at no cost and under strict confidentiality. Additionally, we wanted the agency investigators to have timely access to a multidisciplinary group of investigative experts and criminal justice professionals. It was also important that CCF consultants were motivated with the right heart and mind and were committed to seeking justice for victims by volunteering their expertise to cold case resolution.

The CCF was officially organized twelve years ago on a shoestring budget with a core group of colleagues who were committed to this worthy cause. The response has been both astounding and humbling. Over the years we have grown from a few individuals willing to volunteer their time and talents to over 140 criminal experts. Amazingly, they are always eager to help and responsive to our requests for their expert level of skills, knowledge, and abilities.

The purpose of this book is four-fold. First, it is to introduce the Cold Case Foundation (CCF) to the public. Secondly, it is to educate the reader about the CCF services that are provided by the selfless men and women who donate their expertise to law enforcement agencies, victims, and their families in pursuit of solving cold cases. Thirdly, Greg and Tom have presented a sampling of excellent case examples from the CCF archives that dramatically highlight how uncommon results can be achieved through a collaboration between police, victims and their families, and outside professional resources. Finally, it is to encourage you, the community, to get involved through your participation by passing the word along about CCF, its mission, and the successes that are made possible through collaborating public and non-profit resources. CCF also welcomes any amount of financial donations made in support of this great cause. Your participation at any level allows you to vicariously contribute to solving cases that will answer questions that haunt victims' families while also partnering with law enforcement in support of their efforts to solve cold cases and prevent further victimization.

INTRODUCTION

The Four Keys to Cold Case Resolution

During the forty-five years I've spent in law enforcement, I've done and seen a lot of things. Through that time, there have been plenty of highs and lows. Some of the things I experienced were very difficult while others were extremely gratifying. But the experiences that bother me the most are the cases that have gone unsolved. Or maybe a better way to phrase it is: "The hardest cases to look back on are the ones that haven't been solved—yet."

I qualify this statement with the word *yet* because, as long as I'm alive, I will never stop trying to find resolution to any of these cases. I will never stop thinking about them; I will never stop looking for leads; I will never stop keeping these cases alive through public awareness; and I will never stop recruiting experts in the criminal justice field who can potentially help us solve these cases.

The reason?

I can't stomach the thought of families and loved ones who have been left behind to wonder what happened. Whether a loved one was murdered, kidnapped, was a victim of a violent sexual assault, or has simply gone missing, it's our responsibility as law enforcement officials to advocate for those left behind. It's also incumbent upon us to do everything within our power to honor their memories by finding justice for them. They count on us to do just that and it's heartbreaking to see the desperation on loved ones' faces when investigations stall.

That's why, when I retired from law enforcement several years ago, I knew I couldn't just ride off into the sunset and rest knowing that something still had to be done about so many unsolved cases. Honestly, I don't think I'll ever rest. With more than two hundred thousand unsolved homicide cases sitting out there in the United States alone, how could I?

This has been the case for far too long. A disturbing study of FBI records found that, since 1995, the national average of solved homicides in
the United States is only about 64 percent, leaving 36 percent of murders
unsolved annually. This means that approximately 5,700 killers get away
with murder every year. Such an amount of unsolved cold case murders
takes a devastating toll on thousands of families and their communities.
And it has a compounding financial and workload effect on police departments and the respective personnel assigned to work them.

To address this challenge, some police departments can dedicate cold
case detectives while others simply must do the best they can with limited
resources in manpower and scarce funding.

And, while we can't always control how much funding we get or how
much manpower our police departments are allotted, we can control where
we choose to focus our attention and what we can do to find solutions to
this problem. We can choose to focus on how well we collaborate, communicate, and cooperate, and how well we coordinate the investigations of
these crimes—especially the ones that are largely solvable. The most difficult part of all of this is that we know that many cold cases are indeed
solvable. And the primary key to solving them is that they must be *worked.*

But it is not for lack of interest that cases turn cold and seemingly forgotten. They are never forgotten by victims' families and loved ones or by
the investigators assigned to them. Law enforcement's desire to resolve cold
cases is ever present, but often the resources and budget to solve them are
not. As a society, and certainly as law enforcement professionals, we must
ensure that the victims of these cases are never forgotten. Additionally, we
must insist that such cases are never at the mercy of insufficient funding or
otherwise available resources.

I learned this principle more than thirty years ago as a young FBI profiler.

After two years of serving as a criminal profiler, the Behavioral Science
Unit recruited me to concurrently instruct an "Abnormal Psychology and
Criminal Profiling" course for the FBI National Academy. BSU consisted
of various instructors including FBI agents who conducted various research
projects and instructed select courses to international law enforcement
professionals who were attending the FBI National Academy. As one of
the newer members of the Unit, I was thrilled and privileged to be recruited to instruct at the FBI National Academy, while also continuing my

assignment as a profiler. While I was gathering material and developing the curriculum for the course, I needed a unique and instructive case study that would effectively illustrate an example of a classic serial killer.

I approached Special Agent Roy Hazelwood, who was recognized as both an excellent profiler and one of the premier instructors at the FBI Academy. He was also renowned for his research and respective professional publications on serial rapists and serial rapists who kill. Roy was also one of my instructors who had mentored me in the art of criminal profiling during the first year of required training for newly appointed profilers. I asked Roy if he had a case that I could use in my class as an example of a serial killer. It was then that Roy "introduced" me to Robert Ben Rhoades.

Roy explained that Rhoades, a long-haul truck driver, was a classic example of a serial killer and sexual sadist who was responsible for the torture, rape, and murder of several victims between 1975 and 1990. He related that there was a case that dramatically illustrated Rhoades's method of operation, including victim selection, pre-offense, offense, and post-offense behaviors. Roy presented me with the Regina Walters Case.

Over the last thirty years, I have presented Regina's horrific story to thousands of law enforcement officials and college students. I have given presentations to audiences attending the FBI National Academy, hundreds of law enforcement training courses, several colleges and universities, and a myriad of professional conferences. I have continued to represent Regina by relating her tortuous journey long after retiring from the FBI, and I do it because I consider it a solemn responsibility and privilege to extend her life by relating her legacy to as many people as possible.

My purpose for presenting her case has been to dramatically illustrate the challenges that a roving serial killer poses to the public and law enforcement. I emphasize key components for successfully investigating, identifying, and apprehending these human predators in what I call the "4 Cs": communication, coordination, collaboration, and cooperation of the law enforcement agencies who are investigating homicides, missing persons, unidentified remains, and sexual assaults with serial characteristics. These important principles are also the four keys to cold case resolution.

By relating her account, we allow Regina's story to live on, helping law enforcement solve similar cold cases and preventing other victims. Regina's case is also a stark reminder of how I ended up establishing the Cold Case

Foundation, and more important, why the organization was created in the first place. For me, the foundation represents the full-circle reason behind why I got into law enforcement in the first place.

Even going back to my earliest days, my purpose was never about the excitement of being a cop. Rather, every step of my career has always been about finding justice for the innocent. Whether living or deceased, I believe every victim of a crime—especially crimes as personally reprehensible as violent crimes—deserves to have someone who advocates on his or her behalf. And, from the beginning, that's what I have always striven to do.

I started my law enforcement career as a Provo City (Utah) police officer. Provo is seated along the I-15 corridor at the base of the majestic Wasatch Mountain Range and home to Brigham Young University. After working there in various assignments and completing a graduate degree, I decided to expand my professional horizons. I had applied to the FBI and thought an offer was imminent but was placed on hold due to a federal hiring freeze.

Consequently, I took a divergent path.

At twenty-seven, while looking for an intermediate opportunity, I searched for a challenge that would further my professional aspirations. That opportunity came along when I was hired as the police chief in the small rural community of Delta, Utah. Delta is in Millard County, the state's largest geographical county, covering an expansive southwestern portion of the state. Delta was experiencing an infusion of growth related to the coal-fired energy expansion of the 1980s, which resulted in the construction of the Intermountain Power Project, about fifteen miles north of Delta. I considered this a great opportunity and challenge. As the new police chief, my primary charge was to prepare for the anticipated growth, social impact, and corresponding demand for public safety services by organizing a police department capable of responding to and managing the effects of that impact.

At the time, there were only two police departments in the county—the Millard County Sheriff's Department and the Delta City Police Department. We relied on a close and cooperative working relationship with the Sheriff's Department to augment our resources. Sheriff Ed Phillips was highly respected throughout Millard County and the state of Utah. He was among the first to welcome me in my new job and graciously extended his friendship and department's resources in support of managing the task ahead. It was our department's close working relationship with the sheriff and members of his department, along with the consistent support of the mayor and city council, that was responsible for the effective public safety services during those transition years.

Approximately two and a half years later, Delta was beginning to experience the natural side effects of a "Boom-Bust" cycle that resulted from the completion of the Intermountain Power Project and brought a significant increase in population. In short, I felt that my primary objectives for Delta were approaching completion. We doubled the size of our department, recruited and trained some exceptionally qualified personnel, and completed the construction of a new police facility in the new City Administration Building. Moreover, as a department, we effectively managed the increase for services in a professional and responsive manner while maintaining the historical community atmosphere that the citizens and city administration desired.

Around that time, I attended a three-day "Criminal Profiling for Law Enforcement" course, instructed by two FBI agents, Kenneth Lanning and Bill Hagmaier, conducted at Salt Lake Community College. After attending that course, I was mesmerized by the subject matter and the role of an FBI criminal profiler. I vividly recall that, as I walked back to the parking lot and just before entering my car, I experienced an "aha" moment. I had a distinct impression, an absolute conviction and persuasion, that this was the job for me. From that moment I knew what my principal professional purpose was, and I was committed to pursuing it until I accomplished it. This focus revived my interest in the FBI.

Coincidentally, while considering my options, I received a phone call from the FBI. They told me that the hiring freeze had been lifted and asked if I was still interested in a career with the FBI. The timing couldn't have been more perfectly orchestrated. and that's why I lean more on destiny rather than coincidence.

I entered FBI New Agent's Training in April 1985 and graduated from the FBI Academy in August. As indicated above, in August 1990, five years and two FBI Field Office assignments later, I was selected to fill one of three newly authorized positions as an FBI criminal profiler. In 1995, I retired from the FBI after serving as the acting ISU unit chief, ViCAP national program manager, FBI National Academy instructor, and FBI criminal profiler, and returned to Provo, Utah, as the chief of police.

I continued to present the Regina Walters case to various law enforcement audiences and was invited to give a presentation at an upcoming annual Utah Police Chiefs and Sheriffs Conference held in St. George, Utah. In preparation for the conference, I considered that it may add some additional insights if I could interview Rhoades about Regina. Rhoades had been convicted for Regina's abduction and murder in 1994 and was incarcerated at the Menard Correctional Facility in Chester, Illinois.

Arrangements were made to talk with him over the telephone, and let's just say that it didn't go too well. During our conversation, I brought up Regina Walters and her boyfriend Ricky Lee Jones. It went downhill from there.

He proceeded to rant and rave, spitting out protests and personal derogatory attacks against Regina. He also blamed her boyfriend Ricky for killing her, claiming his own innocence.

I listened to this psychopath for as long as I could, and finally couldn't take any more of his nonsense. I knew I wasn't going to get anywhere with him and so I decided to share with him what I personally thought of him, including that I would do everything I could to make his life as miserable as possible—and much more. The "conversation" ended abruptly by him throwing his phone across the room. The prison guard picked up the phone and asked me *what* I said to Rhoades for him to react that way. I explained that it was "confidential" between Rhoades and me and better left that way. As the saying goes, "Best laid plans . . ."

While my intentions were good, there wasn't much of anything to add after the telephone visit with Rhoades, so I gave my customary presentation. When I was setting up, I was delighted to see the familiar face of Millard County Sheriff Ed Phillips, sporting his customary Stetson hat, among those attending my presentation. It had been over ten years since we had worked together while I served as the Delta Chief of Police.

I proceeded to share Regina's story with the group. She had been a fourteen-year-old runaway from Texas who, along with her eighteen-year-old boyfriend, Ricky Lee Jones, was hitchhiking across the country when Rhoades picked them up in his long-haul truck. Within a few hours, he had shot and killed Ricky, and he then kept Regina captive for several days, raping and torturing her along the way. He eventually killed her and dumped her body in an abandoned farmhouse in rural Illinois.

With the dramatic impact of crime scene photos, I highlighted the maps reflecting Rhoades's long-haul truck route in 1984, 1987, 1988, 1989, and 1990. Just as I was emphasizing that Utah was included among the many states that he traversed in 1990, I noticed a hand raised in the back of the room. It was Sheriff Ed Phillips. He related that he had a cold case of an unidentified female who had been murdered and whose remains were discovered in a rural area of Millard County in 1990.

After the class, we continued our discussion and Ed followed up with the FBI and other law enforcement agencies associated with Regina's case. Not to be distracted, and consistent with their reputation for dogged investigations, Sheriff Phillips and his team of investigators pursued that lead until they solved their cold case.

Through DNA evidence left on a bloody towel discovered in Rhoades's Houston apartment, the victim was identified as Patricia Candace Walsh. Patricia and her husband, Douglas Zyskowski, were traveling in the Southeast when Rhoades picked them up. After killing her husband, Rhoades kept Candace locked in the back of his truck for several days. He raped and tortured her multiple times before killing her and dumping her body in Utah.

We describe her case in detail in our previous book, *Predators: Who They Are and How to Stop Them.* We will also go into more detail about this case toward the end of this book and show how we use it as a training illustration for solving cold cases.

While my role in solving Patricia Walsh's case may not have the investigative flair dramatized in a true crime documentary, that presentation was a critical piece that set things in motion. It further illustrates the principles of the four keys to cold case resolution, particularly when investigating serial killers.

Had Regina Walters's case not been presented at the Utah conference, Walsh's case is likely to have remained among the over two hundred thousand cold case homicides archived in law enforcement agencies across the United States. In an indirect way, Regina contributed to solving the Patricia Walsh case and possibly many more. And as an added personal bonus, little did I know at the time I made the promise to Rhoades, I was able to contribute to making his life as miserable as possible, which gives me great personal satisfaction. This is exactly the type of experience that inspired us to establish the Cold Case Foundation.

It's also the reason we are writing this book.

Publicity can be critical to any investigation, but it is especially important in cold case investigations. If we can publicize the facts of a case that hasn't been worked for a long period of time, it can be like shining a flashlight in a dark room. Sometimes you find things you didn't realize were even there in the first place.

One of the most telling examples of this principle occurred recently when the Cold Case Foundation was asked by ESPN to assist in a case involving a murdered University of Miami football player. He was murdered outside an apartment in 2006 and fifteen years had gone by with no arrests having been made. Because of the hard work of the Miami-Dade Police Department and two investigative journalists who sought us out to help, an arrest was finally made in August 2021.

We will go into this in greater detail later in the book. This is another example of why, in 2014, we established the Cold Case Foundation, a 501c3 nonprofit, to reignite interest and attention for unsolved cases at no cost to the victims' families or to the law enforcement agencies who investigate their cases.

The mission of the Cold Case Foundation is to support law enforcement agencies in their efforts to successfully resolve unsolved cases involving homicides, missing persons, unidentified remains, and sexual assaults with serial characteristics. This is accomplished primarily through private funding, consulting, training, networking, and victim support. I have been amazed by the cadre of retired and working professionals—experts in their fields— who have joined us in this great cause.

When we began in 2014, we only had a handful of retired law enforcement investigators on our team. Today, we have over 150 members on our investigative team of consultants with various levels of expertise and disciplines that include: law enforcement, forensic science, forensic digital technology, forensic psychology, crime analysis, social science, criminal profilers, medical examiner/coroner, fire science/arson, victims advocacy, media, search and rescue, legal professionals, graphologists, statement analogy, and more.

I list them here because each aspect of crime-solving plays a critical role in resolving these cold cases. No single one of them can be done without the others. Collectively, they have provided thousands of hours of case consultation pro bono to law enforcement organizations, victims, and their families. The Cold Case Foundation is supported by private and public donations, and we are pleased that all donations have been devoted to operational case work expenses. All personnel donate their time and expertise to the cause.

We are dedicated to stopping the deadly compounding effect of cold cases and providing hope and resources to families and loved ones affected by violent crime. The Cold Case Foundation is committed to raising public awareness and creating partnerships to assist and provide law enforcement with whatever resources are needed to bring about closure to these cases. We want to communicate the mission of the Foundation to readers in a way that will hit home.

What if this happened to my loved one? Where could I turn if my local police agency didn't have the manpower to find my missing child or to find out who murdered my close friend and bring that person to justice? Who could help and how do I reach out to them? Also, what are some appropriate ways I could help that would not hinder or interfere with the investigation? These are just some of the questions that we address in *The Cold Case Foundation*.

This book will also take readers through the strategies of working cases that haven't been actively investigated over long periods of time—some as far back as fifty years ago and even one that traces back to the days of King Tut, an investigation we did for a Discovery Channel special several years ago to try and determine the identity of the young Egyptian king's killer.

Readers will also get an inside look at how some of the most high-profile cold cases in the country were solved—or not solved, as was the case with Henry Lee Lucas, who was profiled on the Netflix series, "The Confession Killer." We will give a behind-the-scenes look at what our Cold Case investigators do and how we approach cases.

It should be noted that when we revisit highly sensitive criminal cases, one of our goals is to avoid revictimizing the victims and their families as much as possible. Some family members have shied away from the public eye, while others have moved on from the areas where the crimes took place and are trying to start new lives. What we absolutely do not want to do, if at all possible, is to disrupt their attempts to rebuild their lives.

To prevent that from happening, we have done everything possible to protect their identities. In cases where it is feasible, we have changed the names of the victims, their families, loved ones, the names of their assailants, investigating officers, the locations of the crimes, and certain details that could be used to identify the victims and their families. Also, some of the cases we reviewed have not been completely resolved through the court system, including the appeals process in some cases. We don't want to jeopardize the outcome of a case, and this gives us flexibility to teach while telling the stories of our involvement in these cases as a way that illustrates the key principles that we are trying to share with you, the reader.

It is important to emphasize, however, that some of the cases we highlight garnered so much media attention that the identities of key individuals in these cases would be very difficult to conceal. In other cases, however, that were only covered by local news media, we are more general in our descriptions of people and identifying factors, including nonessential details of the case that can be changed without disrupting the integrity of the principles we are illustrating in this book.

We also spoke to a number of criminal experts who agreed to share their investigative strategies for public benefit only on the condition that their identities be concealed. Because we believe that the information they provided is so valuable, we feel it is of the utmost importance that we honor their requests.

It is also important to note that we have taken some creative license in order to reconstruct events not known by anyone other than the individuals involved. Any such dialogue or reconstruction of these events is purely speculative on our part but is based on the facts of these cases. We do this only to give you a more complete picture from which to learn. Our aim is not to sensationalize these crimes, but to use them as a means to teach you, the general law-abiding public, how we can all work together as communities to assist law enforcement agencies in solving them. By so doing, we hope to bring these violent offenders to justice and, consequently, make our communities safer.

Finally, we hope that you will not only find this book to be an informative and fascinating read, but that it will also serve to create a movement that will see a significant increase in the number of current cold cases being worked and, ultimately, solved.

CHAPTER ONE

FIVE THOUSAND DOLLARS
AND A CREDIT CARD

It was the summer of 2019 when I received a phone call from an unusual source.

Two investigative journalists from ESPN had reached out to me about a story they were working on and asked if I would call them back. They had a few questions for me about a nonprofit organization I had started a few years prior, and they were hoping I could help with their story.

Media requests are not unusual for me. I am often tabbed by news organizations who want to utilize my experience as a former FBI profiler to talk about current violent crimes making their way through the headlines. Sometimes, I even get asked by producers to take part in true crimes series or documentaries. But ESPN was a new one for me and, initially, I wasn't quite sure what to think. But I was curious about how I could help, so I called them back.

As it turned out, the two investigative journalists, Paula Lavigne and Elizabeth Merrill, were doing an in-depth investigative piece on the murder of a high-profile athlete in the Miami area. The police investigation had gone several years unsolved, and they wondered if our organization, the Cold Case Foundation, would be willing to look at the case from a fresh investigative perspective.

"We found your organization's website," they explained. "And we think your expertise is exactly what this case needs."

They told me that the victim, Bryan Pata, had been an all-conference defensive lineman for the prestigious University of Miami football team. He was widely considered to be a first- or second-round pick in the NFL Draft, which was just a few months away at the time of his death. They said

1

that, on the night of November 7, 2006, a lone gunman confronted Bryan in the parking lot of the apartment complex in which he lived, then shot and killed the twenty-two-year-old before fleeing the scene.

Since that time, the crime had gone unsolved, and a suspect had not been named.

The reporters told me that the family was frustrated and felt that Bryan's homicide investigation wasn't getting as much attention from the police department as they thought it should.

"The victim's family is desperate," Paula said. "We were hoping that you and your organization would be willing to look at the police records we have in our possession and help us put together some of the missing pieces, based on your expertise. We think this case needs a fresh set of eyes."

They explained that the Miami-Dade Police Department had asked ESPN if they would run a story on Bryan Pata's case in the hopes that, by generating some publicity, some new leads might come to light. But, when the journalists decided to do a deeper dive into the investigation, they were denied access to some of the public records involving the case—even those that fell under the Florida Public Records Act. It had gotten to the point that ESPN actually had to take the department to court in an effort to get those reports.

Essentially, they wanted to know if we would be willing to help them help Bryan's family get some answers after nearly fifteen years of waiting.

Then came the question, "Is this something you and your foundation would be willing to help us with?"

For me, it was a no-brainer.

Helping families like this is exactly why I created the Cold Case Foundation. As a retired profiler in the FBI's Behavioral Science Unit, I had investigated so many homicides and seen so many more unsolved, that I just never felt right about retiring and resting on my laurels.

Despite law enforcement's best efforts, about 40 percent of homicide cases go unsolved nationwide. If there was a way that I could put all my experience to use and help the many families and loved ones who are trying to make sense of the tragedy around them, but are struggling to find answers, then I was going to do it.

The same goes for law enforcement. The vast majority of agencies across the country lack the kind of funding and manpower it takes to be able to keep up with the number of criminal cases they are asked to investigate. It's not uncommon for a single detective to be assigned dozens of cases to work in addition to new cases that come in. It's no wonder that so many detectives feel overwhelmed at times, feeling frustrated that they can't solve them all.

So, I decided to create a nonprofit foundation that would work with law enforcement agencies and victims' families around the country and eventually worldwide. My thought was that we would recruit highly qualified individuals who would donate their time and expertise to try and solve many of these unsolved homicide cases, primarily those that haven't been actively worked for a lengthy period of time due to lack of resources.

The idea came to me so suddenly that, once I had that "aha" moment, I immediately started the application process, then pulled out my credit card and paid the $5,000 in fees and costs to establish the foundation.

And I've never looked back.

It wasn't long before I discovered that I wasn't the only one who felt this way. After starting the Cold Case Foundation in 2014 with just a half-dozen or so of my former FBI and law enforcement colleagues, we have now ballooned to over 150 investigators. Most of them are retired from the FBI or have had extensive experience investigating violent crimes, including some of the country's most prominent homicide detectives. And quite a few members of our organization are actually active-duty detectives who donate their time and expertise on the side to help with some of these cases.

We also have several other volunteers with an array of skills and backgrounds ranging from legal to forensic expertise to public relations and even to web design and research. They are amazingly selfless people committed to this cause and we wouldn't be able to contribute to moving these cold cases forward without them. It truly has been a labor of love for so many and we have been blessed to play a role in helping so many of these victims' families and the investigating agencies.

After talking to Paula and Elizabeth for a few more minutes, I agreed that we would help. Soon after, ESPN sent over every record they had on the case, and we agreed to sit down to go through our findings with them a few months later in February of 2020—just a few weeks before the COVID-19 pandemic would shut the world down.

I had not heard much about Bryan Pata's case, so as soon as we got the materials, Dean Jackson, who serves as deputy director of the Cold Case Foundation, and I pored over the materials and began to investigate.

Dean has a very unique background in law enforcement in that he actually never wanted anything to do with law enforcement in the first place.

To look at Dean, you would never think that. Standing over six-feet-five with a rugged build and a square-jawed goatee, Dean looks every bit the part of a law enforcement lifer. He looks as if he were born to work homicide cases and put bad guys away.

But as a child—and even into his late teenage years—Dean had a severe aversion to death or anything even remotely related to something that would cause serious physical harm to a human being's body.

Dean spent most of his childhood and youth in Japan, where his father set up a ministry as a pastor. When Dean was sixteen, they were using one of the floors of a high-rise building as a meeting place.

One day, Dean's father asked him to retrieve some items from their van, which was parked on the street just outside the building. While Dean was collecting those things from the van, he heard a thunderous crash on the sidewalk behind him just a few feet away. When he turned to look, he was shocked to see that a man had jumped from the top of the high-rise to his death. On the way down, the man's body crashed through an aluminum awning, shredding his body to pieces.

Staring at the scene in a state of shock, Dean could hardly believe what he was seeing. There, in front of him, lay his worst fear—a deceased and dismembered body. As horrific as that experience was for him, Dean remembered the unexpected effect that being forced to face that fear had on him. "The physical death didn't hit me as hard as I thought it would," he said. "But what bothered me the most was that another human being was so desperate that he chose to take his life, and I couldn't help him."

That experience would lay the groundwork for Dean's involvement in law enforcement later in life. But his career journey didn't start there. Instead, Dean chose to follow in his father's footsteps, and he became a pastor.

His work as a pastor took Dean to places like Jackson Hole, Wyoming, and Amarillo, Texas, before eventually landing in Provo, Utah, where he and I would cross paths.

While in Jackson Hole, Dean had become friends with the county coroner. One day, Dean was invited by his friend to join him at an out-of-town training for medical examiners. Dean was invited because the deputy coroner wasn't able to attend, so why waste a free ticket?

Excited for the free trip, Dean accepted and soon found himself watching a presentation he never could have imagined himself sitting through just a few years earlier.

"The gentleman conducting the training was a coroner from Belfast, Ireland," Dean recalled. "He was using one of those old slide show projectors and was showing picture after picture of bombing victims. What fascinated me the most was how they could find bodily evidence from these mass bombings and put everything together to identify victims and solve cases. It was amazing to me and that is when I had that 'aha' moment. I knew I had to be involved with law enforcement in some way." Not long after, Dean would serve on the state's critical response team, doing ride-alongs with police officers and getting to know the ins and outs of law enforcement.

A few years later, Dean was in Provo, Utah, where I served as chief of police. It didn't take me long after meeting Dean to bring him on as our department chaplain. Our relationship developed from there and Dean has been with the Cold Case Foundation from the beginning, serving in so many different capacities that his title of deputy director doesn't do justice to all the things that he actually does on behalf of our organization. He does everything from helping to review the cases that come our way to facilitating all our public relations efforts and everything in between. In fact, Dean was one of the first people I tapped to help lead the foundation's efforts.

His ability to empathize and connect with people, along with his eye for detail, make him the ideal person for the work we ask him to do. Because of his sense of empathy, Dean relates well to victims and their families, making them feel at ease as we talk to them about the difficult experiences they have gone through. And, because of his eye for detail, he notices things in both the cases we review and the operations-related aspects of the foundation that really move our mission forward. He truly makes this engine go and we couldn't do it without him.

Working on the Bryan Pata case with Dean was no different than the many other cases we have worked on together. He was amazing to work with and was a tremendous help to ESPN's efforts in highlighting the circumstances surrounding this case.

We began, as we always do, with what we term "victimology."

Basically, we start by studying the victim and work our way outward from close friends, family, and associates to the victim's general lifestyle. Starting an investigation this way helps us determine what was going on around them and, most importantly, who would have been associating with the victim leading up to and around the time of the murder. By so doing, we get a glimpse into the mind of the victim.

While FBI Profilers are famous for getting into the minds of the killers, it's just as important—if not more so—to dive into the mind of the victim so that we have a strong starting point to work with. In this case, we thought about Bryan and the circumstances surrounding his life during the final months, weeks, and days leading up to the night of his murder. We thought about his final moments as he was confronted by the gunman who would ultimately take his life. We wondered what must have gone through his mind during those final few minutes of his life and how he would have responded in that situation.

After reviewing all the available evidence and crime scene materials, we visualized that November night in the apartment complex parking lot and tried to get a sense for the way the crime might have played out. We could see Bryan pull into the complex and we visualized the killer lying in wait and closely watching Bryan get out of his car before approaching him from behind.

We visualized the crime unfold from beginning to end, starting with the very first words the killer might have uttered to Bryan.

"I told you, man!" a familiar voice would growl from behind as Bryan got out of his SUV. "I told you, you'd better clip up."

In our mind's eye, the angry voice blended into the darkness of the night and coursed through the thick humid air of the Colony Apartments parking lot in Miami, Florida. Humidity was always high in South Florida, but on this night, a light rain had covered the city, creating a palpable density. Just as Bryan could reach out into the night and run his fingers through the misty air, he could also feel the gunman's breath hissing from behind and spraying a light mist on the back of his neck.

The encounter would last a mere two minutes, but two minutes is a lifetime when a life is in jeopardy—especially when another person is at the controls. So many thoughts—an entire lifetime's worth—can flash through one's mind in that amount of time. Every sense is heightened, and time can feel as though it's slowing to a crawl.

Parked next to a nearby dumpster, we could imagine the whiff of odor filling Bryan's nostrils momentarily, slowing the racing of his mind as he tried to formulate a plan to free himself of this situation.

"Don't turn around, man," the gunman would warn.

It was clear to us from the evidence that Bryan most likely would have known the source of that voice and felt its anger. He most likely would have known the man behind the gun and his thoughts would have turned to stopping him.

"What you going to do, man?" we could visualize Bryan saying to the gunman, trying to buy some time, maybe even distract him.

For a lot of people, such an experience would cause fear, trembling, even begging. But, as Bryan's victimology taught us, he wasn't most people.

He was a six-foot-four, 320-pound defensive lineman for the five-time national champion University of Miami football team, and he was a young man who had confronted a lot of violence in his life. He was no stranger to confrontation and, being the larger-than-life personality he was, he came out on top almost every time.

In fact, Bryan cast a large figure wherever he went. On the football field, he was an unstoppable defensive presence slated to be one of the top picks at his position in the upcoming NFL Draft. Off the field, he was the kind of person whose presence you could feel walk into the room no matter where you were sitting. Before he even uttered a word, one could feel his aura just from the responsive buzz emanating from others in the room.

When Bryan spoke, it was big. When he gestured, it was even bigger. Yes, he had the imposing physical size of a defensive lineman, but his personality was even that much larger. He drew people to him. Some of them teammates, some family, and some of them friends. Others, maybe not so friendly. But he embraced them all, friends and enemies alike.

Friends got the warm, gregarious shout out and huge hug of the Haitian-born young man and a smile that was even bigger. Those who weren't friends got an opposite reaction that was no less that size. Bryan Pata was a defender of all those in his circle. And, like everything else he did, he was a passionate defender of those he cared about.

That's one of the reasons he cited when he announced his decision to stay near his hometown of Miami and play for the Hurricanes when he could have played for any college in the country. He wanted to be near his mother so he could watch over her. Same with his eight brothers and sisters.

Never one to shy away from conflict, he was not afraid to get in someone's face. Regardless of who you were, he had no problem telling you how he felt and no qualms about telling you publicly. If humiliation was the result, then so be it. Bryan was not concerned about your feelings. His biggest concern was for those he loved and cared about. And, like everything else he did in his life, he loved large.

As we looked through various accounts of Bryan's life, we noted that one example of his huge generosity actually occurred within an hour before his murder. The gregarious young man had been laughing and joking with some of his teammates on the way home from a team meeting. He had seen them—most of them underclassmen—waiting at the bus stop and he pulled over to offer them a ride to their dorms, as he often did, taking them under his wing.

He and his young teammates laughed and joked about the team meeting, talked about practice and about life in general. Bryan offered encouragement to them, telling them that good things would come if they just stuck with it. Just keep grinding.

"Things will work out," he said to them. "Just keep putting in the work and good things will happen. You'll see."

When the SUV pulled up to the dorms to drop them off, Bryan gave one last call-out to his teammates.

"All right, ya'll boys take it easy," he hollered, as they piled out of the car. "We'll see y'all tomorrow!"

Yes, Bryan was a giant in more ways than one. But big men attract a lot of attention and not always the desirable kind. Just a few minutes after his jovial exchange with teammates, Bryan's life would hit a crossroads in that dark parking lot. But he wasn't about to quit—even with a gun pointed to his head.

"You don't want to do this man," we could visualize him telling the gunman in another attempt at distraction.

"I told you to stop disrespecting me and you just wouldn't leave it alone," the gunman would bark, closely watching Bryan's every move. "Don't turn around!"

Being the protector and standing just a few yards from where he and his girlfriend, Jada, shared an apartment, we wondered what he might have been thinking about her. It wouldn't be out of the question to think that his first instinct was to protect her. If the gunman was someone he knew, someone who probably had an axe to grind with Bryan, wouldn't it stand to reason that he might target her next?

If those were Bryan's thoughts in that moment, it's not out of the question that he would make a sudden move to defend his girlfriend.

The couple had met a year earlier when she was a freshman, and he was instantly smitten.

"I'm going to make her my girl," he declared.

And he did.

Over the next year, theirs was a very passionate relationship that ran hot and cold. Good times frolicking on the beach and dancing at clubs. Quiet nights at the apartment where they would talk about life and their futures together.

There were also those times that one often regrets in a relationship. Arguments over things that, in that moment, probably seemed so inconsequential. Arguments over petty things that really weren't that important. Jealousy over ex-girlfriends and ex-boyfriends.

One of those ex-boyfriends was a teammate of Bryan's, Rashaun Jones. On occasion, he would make it a point to let Bryan know that he dated her first. His comments would get under Bryan's skin and sometimes end in fist fights in which the larger Bryan Pata got the best of his smaller foe. On one occasion, Pata wrestled Jones to the ground and head butted him several times in succession before teammates rushed to break up the fisticuffs.

During their latest physical altercation, Jones reportedly yelled out threateningly at Bryan, "You'd better clip up!"

It was a threat that Bryan may not have taken seriously at the time, but over the course of the next few weeks, we were told that he began to have nightmares that his life would be coming to an end prematurely. He confided these dreams only to a small circle of people, including Jada and his brothers, Fednol and Edrick, brothers he spent countless hours with restoring classic cars.

He and his brothers were planning to make a lifelong partnership of the car restoration business and had already been fairly successful in doing so. Bryan had even had the opportunity to showcase his work for a *Miami Herald* feature story and occasionally showed off his work via videos that his family would make. Life seemed good, but the young man's nightmares caused him to fear that something ominous loomed on the horizon that would take all his success away. The twenty-one-year-old told his brothers and others close to him that sometimes the dreams felt so real that he would sleep in his closet where he kept a stash of firearms.

In the tense moments with the gunman, was it possible that he was thinking about some of the most recent conversations he had with his brother, Edrick?

"Man, they keep chasing me," he told his elder brother. "These people, somebody, keep chasing me in my damn dream."

Edrick tried to comfort him by assuring him that nothing was going to happen. "It's just a dream, man. Everything's going to be alright."

In the end, Bryan's soul refused to be comforted. All he could think to do was ask Edrick to pray for him.

Of course, his brother would.

It is common for victims of these kinds of violent crimes to see their lives flash before their eyes. Thoughts of significant life events, achievements, and loved ones can often pass through a victim's mind in a split second. If that was the case with Bryan, then as quickly as those thoughts may have raced through the young man's mind, in all probability, they were also just as quickly interrupted.

"Now you're going to get what's coming to you!" we could visualize the gunman telling Bryan.

Then, holding the gun to his head, the assailant pulled the trigger.

In an instant, a young man's life was taken along with all his hopes and dreams and his future.

As I visualized what transpired in those final minutes of Bryan's life, we also considered the possibility that Bryan's initial reaction might have been to be dismissive of his assailant's resolve. After all, the gunman was more than likely someone Bryan knew, someone he was familiar with.

He had also been known to laugh off threats before, as he did when an enraged ex-girlfriend barged into his apartment while wielding a knife and threatening to kill him. Seemingly unfazed, he easily wrestled the knife from her, walked her out of the apartment, calmed her down, and sent her on her way.

Maybe he was simply calling her bluff or maybe he just sensed that she needed to blow off some steam and was not serious about stabbing him with the knife. Either way, he found a way to diffuse the situation and his actions kept it from becoming something much worse. Perhaps he thought he could take the same tack with the gunman.

Unfortunately, this threat in the parking lot—an angry, desperate man holding a gun on him—was a different story. This was much more serious. Still, it wasn't hard to envision this confident young man, who had endured life-threatening confrontations before, attempting to end the conflict in his favor by taking matters into his own hands.

I could see a scenario in which Bryan may have turned around to see the assailant and thought—or said—"You don't have the guts to pull the trigger. You aren't serious. You aren't going to shoot me."

I could also visualize Bryan turning around slightly and suddenly flinching in a motion that suggested he was going to attempt to wrestle the gun away from his assailant. A movement like that—no matter how subtle—may have been enough to cause the gunman to shoot.

Whatever the circumstance, in an instant, the assailant pulled the trigger and Bryan Pata was lying face down on the ground of the dimly lit parking lot, having been shot in the back left side of the head. Just as quickly, the shooter fled the scene before anyone could get a good look at him.

From the outside, it might seem unusual for a homicide investigator to be focusing on the victim's thoughts and feelings around the time of a murder. Why not focus primarily on the killer? But this is exactly where we should be focusing our attention—on the victims, their lives, the people they were surrounded by, and especially their families and loved ones.

Whenever we are presented with violent cold cases of any kind, the first thing we do is get to know the victim as intimately as possible. As I said earlier, the foundation of each investigation is victimology. And not just the circumstances surrounding their lives around the time of the commission of the crime.

For me, homicide investigations are much more personal than that. When I study the victim I see a person who had hopes, dreams, and aspirations. I see someone who has left a family behind, who has left friends and loved ones grieving for them, for the person they miss and will never get back. I look at the life they led well before the point they crossed paths with their assailants. I truly want to get to know them—their strengths, weaknesses, personalities, and dispositions.

And I think about what might have been had they not been taken from us so prematurely. What would have become of their lives? What dreams would they have achieved?

In my experience, the more we focus on these questions, the closer we come to answering the question of who took it upon themselves to end all the potential of a human life. It's the criminal investigator's equivalent of starting with the end in mind. In Bryan Pata's case, he almost assuredly would have achieved his dream of playing in the NFL, a dream so many boys want to live, but so few men ever really get to. What would that have looked like? How well would he have done?

Beyond the football field, what kind of personal influence would he have had on people? Would he have married his college sweetheart or maybe someone else? Would he have become a father, and if so, what kind of kids would he have raised? I think about how long fifteen years is in the perspective of a life, and I think that, if he would have had children, he might be retired from playing football by now and coaching his own children's teams.

The losses also extend beyond Bryan Pata's life. If not for this gunman, this young man's parents might have been grandparents, and his siblings would be aunts and uncles.

In 2017—eleven years after his murder—Bryan's family spoke at a press conference organized by the Miami-Dade Police Department and the immense pain of their loss was agonizingly evident as Bryan's mother, Jeanette—a Haitian immigrant who had raised nine children largely on her own—spoke to the press.

"This hurt me! This hurt!" she sobbed. "I can't imagine ten years ago we don't hear nothing for my son. They are not working the case. . . . I don't feel they're even working on the case anymore. The case is closed. The system doesn't work."

The images of that press conference were burned into my mind.

I've been in law enforcement for over forty years and, no matter how many cases I investigate, it never gets easier to see a grieving mother. In fact, it just gets harder. So much is taken from a family left behind.

Bryan and his brother Fednol famously worked on and restored cars together. I imagine that every time Fednol works on a car, there might sometimes be a melancholy undertone to his work as he thinks about what might have been with the brother who spent so much time working with him.

And what of the community he might have lived in and given back to? What might have been there? Bryan grew up in a low-income area in South Florida. We see so many professional athletes who have grown up in similar situations give back to the kids in their communities, providing much-needed resources to schools and, in turn, providing hope to a new generation of young women and men. It seems likely, given what I learned about Bryan's personality, that he would have been one to do that kind of charity work.

So much is lost when a single life is taken that extends well beyond that one life or even a victim's inner circle. So many lives are affected. So many of those types of questions remain unanswered and will remain unanswered forever.

That is why I organized the Cold Case Foundation. I don't want any murdered loved one to be forgotten, and I don't want any of their families to feel abandoned—especially by those of us who have the training and skills to help them find answers.

As I said earlier, in the United States, about 40 percent of homicide cases currently go unsolved. It's devastating, and I—along with my fellow colleagues—have always felt that we can do better, that we must do better. People need to know that their lives are important and that the lives of their loved ones matter. And the best way for us as law enforcement to show them that is to continue looking into their cases and earnestly trying to solve them. We owe that to every victim's loved one who has lost and suffered so much.

That's why Bryan Pata's case meant so much to us at the Cold Case Foundation and why we were willing to assist ESPN, Miami law enforcement authorities, and Bryan's family with his case.

So, we kept digging.

As we continued to work through the evidence, we expanded the victimology from Bryan and his family to his close circle of friends and acquaintances. Our focus shifted to that parking lot the night of the murder. I thought about the people who heard the shots and found Bryan on the ground, bleeding from the gunshot wounds—Bryan's girlfriend, Jada, and his roommate, Dwayne Hendricks. That is a horrifying experience that leaves a person forever changed. How were their lives altered as a result of that experience?

The police report showed that, just a few minutes before the shooting, Jada was cleaning out her dog's kennel. Thinking she had heard an argument downstairs, she left the apartment and walked down to the parking lot where she saw her boyfriend lying on his back and bleeding on the walkway near his car.

She ran back up to her apartment to call 911, screaming to a dispatcher for help. About that time, Dwayne drove up in his Dodge pickup. When he saw Bryan on the ground, he initially thought it was a prank.

"Get up," he jokingly said. Then Hendricks noticed a puddle of blood behind his roommate's head. He took the phone from Jada, who had returned to the scene and was panicked. The call dropped, after which Dwayne called back. He had the following exchange with the 911 dispatcher, as per the official report:

Dispatcher: "Miami-Dade Police and Fire, what is your emergency?"
Hendricks: "Hello? Hello, we need help!"
Dispatcher: "At what address?"
Hendricks: "9315 Southwest 77th Avenue."
Dispatcher: "What happened there?"
Hendricks: "Somebody got shot. The guy's on the ground. I don't know where he's bleeding from, but he's on the ground, Miss."
Dispatcher: "Okay, if you will stay with me on the line, did you see what happened?"

Hendricks: "No, I did not see what happened. Nobody seen what happened, Miss."

Dispatcher: "And you don't know where he's shot?"

Hendricks: "He's not breathing, Miss!"

Listening to the 911 call, in the background screaming can be heard and the person, presumably Bryan's girlfriend, sounds understandably emotional. A man working on his car nearby heard the commotion and ran to help, performing chest compressions as Bryan lay unresponsive. Minutes after the initial 911 call, rescue personnel arrived and took over. They pronounced Bryan dead at approximately 7:07 p.m.

As I said, when I look at a case, I think about the victims, their families, and their loved ones. And these life-changing moments are what I think about on their behalf.

According to the medical examiner, Bryan was shot about three inches above and a half inch in front of his left ear with a medium-caliber lead bullet that left a six-millimeter wound. As I looked at the evidence and autopsy photos, the angle of the bullet entry wound is why I think that it's possible that Bryan may have started to turn toward the gunman, who was in all probability standing behind him. It's possible that Bryan may have turned to say something to him or even possibly to attempt to try and wrestle the gun from him. When we look at Bryan's victimology, in conjunction with the physical evidence, there is a good chance that he made a motion to turn toward his assailant in an attempt to, in some way, stop him.

The one thing that became apparent to us as Dean and I looked at all the surrounding circumstances, was that Bryan most likely knew his killer and that there was a high probability that the killer was pretty familiar with him. That's when we turned our focus from the victim to the perpetrator of the crime. Given everything we knew about the victim and his life, who might the offender have been and what would have driven that person to do such a thing?

With those questions in mind and, with all the investigative information in hand, we began developing a profile of the killer.

From a physical evidence standpoint, we knew this was not a robbery gone bad. Bryan's wallet, which contained several $100 bills in it, and his car keys, were left behind. Nothing of monetary value was taken, and when we put the timeline of the actual crime together, from when Bryan pulled into the parking lot until the trigger was pulled, we were looking at about two minutes.

Because there was no evidence that the motive was robbery, and because of the short amount of time it took for the murder to be committed, one other aspect of the crime jumped out to us.

"The behavior of the offender tells us that the offender knew the victim's life very well," I observed as we were discussing the timing aspect of the case. "He knew where the victim lived, and he had a specific idea of when he would arrive home and even where he would park. That tells us that he's familiar with the victim's schedule on a specific level."

Besides that, between the time anyone nearby heard the gunshot and then came out to see what happened, the shooter had fled. No one could even see someone fleeing the scene of the crime.

As we pored over the police reports, all indications were that the shooter might have been waiting for Bryan, possibly in the bushes or behind a nearby dumpster. Police detectives never found any witnesses to the shooting, and there were no security cameras in the area that captured it. Some people interviewed at the apartment complex reported hearing loud voices, while others heard gunshots, but all those statements have one thing in common: the commotion they heard was over very quickly and no one saw the shooter arrive or leave.

The killer was fast and precise.

"That suggests a very well-planned entrance and exit to avoid detection," Dean pointed out. "That kind of detail can only be planned and executed with this kind of efficiency if the offender has an intimate familiarity with the victim and his life habits."

"Absolutely," I agreed. "And he had to have been extremely familiar with the apartment complex layout and the surrounding area. This suggests that the offender had been there before, and it's highly likely that he had been there multiple times."

During our discussions, we talked about the probable mental and psychological mindset of the gunman. We were sure he knew Bryan, but how well did he know him? What kind of circumstances surrounded this person that he would feel compelled to kill him? And why was the way he committed the homicide so personal?

As we sorted through the case files and the information we had, it became apparent that the offender was most likely someone Bryan knew and who knew him well. All of this led us to believe that this was planned out by someone who would have known where Bryan would be and when he would be there. Add to it that that someone was so enraged with the victim that he shot him in the head at point-blank range, execution style.

"The way the offender commits the crime," I said, "typically, that's not the kind of angry outburst that comes from a random two-minute encounter. It's the kind of rage that builds over time and turns into a personal vendetta."

I could visualize the shooter trembling with rage—and fear. Bryan was a large man and, by all accounts, was not one to back down from confrontations or fights. That kind of brashness can sometimes bring with it hostility and resentment—especially if that person felt he had been publicly humiliated but didn't have the means or size to physically best a man with the stature of Bryan Pata. Confronting a man with Bryan's size and strength can be a very scary proposition for an assailant, even if he is carrying a gun. One missed shot, untimely delay, or miscalculation, and a young man the size of Bryan Pata could quickly take the gun and end the conflict.

"That's why this crime had to be planned out precisely," Dean noted. "He couldn't afford to give the victim the slightest window of opportunity to turn the tables on him."

As we looked at the circumstances and people surrounding Bryan, as well as the circumstances directly related to the events of that night, our thought was to identify anyone who would have had an axe to grind with him and who would have known him so well that they would know where he was going to be and when he was going to be there. Aside from Bryan's girlfriend, roommate, and a handful of teammates, he had told no one where he was going and what time he would be there.

After having combed through pages and pages of police interviews, we listed people who should be named as people of interest, and we provided a recommended course of investigation based on the information we had. As we always do when we are looking to identify people of interest in a murder investigation, we started with the victim's background and took note of the people he associated with.

We had a bio on Bryan's life from childhood up to the night of the murder and we knew the things the twenty-two-year-old college senior had accomplished. We also studied statements detailing the kind of life he lived and some of the situations he had been in that may have increased the risk of his homicide.

Having arrived in the United States with his family from Haiti, Bryan was an energetic child and, by all accounts, had always been larger than other kids his age. By the time he reached high school, it was apparent that his football talents would lead him to great achievements. He was recruited by some of the most prestigious college football programs in the country. But, wanting to stay close to home, he chose the University of Miami in hopes of helping them win another national championship. Most notably, though, he chose his hometown college because he wanted to be near his family.

On the football field, it wasn't long before Bryan started getting regular playing time and then became a starter. In his final year of college, coaches moved Bryan to defensive tackle, hoping the move would build his prospects of an NFL future. The move worked, and soon, Bryan was widely regarded as a lock to be selected in the first round of the upcoming NFL draft.

While his prospects on the field were moving forward, Bryan's personal life was more complicated. This is where we shifted our focus to risk assessment. When ESPN interviewed us, I told them that the key to solving this case was determining the relationship between the victim and the offender.

"The individual is waiting for him, hiding, has the weapon," I explained. "The weapon is loaded, and the individual is prepared to use it, and to use it immediately. There's no outside threat (to the perpetrator). The offender has to know Bryan is going to be by himself and that person has figured out the short window of time Bryan would be alone—while walking from his car to his apartment. Bryan is a larger-than-life type of guy, and any conflicts he has had are the key to finding his killer, or the person who hired the killer. That's why the key to finding who did this is to identify people who potentially had contentious relationships with Bryan Pata."

And those relationships, as I pointed out, go directly to the kind of lifestyle an individual lives. So, we needed to ask ourselves, what kind of activities was the victim involved with? And, most importantly, who were the people he surrounded himself with while engaging in those activities?

As Dean and I looked for the answers to those questions, we determined that Bryan's lifestyle was medium risk and was often elevated to a level approaching high risk based on his extracurricular activities. What does this mean? Quite simply, when determining a lifestyle's risk level, we are looking for activities that would put a victim in harm's way. We also look at the frequency of those activities.

Homemakers in the suburbs, for example, would be individuals who live low-risk lifestyles because they tend to stay close to home and they frequent areas that are typically low-crime areas. In short, they usually avoid putting themselves in high-risk situations. In Bryan's case, we could see that he engaged in a number of activities that would put him in what are typically considered medium- to high-risk situations, and we compiled a list of them, which included:

- "Clubbing" and reports of fighting.
- Questionable business dealings related to high-end cars. For example, there were reports of Bryan being accused of shorting someone on a vehicle with a bad transmission.
- The purchase of known stolen rims that he then put on his own vehicle (estimated value of about $5,000 each). He was eventually confronted by the owner of the rims, which led him to remove and sell them.
- His demeanor could also be considered high risk at times. For example, he often dressed in a way that elicited a lot of attention (gold medallion and chains, dental grills, and high-end clothing choices).
- His personal demeanor and approach was outgoing and confident, and, combined with his overbearing physical presence, could be interpreted as abrasive and offensive by some people.
- He would sometimes flash several hundred dollars in cash at the clubs he went to, which drew a lot of attention.
- He had a domestic relationship with his girlfriend but would engage in relationships with other women, which caused jealousy and heated arguments with several of the women he dated, including his girlfriend.

- Bryan had a propensity to escalate conflicts to physical altercations. In one instance, he head-butted a teammate in a dormitory during a dispute over a woman they had both dated. This is important to note in that Bryan's ability to defend himself due to his size and athleticism gave him confidence to escalate those conflicts because his risk of serious injury during a physical altercation was low—unless the opposition introduced weapons into the conflict.

Once we had established Bryan's common activities, Dean and I then turned our attention toward any potential or significant triggering events that could have led to Bryan's murder, including:

- Bryan was confronted by the alleged owner of stolen car rims.
- He received a contentious phone call prior to leaving practice the night of his murder.
- Bryan was in a fight in a club and was told that an unidentified person had put a hit on him.
- Upcoming NFL draft and his status, which could draw jealousy or undesirable attention.
- He and his girlfriend's one-year anniversary, a milestone that could potentially draw attention to him.
- Fight with a teammate, who was heard yelling, "You'd better clip up!"

With the list finished, yet incomplete because we did not have access to the entirety of evidence and interviews that the Miami-Dade Police Department had gathered, we began to formulate some recommended actions based on plausible theories that had been developed from the information ESPN had sent to us.

Before I go into those theories, I do want to note something important in regard to our categorization of the risk level of victims. In no way is our assessment of the risk level a judgment of the victim's life choices or character. It is simply a series of observations that helps us establish a baseline for the investigation. Determining risk level helps us develop a criminal profile of the offender. The more we can narrow down the characteristics of the person responsible for the crime, the more likely it is that we will find who committed it and make an arrest that hopefully ends in a conviction.

That all has to start with the victim—in this case, Bryan Pata—and the circumstances surrounding the life he lived. But in no way is the risk level a means of judging victims' morals or implicating them in the crime that was committed against them. That responsibility rests with the perpetrator and the perpetrator alone.

In Bryan's case, we narrowed down the circle of potential people of interest to a few theories and recommended actions that investigators could take to follow up on each one.

The first theory—and the one we thought was the most likely, given the information and evidence we had at the time—was called "The Rashaun Jones Theory." When teammates and coaches heard the news of Bryan's murder, they immediately reached out to everyone on the team and brought them together for a meeting at the University of Miami practice facility later that night. The following excerpt from the ESPN story describes that meeting and the suspicious circumstances surrounding the absence of one of Bryan's teammates. That teammate, a skilled position player from the state of Florida, was the only member of the team who did not attend the meeting. The story reads:

As word of Pata's death spread, players jumped into cars and raced toward the apartment complex. A text from Miami's football office appeared on their cellphones: Head to the Hecht Center immediately for a mandatory team meeting.

Hendricks came in late, dazed and with his shirt covered in Pata's blood. The room was dark and eerily quiet. Coaches spoke in reassuring tones, but Clint Hurtt was full of rage and had to leave the room. He punched a hole in the hallway wall.

One teammate was noticeably absent: Rashaun Jones, a 6-foot-1, 195-pound defensive back from Lake City, Florida. He'd been suspended that day after testing positive for marijuana, his third failed drug test, but he was still expected to be at the meeting.

Jones would later tell police that he was home alone the night Pata was murdered, and that when he heard of Pata's death, he headed to the Hecht

Center, presumably for the meeting. But other witnesses told police, and more than a dozen ex-players told ESPN for this story, that they had no recollection of Jones being there.

ESPN reviewed police notes that indicate Jones called a fellow student-athlete to borrow money that night to go out of town. Police subsequently interviewed the person who received the call from Jones. That student spoke to ESPN on the condition that he not be named but confirmed that Jones did ask for money; he declined to comment further.

Jones had been dating Miami student Sherry Abramson that semester in what Abramson described to ESPN as an on-and-off relationship.

She said she was working at Pottery Barn on Nov. 7. As she left work, Willie Cooper called to tell her the news that Pata had been killed. Cooper asked where Jones was, and Abramson began to panic. She didn't know where he was. She called Jones's phone repeatedly after that, but said she couldn't reach him. She said she was worried that Jones was hurt, too.

Desperate, Abramson called Jones's grandmother and sister and asked if they'd heard from him. Nobody had. When he finally called a couple hours later, she said, he was upset. Jones already knew of Pata's death from team-mates. "He was shocked," Abramson said. He told her about his failed drug test and suspension. She said he shut off his phone to be by himself for a while and process the news of his dismissal.

Former team chaplain Steve Caldwell, who was talking to players at the Hecht Center that night, told ESPN that Abramson called him "in a panic about Bryan being dead . . ." he said, "and she immediately asked me, 'Where did . . . what . . . is Rashaun there?'"

"And I said, 'No, he's not here.' And I think he was the only player that didn't show up," Caldwell said.

In high school, Jones had been considered one of the nation's best defensive back recruits. But he did not live up to his promise at Miami and was relegated mostly to special teams. In some ways, he was like Pata, trying to better his life through football. But Jones and Pata were not friends.

Jones dated Brody first, and, witnesses said, he reminded Pata of it constantly. Teammates could sense the friction. Moncur recalled an incident in summer 2006 when he and Jones got into an argument. Two other teammates, including Pata, were in a nearby room.

"Bryan just came out of nowhere. He started getting in Rashaun's face, and then their argument escalated and they started fighting," Moncur told ESPN. Moncur said Pata got on top of Jones and started head-butting him, "Five times. Boom, boom, boom, boom, boom."

Moncur jumped in to break up the fight. As the two were separated, Moncur said, Jones issued a warning to Pata: "Boy, you might as well go ahead and clip up."

Teammates said that one time, Jones was taunting Pata about Brody, which led to a fistfight in the locker room.

According to partially redacted police documents, there were other reasons for detectives to focus on Jones. At some point on the night of Pata's death, Jones went to Abramson's house, and Abramson told receivers coach Marquis Mosely on a phone call that Jones was "out of it." Police also noted that Jones changed his phone number that day.

Coral Gables Police Chief Ed Hudak, a law enforcement liaison for the Hurricanes at the time, told ESPN it wasn't uncommon for players to have beefs. He remembers Jones as someone who had "issues with a bunch of people."

Hudak said he didn't remember Jones and Pata tangling, but as he spoke with players at the Hecht Center on the night of Nov. 7, Jones's name kept coming up. "There was a very strong sentiment [Jones] had something to do with it," Hudak said. "When that was brought up to me by the players, I made sure that the detectives had that. What came of those leads, I don't know."

As you can see from these statements, there was reason to, at the very least, want to interview Jones. Based on the facts of the case as we had them, our recommendation was to do a series of interviews, both with Jones and several other people who associated with both Jones and Bryan within a short time of his murder.

In reinterviewing Jones, the strategy we recommended was to initially take a soft approach with him so his guard would come down as much as possible. "We want him to think that, because of the recent publicity around the case, detectives were just doing their due diligence in reinterviewing everyone who knew Bryan—teammates, associates, etcetera," Dean pointed out as we discussed the case. I agreed. In a case like this, you don't want the main suspect to feel singled out. We thought it would be best to give him the impression that he was simply part of a large group of people that investigators were talking to. Standard procedure in a cold case. Nothing out of the ordinary.

Once his guard was down, that tack would abruptly be followed by an accusatory confrontation, implying that there was now sufficient evidence of his knowledge, participation, or awareness of what happened to Bryan Pata. "The hope behind implementing this particular strategy would be to create panic within him," I explained, "which would cause him to slip and tell investigators something that only the killer would know about the night in question."

We also recommended that police interview any and all girlfriends *Jones has dated* since Bryan's death. "If there was a chance that he told at least one of them something incriminating," I said, "we wanted to be able to get it on record and have the potential testimony of perhaps multiple witnesses that could aid in a conviction."

Our final recommendation in regard to this theory was to talk to as many of Bryan Pata's teammates and associates as possible. We felt that the best course of action would have been to question them individually, which from what we could tell in looking at the records ESPN gave us, was not done on as comprehensive a level as it could have been. By doing separate interviews, detectives could then compare and contrast their individual accounts and build a single account based on the commonalities among their statements. Additionally, if detectives interviewed them individually today, it's always possible that someone or something was overlooked and could point detectives in the right direction.

Once we made those recommendations, our attention turned to the only other real plausible theory, which was that the individual who was angry with Bryan about the alleged stolen rims, might be the killer. I personally didn't think this theory held much water, given the intimate nature of the crime, but I did feel that we needed to vet out every possibility. And to be completely honest, I didn't feel like any of the theories had been adequately vetted enough to rule any of them out. But, mostly, I felt like we owed it to the family to say that every possible stone was turned to find Bryan's killer.

Dean and I thought that the best course of action would be to interview the person who sold the rims to Bryan in the first place, a man known as Dimitri. Once police interviewed him, they could cross check his statements by checking for insurance claims or old police reports for stolen rims that fit the description of those that Bryan had purchased. That would have been an easy cross check given the unique features of the rims. We also recommended pulling Bryan's financial records to see if there was anything connected to the rims.

Another necessary step would be to question anyone else who would have had knowledge of the rims, including Bryan's brother Fednol and his then girlfriend, Jada. Perhaps they would remember something that would help with the investigation.

Finally, we recommended that detectives check with officers who were assigned to gang units around the time of the murder to identify any relevant gang members who could be interviewed regarding the circumstances surrounding the rims. The possibility, however remote, still existed that someone could have contracted with the killer to have Bryan murdered.

All that said, while we definitely wanted to vet out all the reasonable options, we were pretty convinced that there was more than enough evidence—both physical and behavioral—to point to Jones as the primary suspect. Our recommendation was that investigators focus most of the investigation on looking into him. He was by far the most plausible suspect in this case, and we thought it should be investigated as such.

Toward the end of our interview with ESPN, Dean summed up what we were both feeling. "This case, it was solvable," he told Paula Lavigne and Elizabeth Merrill. "The pieces were there. Unfortunately, it's become a mystery, but I don't think it should have been a mystery."

At the conclusion of our interview with ESPN, we left a report of our findings and recommendations with the producers of the story and recommended that they be sent to the Miami-Dade Police Department for their review. As it turned out, detectives did end up arresting Jones for Bryan Pata's murder just a few months later on August 19, 2021.

At the time this book was being written, he was still awaiting trial.

Our greatest desire is that justice will be done on Bryan's behalf and on behalf of his family and loved ones. And we hope the truth of what really happened to Bryan that night will be revealed so that they can all begin to find some level of healing and live the lives that the young man with so much promise would want them to live. We wish the same for the families and loved ones of every homicide victim and it is our mission to do everything we possibly can to contribute to the investigations of these unsolved cases.

Ultimately, we know that solving cases can never cure the heartbreak that these families experience when losing a loved one. But we hope to contribute to them, at least finding some kind of justice on behalf of their departed loved ones.

Part of the unrest that comes with losing a loved one to an unsolved homicide is knowing that the person who murdered your loved one has not been brought to justice and that the killer is still out there potentially taking the lives of other individuals and causing the same pain and heartache to other families. And, while an arrest and conviction of their killers isn't going to bring them back, we hope that there is at least a measure of peace associated with knowing that justice has been served and that one less killer will be free to cause this kind of pain and suffering to someone else.

As we sit down and talk to these family members, we see the toll that the time gone by without knowing what happened—years in many cases—has taken on them. There has never been a time that I have met with a family that I didn't wish I could do more. So many of these families are so desperate for answers. The torment on their faces almost always tells the story. They want to know who would do this and why. It's almost as if their lives will be in a permanent state of paralysis if they don't get those answers, that, until they get answers to those questions, they won't be able to move on and complete an already excruciating grieving process. Many feel stuck and helpless, often feeling that they are at the mercy of legal authorities to find the responsible parties and bring those monsters to justice.

And, as much as we would love to promise that we will, there is so much more to a homicide investigation than police detectives simply finding the killers and locking them up forever. The truth is, in the majority of cases, it really does take an entire community that extends beyond detectives and prosecutors. With resources largely being limited in police departments throughout the country, there needs to be involvement beyond law enforcement. Having been a police chief twice and head of the FBI's Behavioral Sciences Unit, I can tell you from experience that there is almost always a shortage of funding and resources on the law enforcement side of the ledger.

So, we have a choice. We can either throw our hands up in the air and complain or we can get creative and find ways to maximize our resources in ways that safely and effectively involve the law-abiding members of our communities. Like the Bryan Pata case we just reviewed, it sometimes takes the involvement of those who are most closely associated with the victim to help move an investigation forward. They need to come forward. That can be a scary thing to do, and it takes a lot of courage sometimes to approach law enforcement. In this case, many of Bryan's family and friends were actively involved in contributing information to detectives throughout the years, and that was likely a key factor in the agency's ability to make an arrest.

Quite often, solving these cases requires public awareness. Where possible, we need to keep the public abreast of what we are looking for and specifically the kind of information that will be most helpful in working an investigation. For instance, it wasn't until two diligent journalists at ESPN, Paula Lavigne and Elizabeth Merrill, wrote an in-depth story on Bryan's then fifteen-year-old case, that the investigation regained momentum and an arrest was made a few months after the story came out.

Also, credit goes to the Miami-Dade Police Department for reaching out to ESPN a couple years prior to that story coming out. Granted, there was a conflict over what information to release to the network, but the detectives did the right thing in enlisting the public's help. Most important, friends and family were willing to go on record on behalf of Bryan to rekindle interest in the investigation. This case teaches us a great lesson. If we hope to gain traction in bringing resolution to any of these unsolved cases, then communication, coordination, collaboration, and cooperation will be essential in accomplishing that design.

This case is a perfect example of what can happen when those things come together. Paula Lavigne was kind enough to say so when she spoke about the Foundation's role in this investigation. "When ESPN needed help assessing the records and materials we had gathered on a long, unsolved homicide, we enlisted the help of the Cold Case Foundation," she related. "We were impressed with the time they took to read through police documents, analyze the work that had already been done with the case, and meet with us in person to discuss the results. Gaining insight from experienced investigators helped us ask probing follow-up questions and request additional records and information."

This is exactly why the Cold Case Foundation was created. We hope to promote a better, more effective way of working these cases and bringing more killers to justice. Most important of all, we hope to contribute in some small way, to bringing some peace of mind to the families of the victims of these cases.

Throughout the rest of this book, we will take a deeper dive into this process in a way that illustrates how legal authorities, victims' families, loved ones, communities, the media, and other key organizations can come together in a way that makes us all better and all safer.

CHAPTER TWO

THE CASES THAT HAUNT

When people hear about the Cold Case Foundation, one of the questions I get the most is, "Was there a specific case that inspired you to establish this foundation?"

People understand why it exists and what its mission is, but I find they are most curious about what actually drove me, from the deepest chambers of my heart, to go to all the work to establish an organization with so many moving parts and so few guarantees that it would actually succeed.

"You had a long and distinguished career," they sometimes say. "Why not just retire and rest on your laurels? Why go to all that work?"

My answer, simply put: It's the cases that haunt.

It's the same reason that so many of our 150-plus investigators—many of them retired FBI and homicide detectives—have joined the cause and give so generously of their time with nothing in return except for the potential satisfaction of contributing to the resolution of some of the most heinous unsolved cases imaginable. When you have spent a good deal of your life standing in the midst of bloody crime scenes, surveying so much senseless loss of life, it takes its toll. And not just in the moment, but for the rest of your life. The impact that it has—spending hours on location of some of the grisliest murders imaginable, working with the justice system, trying to get answers for families, talking to them and seeing their grief—you feel like you are up to your ankles in blood.

And, in some cases, you literally are.

Add to it that, as an FBI profiler whose job it is to immerse yourself in the minds of both perpetrator and victim, you vicariously experience the horrific worlds of both simultaneously. It's a whole other level. Sometimes, you reach a point that you just want it all to stop. You just want it to go away. It can feel like, no matter how many killers you find and put away, ten more spring up for every one that you catch.

If you think about it too long, it gets demoralizing. There is so much mental, emotional, and physical impact associated with what we do. And all the while, you realize that the toll that these cases take on you is just a drop in the bucket compared to what it does to the families and loved ones of the victims. Aside from the victims themselves, they're the ones who pay the steepest price.

As investigating officers, all we are trying to do is bring their loved ones' killers to justice in the hope that it will remove just some of the heavy burden they carry, that they might be able to start the process of working through an immense amount of pain and find a way to move forward with their lives. In my experience, most families just want to see justice done. They want the people responsible to be held accountable so that these perpetrators won't be able to do to another what was done to their loved ones.

Sometimes that is their sole focus and, understandably, they become obsessed with seeing justice done. It's as if they are emotionally paralyzed and they feel that, if they can just see the killer put away, then they will be able to get out of that state of paralysis and move on, that a switch will somehow be flipped, and all will be better. We hear the word closure a lot. People sometimes say things like, "If the killer is brought to justice, the family will get closure and the weight will be lifted." Unfortunately, that's not typically the way it works. For families and loved ones, seeing justice done is often just the beginning of the long, arduous process it takes to work through an unimaginable emotional toll.

As law enforcement, it's satisfying when we can help solve a crime and lift the part of the burden that comes with wanting justice to be served, but it is also very humbling when you realize that, while your part is grueling and sometimes very public, it is also just one step in what will be a seemingly infinite series of steps in a very long journey for those families and loved ones. During my career, I worked several cases that taught me this lesson. But it was a realization I had in the hallway of a North Carolina courtroom when I was a young FBI Profiler that sticks with me the most.

I had been asked to testify in two separate homicide cases in which the killer took it upon himself to prey on mildly learning-disabled young women in their early twenties. In both cases, he met the girls at a dance club and befriended them before taking them for a ride to a secluded area where he brutally raped, tortured, and murdered each of them. To this day, they are among the saddest and most harrowing murders I have ever seen.

Because the murders took place in separate counties, each county's district attorney requested FBI assistance in an effort to link the two cases to the same offender. They were sure that both homicides were committed by the same perpetrator, but because the crimes were committed in separate jurisdictions, prosecutors needed an independent investigator to corroborate the physical evidence and tie them together with an additional type of evidence—behavioral evidence.

At the time the call first came in, there were only a dozen of us working in the FBI's Behavioral Science Unit, and I happened to be in the office when the call came in. It had been a little over a year after being promoted as a criminal profiler in the Investigative Support Unit (now referred to as the BAU). I was finishing out the week on Friday afternoon and happened to be the only profiler in the office at the time.

Wynn Norman, a ViCAP (Violent Criminal Apprehension Program) major case specialist, dropped by my office and advised me that a prosecuting attorney from North Carolina wanted to speak with a profiler regarding the possibility of linking two homicides to one offender. Wynn joined the FBI after retiring as a veteran homicide detective for the Washington Metropolitan Police Department. He shared that, from the brief discussion he had with the prosecutor, he did not see any linkage based upon the four traditional forms of evidence (confession, eyewitness testimony, forensics, and circumstantial).

Then he said to me in jest, with a smirk, "Maybe you can find a behavioral link. You're the profiler."

Ironically, I didn't actually think I would be the one doing the final analysis, much less giving testimony.

As it turned out, the profiler who was assigned to cases in North Carolina was out of the country on an assignment, so I called the prosecutor and, after a discussion about the case, I felt that the two cases were linkable from a behavioral perspective. I assumed that when the other agent returned to the office, I would be able to brief him on the case and that he could take it from there.

On Monday I met with my unit chief, John Douglas, to brief him on the situation. I thought that would be the end of my involvement.

To my surprise, John asked me, "Did you give your opinion to the district attorney?"

When I told him that I did, he asked, "What was your opinion?"

"I told him that I thought the cases were linkable," I answered.

"So you told him that you believed that the cases were linkable and now the DA has an expectation that he can use your testimony to link these two cases behaviorally as an expert witness," he said. "Well guess what? This is your case now!"

I was shocked.

In addition to realizing the weighty scope of the task ahead, I was beginning to feel the immense weight of responsibility descending upon me—not only for my personal career, but also for the reputation of the FBI. At that point I tried to convince him with every reason in the book why I shouldn't be the one to proceed with this case.

"Well, you are the one with the big mouth who has raised the DA's expectations!" he joked. Then, to reassure me, he told me that he agreed with my analysis and that I was more than capable of shouldering the responsibility.

"You're going to be just fine," he said.

If John's name sounds familiar to you, it's because John would famously go onto become known as "The Mindhunter." Essentially, he was the man who pioneered criminal profiling as we know it today and wrote the manual that the FBI and so many law enforcement investigators around the world use to investigate violent crimes. After his retirement, he wrote a *New York Times* bestseller by the same title as his nickname, and he and his work have inspired movies and TV shows, such as the Academy Award–winning movie, *Silence of the Lambs*, the recent Netflix series *Mindhunter*, and the long-running television series, *Criminal Minds*.

I respect and admire John's success. He definitely deserves it. But, most important to me is his mentorship and the friendship we continue to share to this day. In fact, John served as the original chairman of the board for the Cold Case Foundation and currently serves as chair emeritus. I will always be grateful to John for the many things I learned from him and the encouragement he has given me throughout the many different stages of my career. Of all the great many lessons I learned from John, none were more impactful than what I learned the day I met with him to talk about how I was approaching these cases. As a young profiler, his confidence in my ability to come through meant the world to me and I was eager to get to work.

The first thing I did was a thorough study of both of the victims—the victimology, if you will. I looked through each of their lives and what I found were two very kind, innocent young ladies who were just out having a good time with friends. Donna Hansen and Denise James were enjoying the social side of young adulthood. Each had had a difficult time socially during their youth, but now in young adulthood, they were beginning to develop social lives. They each had befriended some ladies at their respective places of work and would occasionally go out on the weekend to a local club. Both of them lived in very safe communities and were from solid, loving families. Neither of them had been involved with anything that would even remotely be considered troublesome. It quickly became apparent to me that neither were living what we would consider high-risk lifestyles. There was nothing to suggest that their day-to-day activities put them in harm's way. In my experience, if someone who lives a lifestyle of this nature becomes a victim of such a personally ferocious attack, that typically means that they unexpectedly found themselves in a high-risk situation. And, after studying all the evidence, I was convinced that was the case here.

Having all the background on their lives, I began to visualize the events that led up to their murders from their respective points of view—what their lives were like, how they saw the world, and what they were anticipating that day. I started with Donna Hansen. I pored through all the files about her and was ready to find a quiet space where I could turn off the lights, close my eyes, and put myself in her place. I wanted to vicariously experience what her life was like and especially what she experienced throughout that last day and through the night up to the point when that horrible crime was committed against her. I began by visualizing an excited young lady getting ready to go out with her friends.

"Do you think this outfit looks cute, Mama?" I could see her asking in my mind's eye.

"Yes, you look wonderful in that skirt," her mother replied. "It matches your purse perfectly and brings out your beautiful eyes."

"You really think so?" Donna asked coyly, knowing her mom would give her the validation she was looking for.

"Of course!" she responded, knowing her daughter could use all the validation she could get.

Socially, she had had some challenges growing up, and some of her classmates could be very cruel about her speech delays. But she could always count on her family for support and, now that she had entered her young adult years, she had found a better life and a much kinder group of friends from the office. At first, Donna's parents showed concern about her newfound social life, but seeing a bounce in their daughter's step offset any worries they had. Besides, she had gone out with these ladies a few times before, and things had always turned out fine.

With a few more encouraging words, Donna's mother sent her on her way, grateful that she was now associating with people who cared about her daughter and were kind enough to include her. It was good to see that she had found a place she felt welcomed.

"I'll be back at eleven," the young lady told her parents as she walked out the door that night.

"Okay, sweetheart," said her mother. "Have a nice time."

"It's good to see her happy, isn't it?" her father said.

"It sure is a far cry from high school," she replied. "The girls there could be so mean to her. I'm so grateful for those people she works with. They've really taken her under their wing and included her."

The story was very similar with Denise James's situation. She too had a slight speech impediment but had found some sanctuary in her friendships at work. In many ways, it was uncanny how similar these two young ladies were.

The victimology indicated that, if the person who took their lives was indeed the same killer, it was certainly not by chance. Though they lived several miles apart in separate counties, they lived close enough to each other that it was feasible that the same perpetrator could have crossed paths with both young ladies at the same club. It was also likely that he was looking for a certain type of individual that he could easily dominate.

That's when I began to take a deeper dive into the crimes themselves. I was looking for a signature behavior that would show whether these murders were indeed committed by the same person. In the FBI, we use the term *signature*, which is consistent, unique ritualistic behavior that some violent serial criminals display when committing crimes.

Signature behavior can be anything from the unique manner in which killers murder their victims. This can include their methods of control, disposal, and how they display the victim's bodies afterward. These behaviors can be manifest separately or in multiple combinations. Either way, whatever the specific behavior is, it typically leaves behind some clue about who that individual is psychologically. It is literally their behavioral signature.

As I studied the details of these murders, I wanted to gain an intimate knowledge of who this person was and what made him tick. What I sensed was a predator who was on the hunt for just this type of young lady. He was looking for someone he could easily dominate, manipulate, and control both physically and psychologically. He was in pursuit of a victim who would be vulnerable to his charms and feigned interests. She would be trusting and responsive, someone he could lure into his trap wherever he wanted—and with minimal resistance.

I could also visualize the killer the day of the murder. I could see him smugly looking at himself in the mirror. "Tonight's my night," I could visualize him arrogantly saying aloud to himself.

As I reviewed the evidence and photos of the crimes, I could see that this guy was a sexual sadist who was seeking absolute power, domination, and control over his victims. He was looking to achieve gratification from inflicting pain and suffering on his victims and seeing in their eyes the terrifying acknowledgment of his utter control over their destiny.

This was manifest in the way in which he committed his crime while torturously inflicting physical and sexual injuries. In the cases of both Donna and Denise, their bodies were brutally bludgeoned, and they had been strangled. This type of rapist is classified as an "anger excitation rapist," who achieves power and gratification over his victims through committing a sexual homicide. His strategy would have included preselecting the who, what, when, where, and how to successfully execute his crime.

The more I studied the crime, the more evident it became that he hadn't targeted a specific person as his victim. However, he was keenly aware of the vulnerable personality *type* he was seeking—naive, unaware, and easily dominated. Before he left for his night out, he would have practiced his approach and would have been comfortable in his selected environment for the hunt.

Most important, this type of offender would have fantasized about what he would do and the methods he would use to possess his victims. His ultimate satisfaction would be achieved by inflicting the greatest physical and psychological suffering through torture, rape, and murder. In his mind, victims were objects, holding no value; they were merely a necessity in the fulfillment of his fantasy.

He would disarm his victims by his approach and attention. The young ladies most likely never felt intimidated, alarmed, or threatened. In fact, they probably looked upon him as a gentleman who would safely escort them home. But, once alone in a pre-determined location, he would transform from the kind and benevolent Dr. Jekyll to the ferocious Mr. Hyde. Unfortunately for Donna Hansen and Denise James, this is who they unsuspectingly came across on the last nights of their lives.

As bad as the details of these crimes are, the thing that makes this kind of offender most dangerous to society is the lust to repeat the crime again and again on other unsuspecting victims. While this type of sexual sadist often goes through a period of post-offense repose, basking in his success and reflecting on and reliving each aspect of the crime, as the psychological high begins to wane, he begins making plans to repeat the process.

As I continued to look at photos of the crime scenes and dug into every gruesome detail, I could envision what had happened in both of these cases, from the planning stages to their initial meeting and progressing through the commission of the crime and its aftermath. I had to look at these crimes from all angles, from the perspectives of both the killer and the victims. And for me, this has always been the most difficult part.

The visualization process takes so much out of me emotionally, mentally, and even physically. But it has to be done. As a criminal profiler, I need to focus on this key element of analyzing violent crimes.

From a behavioral perspective, you have to get to know both victim and assailant on the most intimate psychological levels. That means you do everything you possibly can to walk in their footsteps, which is what I did in this case.

I had begun that process by retracing the steps of the first victim, Donna Hansen. I could visualize her anticipation for a fun night out on the town. I could feel her giddy excitement.

On the opposite end of the spectrum, I could also feel the killer's anticipation of the hunt and initial thrilling encounter with his prey. I could visualize him locking in on a potential target, experiencing an elevated level of focus and excitement as the stalking began. Each calculated move set the stage for the predator's succeeding acts, culminating in the victim's suffering and death. This was his MO with both Donna Hansen and Denise James.

I closed my eyes one last time, leaned back in my office chair and turned my attention to visualizing the crime itself—from the moment the paths of the perpetrator and victims crossed to the horrific crime itself. At the club, I could visualize Donna and her coworkers having a great time.

"You're quite a dancer, Donna," said one of her friends as they headed back to their table. "Where did you learn to dance so well?"

"I don't know," the embarrassed young lady said. "I like to watch dance shows on TV and dance along to them in my room."

"Well, you must have watched a lot of those shows," her friend gushed. "Because I'm not the only one who noticed your moves. Look over there. I think that guy is checking you out."

"No, he's not looking at me. He's looking at you," Donna said coyly.

"I don't think so. In fact, don't look now, but I think he's making his way over here as we speak."

"Hello," said the young man to Donna. "Mind if I buy you a drink?"

"Uh, yeah, I guess. Sure."

"What's your name?"

"D-Donna," she stuttered, taken aback. "But my friends call me Dawn."

"Ask him his name," Donna's friend whispered in her ear.

"Oh, yeah," she said, giggling. "What's your name?"

"Kenneth," he said. "I'll tell you what. Why don't we grab a dance or two first, then we'll get that drink. What do you say?"

"Sure," she said, and off they went to the dance floor. The surprised young lady looked back at her coworkers, who were waving her on to go have a good time with the young man.

"So, what do you do?" he asked her as they danced.

"I'm a receptionist for a real estate agency," she answered. "How about you?"

"Oh, I'm in business for myself," he said. "I do mostly consulting work for general contractors."

As the night wore on, Donna's friends could tell she was enjoying herself, but it was time to go.

"Should we grab Dawn and give her a ride home?" one coworker asked.

"I don't know if she wants to be grabbed," giggled another. "At least not by us."

The group of young ladies howled with laughter.

"Well, let's at least let her know we're going."

"Okay, I'll go tell her."

"Hey, Donna," the young lady interrupted as the couple danced, "we're going now. Do you want to come, or will you be okay?"

"I'll give her a lift home," Kenneth quickly interjected as Donna nodded in approval.

"Okay. Have a good time. We'll see you at work."

With that, the group—minus Donna—headed home.

The young lady, meanwhile, was having the time of her life. Finally, she thought, a relatively good-looking young man had taken an interest in her and wanted to get to know her. Not only that, but he had also singled her out from among dozens of other women at the club. She couldn't believe it. Here she was dancing with someone who thought she was fun and interesting. After all those cruel years during adolescence when she didn't feel like she had a prayer in the world of getting this kind of attention, now someone found her interesting enough to talk to. And it wasn't just anyone. It was a handsome man with an irresistible smile. At that moment, she felt like she was living a dream.

Unfortunately, that night would soon turn into an unimaginable nightmare.

"Hey," Kenneth called to Donna over the loud music. "Why don't we get out of here and go someplace where we can talk without all this noise?"

"Okay," she hollered back.

Soon, they would be in his car, driving down the moonlit highway. Donna was on cloud nine. Had she finally broken out of her shell? She couldn't wait to tell her mom and dad about her magical night.

Suddenly, Kenneth abruptly pulled onto a dirt road and parked the car behind a row of tall bushes. In an instant, the young man's friendly smile disappeared, replaced by a monstrous look.

"Get out of the car," he demanded. "We're going for a walk."

"Huh?" she said, startled. "Why? What's wrong?"

"I said, get out!" he shouted as he reached across her lap, opened the door, and shoved her out of the vehicle.

She tried to get up and run, but he rushed around the car and grabbed her.

"Where the hell do you think you're going?" he barked, squeezing her arms.

"Ouch! Stop, you're hurting me."

"Oh, am I hurting you?" he queried sarcastically. "Then how does this feel?"

With that, he shattered her nose with a single punch to the face.

"Did that hurt, too?" he mocked.

All Donna could do was sob, and the more she sobbed, the more he hit and tore at her.

"What are you crying about?" he continued. "Oh, I know. I must not be the nice guy you thought I was. Is that it? I thought you wanted a good time. Well, let me show you what a good time is."

He ripped her skirt off her body. Then, he tore her panties, blouse, and bra off, taking chunks of skin with them. Then, he beat her some more.

"Why are you doing this to me?" she cried.

"Why?" he screamed at her. "Because you're disgusting, that's why!"

Then he kicked her repeatedly between the legs. All Donna could do was tremble and try to control the sobbing that seemed to draw more of his ire. At this point, she could only hope to get out of this alive.

"Why is this happening to me?" she thought. "Why is he being so mean? I didn't do anything to him. I should have gone home with my friends."

"Please don't hurt me anymore," she mumbled to her attacker.

"Don't hurt you?" he mocked. "Don't hurt you? You should be thanking me. You're finally gonna get laid."

He knelt on top of the terrified girl then wrapped his hands around her throat before repeatedly slamming her head against the ground until he had strangled the life out of her. Then he raped her and savagely beat her some more.

He repeated his crime three months later, following nearly the same MO with Denise James. The crime occurred in a nearby county just a few miles from where he had dumped Donna's body.

At the end of my analysis, I concluded that these individual atrocities were committed by the same killer, who was most definitely a depraved sexual sadist. It was sickeningly uncanny how similar the circumstances between the two murders and victims were.

With the instinctive skill of a wild predator, he had hunted for and found two young women he knew would be easy prey. Within minutes of entering the club, he had identified victims he knew he could lure into his hands and have his sickly way with. But it wasn't long before the authorities caught up with this monster.

Witnesses who saw him with Donna and with Denise were able to place him at the club during the nights in question, while others had seen him drive away with each girl, including a man whose car he had borrowed to "take Denise home."

Combined with the physical and circumstantial evidence collected and, having been seen with both victims at the club, Kenneth Dean Malstrom was identified as a suspect and subsequently arrested for both murders.

But, in order to link both crimes to Malstrom, prosecutors needed to introduce behavioral evidence to tie them together, and that's why they contacted our unit at the FBI. Even though the homicides took place so close to one another, they were committed in separate counties, and in a prosecutor's world, jurisdiction is everything. That meant that they would have to find a way to connect the homicides in order to try Malstrom as a serial killer instead of trying the cases individually. Without the ability to link Donna's case to Denise's, the evidence that the state could present against Malstrom wouldn't be as strong as they wanted it to be. That could mean reduced sentences, and no one wanted to see this guy walk—ever.

That's where I came in.

It took weeks to put together all the pieces in a way that I would be able to testify effectively and clearly enough for the jury to easily understand why signature was so important and how it pointed to Malstrom. I had to be extremely detailed but testify in a way that wouldn't lose the jury in so much scientific minutiae. Missing even one tiny piece of the puzzle could lead to this man's acquittal, and I wanted no part of that. A mistake that resulted in anything other than a conviction was something that I did not want to have to live with.

Working on this case was both exhausting and heartbreaking. As the weeks wore on, I began to grow more and more tense, and the stress was beginning to get to me. In addition to this being a harrowing murder case, it was also another potential landmark case for the FBI in that it was only the second time that the FBI Investigative Support Unit, as it was called at the time, was called upon to provide expert witness testimony identifying signature criminal behavior in an effort to link cases from a behavioral perspective in open court, so it was almost unprecedented.

John Douglas was the only other agent who had done so—in the George Russel case in Renton, Washington. My career as a young profiler and the reputation of our unit would be heavily scrutinized through both of these trials, and I was feeling the weight of it.

Feeling the pressure, I decided I would call John from my hotel room in North Carolina the night before I was to appear in court to discuss my approach to these cases. He could sense the mounting pressure, and he graciously allowed me to once again walk through the key points of my anticipated testimony. I was expecting to get a play-by-play discourse on exactly how to testify about signature, what to say, and how to say it. After all, since I was only the second FBI profiler to ever testify in this manner, it would only make sense to get the playbook from the only other person on the planet to have done it successfully.

With that, I dialed John's number and got ready to hang on his every word and write verbatim each and every point he made. Much to my surprise, however, instead of the detailed analysis I expected, I got a five-minute lecture on not making more of this than it really was.

"Relax," he said in a calming tone of voice.

We were hundreds of miles away from each other, but John's encouragement made it feel as if he were right there in the room with me. I could almost visualize him casually leaning back in his chair sporting that signature half grin of his. "Greg, you teach in the FBI Academy. This isn't anything you haven't done before. You're just teaching the judge and jury about the behavioral principles of criminal profiling and the specific application to this case. So, just go in there and teach. You do that and all the other stuff will take care of itself. You got this!"

With that, he gave me a few more words of encouragement before sending me on my way and wishing me a good night's sleep. John has always known just the right buttons to push.

A few hours later, I was standing in the hall of that North Carolina courthouse when Aaron Simpson, the prosecuting attorney, approached me and introduced me to the parents of Malstrom's first victim, Donna Hansen.

"Greg, it's good to see you," Simpson greeted me with a slight southern drawl. "I want to introduce you to some folks. This is Mark and Deanna Hansen. They are Donna's parents. Mr. and Mrs. Hansen, this is Special Agent Greg Cooper. He will be testifying today as an expert witness in Donna's case."

"Pleased to meet you," I said as I shook each of their hands. "I am so sorry for your loss."

It was the only thing I could think of to say in that situation. I think it's the only thing anyone can ever think of to say because what other words are there?

"It's a pleasure to meet you, Mr. Cooper," they each responded. "Thank you so much for all you are doing on behalf of our Donna. We can't thank you enough for all the time you have taken on her behalf."

In that moment, I was so moved by how gracious, kind, and sincere they were that I really didn't know how to respond. Standing in front of me were these sweet parents who had lost their innocent young daughter in one of the most horrific ways imaginable and all they could focus on was their gratitude for me taking my time to help their family. Essentially, it felt like they were going out of their way to thank me for simply doing my job.

I was so blown away to the point of almost being speechless that I simply said, "I am going to do everything I can to get justice for your daughter."

They looked at me and graciously said, "We know you will. We will be praying for you, Mr. Cooper. Thank you."

Every time I look back on this experience, I am amazed at the simplicity of such a life-changing event. There really weren't any profound words uttered during this exchange, nor was it a long conversation, but for me, this specific scene in my life is burned into my memory because it was one of those moments in time when life teaches you a poignant lesson. But the lesson didn't come in their words as much as it did in their collective demeanor, in the expressions on their faces, and in their kind-mannered behavior toward me.

There was something about those expressions that quietly said, "We are hoping to get justice for our daughter. We have faith in you, and we are so truly grateful that you have put your heart and soul into doing this for us. But, even if this man goes to prison for life, it will never bring our sweet little girl back, and we will have to somehow find a way to pick up the pieces and live with that forever."

That's when I realized that I was never going to be the hero in any victim's family's story. I could never bring a loved one back to them or anyone else. The best I could ever do would be to help open a door for them and hope they had the strength to walk through it—one foot in front of the other. By so doing, maybe these people would be able to find a little peace.

In that moment, I was keenly sensitive to all the hours and hours of work invested in this case by all of us in the law enforcement community. Imagine a symphony orchestra ready to step onto the stage for their performance. All the preparation, planning, and rehearsing has been completed. Now the time has arrived for each of the musicians to take their place in the orchestra pit and the conductor raises his baton to begin the concert. In this case the DA was the conductor, and each expert witness would take their turn presenting their solo testimony. With a cue from the DA, I would be called upon like the first chair violinist to tie all the behaviors together.

A few minutes later, I prepared myself to testify on the stand and do what I promised these sweet parents that I would do—my job. If it meant that my role was to play a small part in helping this good family find their way forward after this tragedy, then that's what I was going to do. And I was going to give everything I had to them over the course of my time in that courtroom that day.

With that, I took the stand, immediately fixed my gaze on the defendant and never looked away. I was not going to let this family down and I was determined to make sure that everyone in the courtroom knew it—especially the man responsible for creating this senseless pain, Kenneth Dean Malstrom.

After Deputy District Attorney Simpson began with a few preliminary questions, he then moved on to queries that led to my investigation of the crime.

"Mr. Cooper," he began, "by whom are you employed?"

"The Federal Bureau of Investigation," I stated.

"In what capacity, sir?"

"I am a criminal investigative analyst assigned to the National Center for the Analysis of Violent Crime at Quantico, Virginia, at the FBI Academy," I answered.

"And as an agent in the Investigative Support Unit, can you tell the court what some of your duties are there?"

"We provide consultation services for any legitimate law enforcement agency internationally. Specifically, with regard to repetitive violent crimes, we provide any type of services from investigative techniques, prosecution strategy, interrogation techniques, and the analysis of the crime to identify particular personality characteristics of an unknown offender."

"What does that entail?"

"When we analyze a crime, we request specific information on the crime to assist us in re-creating that crime so that we can vicariously experience being both the victim and the offender," I explained. "The procedure involves the basic following process: We will request initial police reports of the crimes and investigative reports, including the crime scene photographs, the autopsy photographs, and forensic medical examiner's reports. In addition, we'll request, at times, maps to identify the locations of the crime scene, the abduction, or the initial contact site, as well as the disposal site."

"And what are you hoping to determine from that analysis?"

"What we attempt to determine," I responded, now staring straight at Malstrom in an attempt to gauge his response, "are specific behavioral characteristics that we see at a crime scene to assist us in interpreting the personality characteristics of an unknown offender. It's one of the services we provide."

As I continued speaking, I could see that Malstrom was growing a little uneasy, but he still had an air of smugness about him. I was determined to systematically remove his mask and expose his true identity.

"In addition to that," I continued, "we attempt to identify common characteristics between crimes to assist agencies in identifying whether or not there may be a serial offender in the community, identifying unique characteristics of a crime scene to determine whether or not they suggest that the same person may have committed those crimes."

Over the next several minutes, Simpson asked me about the criminal profiling procedure. I could tell that Malstrom was interested, but he didn't seem overly concerned about my testimony, at least not until Simpson began asking me about the victims.

"Did you study the victimology of Donna Hansen and Denise James?"

"Yes, I did," I answered.

"Would you tell the court what you found?"

"Yes," I replied. "Both the victims were very small in stature. Both also possessed birth defects affecting their speech patterns, and both received medical treatment previously in their lifetime for that particular condition. They also were both living at home in a somewhat dependent relationship with their parents."

As I continued talking about the lives of these young ladies, I could almost see a smirk forming across Malstrom's lips. He obviously had no remorse for what he had done, and I wanted to wipe that underlying smirk right off his face. But I knew I had a job to do, and I couldn't let myself get caught up in my own emotion if I was going to give an effective testimony, so I calmly continued with my answer in a matter-of-fact fashion. Besides, I knew that the best way to rattle him was to expose his innermost thoughts and intentions in open court—and that is exactly what I intended to do.

"Both had no steady serious relationships in terms of a boyfriend," I continued. "Both attended the nightclub unattached, and both were considered friendly and trusting and unsuspecting. As an example, James, as I recall, was asking strangers for a ride home the evening of her disappearance. In addition, Hansen was dancing with people whom she was not known to have known before that evening."

"And what did that tell you about the victimology between the two girls?" Simpson asked.

"From the perspective of the offender, looking for a particular sort of victim he could commit this type of violent crime against," I answered, now glaring at Malstrom, "he's looking for somebody he can easily dominate, control, and manipulate—somebody who is at high risk, as far as he's concerned, when they cross his path."

As I talked about the victims, I added commentary about the offender.

I spoke about what kind of a small man would do something like this to two friendly, innocent girls. I could see beads of sweat start to form on Malstrom's forehead. His jaw began to lock, and his nostrils flared.

I was beginning to get to him.

He was taking my comments personally. If he could have jumped over the table and punched me in the face—or worse—he would have.

Everything about his demeanor during this part of my testimony told me what my analysis had already confirmed—that he was definitely the perpetrator. Why else would he take general testimony about a customized criminal profile so personally?

"The offender in a case like this is typically referred to as a predator," I continued, still staring straight into Malstrom's eyes. Now I was the one with the invisible smirk.

"Predator?" Simpson asked. "Why a predator?"

At this point, I paused for effect. I wanted to make sure Malstrom hung on my every word as I dissected him psychologically. Nothing elevates the stress level of a serial killer more than being told exactly what he was thinking as he planned and carried out his crimes. Serial killers are notorious for their arrogance in this regard.

"Because he's out stalking, looking for somebody, for a victim that fits his particular profile. He wants someone who will reduce his risk of identification yet enhance the exposure to his crimes. Basically, he wants to make news, but he wants to remain anonymous, mysterious if you will. He doesn't want to get caught. And he gains satisfaction from the illusion that he has control over an entire community."

As I was speaking, I noticed Malstrom becoming increasingly uncomfortable in his chair. I knew it was time to turn up the heat, and my goal was to shatter his self-image, to utterly destroy the world he had created for himself.

Simpson's next question opened the door for me to do just that.

"In addition to identifying the person the offender is looking for, how does the victimology affect the individual victim?"

"From our perspective, the victim is trusting, unsuspecting. There is no reason for her to believe she is exposing herself to any particular kind of risk," I said before pecking away at Malstrom's self-image.

"Typically, the offender in these types of cases will use what is referred to as the 'con approach,' meaning he will appear to be very innocent. He will use the ruse that he wants to help the victim, which helps him manipulate her into his own environment where he can control her."

As I dissected Malstrom's cowardly strategy, I could see that I was destroying his self-image. In his mind, he was an ingenious giant. In the dark agricultural fields of North Carolina, he could dominate two helpless young ladies.

But in open court? He didn't stand a chance.

He could only sit and listen as I laid out—and professionally belittled—what he thought was a clever plan.

In court, he had power only to sit—sit and listen to the truth, which was simply that he was nothing more than a cowardly bully. With each piece of testimony I gave, his self-image was imploding for all to see—and it was eating him up inside. Every word I uttered cut out another piece of his twisted illusion. He was no genius outsmarting the law. He was merely a psychopathic bully who preyed on the helpless.

I concluded my testimony by hammering the final nail in his coffin. My last answers explained how a predatory criminal garners all his self-esteem from thinking he can destroy lives and terrify a community while never being held accountable for it, how he views himself as a puppet master—an unknown entity who controls an entire community at the push of a button.

"But in reality," I testified, "he is just a small man who has accomplished nothing of any consequence in his life and therefore has to resort to taking the lives of innocent people. And most often, he is so inept that the only people he can prey upon are those members of the community who have the least ability to defend themselves—in this case, two petite, naive, trusting young women who had overcome childhood speech impediments finding themselves vulnerable in the presence of a sexual sadist."

By the time I concluded my testimony, Malstrom was red-faced, and beads of sweat poured down his brow. He wanted so badly to hop over the table and come after me.

Of course, he never would have. Even if there had been no armed guards in the courtroom, he wouldn't have. He didn't have enough depth of character to ever go after someone out in the open, face-to-face. That's why he committed his crimes in such a cowardly way.

In fact, my testimony shook him so much that the guards who ushered him to and from court told me that when he saw me several months later at his trial for the second homicide of Denise James, he said, "That's the SOB who's gonna try and get me for this one, too!"

As it turned out, we did get him.

The physical evidence, combined with the behavioral evidence during the commission of the first crime resulted in the first conviction. The behavioral evidence during the commission of the second crime, combined with the circumstantial evidence linking Malstrom to the victim, enabled prosecutors to obtain a conviction in the second case. Not only did I give my all to Donna's family that day, and to Denise's family a few months later, but I have given everything I've had to every victim's family I worked on behalf of during my entire career—and beyond, as it has turned out.

And I'm not the only one.

So many put in so much effort on behalf of Donna, Denise, and their loved ones. None more than the investigating officers. Detective Craig Thompson, who was the lead detective on Donna Hansen's case, did a stellar job with that murder investigation. He left no stone unturned and, largely because of his painstaking efforts in collecting every detailed shred of evidence, prosecutors were able to make a case for linking Malstrom to both homicides from both a physical evidence perspective as well as the behavioral aspects of the crimes. In fact, if it hadn't been for the work of both counties' homicide investigators, my job in identifying signature behavior in these murders would have been far more difficult.

Just as important—and probably even more so—was the way in which these detectives treated the families of these victims. They were kind and sensitive to the families while still conducting the investigation in a professional and thorough manner.

Being the lead detective at the scene of Donna Hansen's murder, Thompson told me about his first visit to the Hansen family residence. The family knew what had happened and had already been to the morgue to identify the body. After Craig pulled up to the front of the family's quaint North Carolina house, he spent the next few minutes sitting in his car trying to compose himself. "I've got to keep it together," he reminded himself while trying to repress the fresh images in his mind of the deceased young lady. "Can't let emotions get the best of me. I've got to be strong for this family." As he took a few deep breaths and looked around the neighborhood, he couldn't help but marvel at the setting. The small four-bedroom home in this suburban southern community was a scene straight out of Mayberry from the old Andy Griffith show. Gazing at the front yard with its perfectly manicured lawn, shade trees, and pristine flower beds, he couldn't help but think what a wonderful place this would have been to grow up. Every home in the neighborhood seemed to bring such calm to the soul that he envied anyone who spent their childhood in such a calm, peaceful setting. Not only was it picturesque, but everything about it felt so safe.

That made the task of getting out of his car and knocking on this family's door that much harder. He couldn't help but think that he was going to be yet another disruption to the calm lives these people once lived. With a simple tap on the beautiful oak wood door, he was going to be yet another reminder of the horrors this family had been confronting over the past couple of days.

After saying a short prayer to himself, he slowly exited his police-issued vehicle and dragged himself up their walkway and to the front door. He told me how he stood at the door and looked back longingly at the walkway, which was beautifully landscaped with an array of brightly colored flowers and shrubs adorning each side of its path. In that moment, he said he wished he could have just turned around and walked right back to his car, pretending none of this had ever happened.

I knew exactly how he felt, having been there many times myself. You say to yourself, "Maybe this is just a bad dream. Maybe this didn't really happen, and I won't have to bother this family after all." But then you steady yourself, get your mind straight, and prepare yourself to do your job. Because if you don't talk to this family, who's going to?

And that is just what Craig did. He gathered himself for a moment, took his hand out of his pocket, and gave three taps with their decorative door knocker.

A pleasant middle-aged woman answered the door and greeted him warmly.

"Hello," she said somewhat hesitantly. "Can I help you?"

"Yes, um, I'm Detective Thompson," he answered. "I spoke to your husband on the phone yesterday and made arrangements to come by and meet with you today. Did he get a chance to talk to you about that and let you know I was coming?"

He pulled his badge out of his pocket to show her he was legitimate, and she politely acknowledged it.

But she didn't need to see it. She had already met with so many law enforcement officials since her daughter's murder, and she unfortunately knew all too well how this worked. Despite that, her demeanor remained pleasant and polite, though her expression a little more hollow now that she realized who he was and what he was there for.

"Yes, my husband did tell me you were coming. Please come in, Mr. Thompson."

With that, Craig asked a variety of questions, most of them intended to obtain background information on Donna to determine whether her killer had known her previous to the murder. Or, at the very least, maybe he had come in contact with her in some way before the night she was killed. The meeting lasted about an hour, and throughout the entire time, Craig had a difficult time keeping his mind off the pain these people were going through. He maintained his professionalism and he asked all the necessary questions, but with each one, he felt the heartache emanating from their answers.

The parents tried to keep their emotions in check, but that was an impossibility. They remained polite, but it was clear that they were just trying to make sense of it all. How are you supposed to respond when a police detective sits in your living room and asks you background questions about the daughter you just learned was brutally raped and murdered? Each question and subsequent answer evoked new waves of emotion for Donna's parents. And for Detective Craig Thompson, as well.

When Craig had completed the interview, he thanked the couple for their time before once again expressing his condolences for what seemed to him like the thousandth time. Much like my experience in the halls of the courtroom the day I testified on behalf of Donna, Craig was at a loss for what to say to them. That's because there is nothing you can say. All you can do is try to do your job and do your best to bring the perpetrator of that horrible crime to justice.

In the case of Kenneth Dean Malstrom, we were successful in linking the murders together through behavioral signature, for the second time in judicial history.

Malstrom was convicted for both crimes and received the maximum penalty under North Carolina law—the death sentence.

For my part, I was told I would be notified when a date was set for that penalty to be carried out and that I would be invited to witness his execution. But that day never came. After several years in prison, Malstrom died of stomach cancer.

Maybe that was nature's way of serving justice. Some may believe that's the case. But, if I'm being truthful, after seeing all the terror he imposed on those innocent young ladies and the subsequent suffering on their families, I was prepared to see this case through to its legal conclusion. I don't know if that's right or wrong, but at the very least, it's human. I truly cared about those young ladies. My heart ached for them and for their loved ones. I guess I just wanted to tangibly see justice carried out in some form.

In terms of how bringing a killer to justice helps those left behind, it's different for every family and for every loved one. It doesn't bring any of the victims back, but in talking to so many families and loved ones, I have found that, on some level, it does bring some sense of peace knowing that your loved one's assailant won't be able to inflict that kind of pain on anyone else.

And, at the very least, it does remove a major obstacle that stands in the way of a family's ability to deal with the loss and find some way to try and heal.

At this point, you might be asking yourself why a case that resulted in a death penalty conviction would be the one I would identify as the case that haunts me among all the violent criminal cases I've worked during my career. Why would a successful conviction be the one that stands out instead of the ones that I wasn't able to solve?

I've asked myself that very question a number of times, and I've come to this conclusion: Getting justice for a family, for loved ones, and for a community is a fragile thing. All the work that goes into it from following the leads to finding the perpetrator to gathering enough evidence to make an arrest and assuring that you have arrested the right person to working with prosecutors to satisfy their burden of proof enough that it will convince a jury to convict and sentence the guilty party beyond appeal is extremely fragile in a system where we are innocent until proven guilty. And it should be fragile when the justice system is founded on citizens being innocent until proven guilty.

But, when you add to this list that innocent people still get convicted— even have been sentenced to the death penalty on occasion—then that compounds the fragility of the entire legal system and investigative process.

In the case of Donna Hansen and Denise James, it's overwhelming to think that one missed detail could have set a murderer free to kill again. I'm grateful that it didn't, but I think the reason that this case stands out to me as the one that drove me to create the Cold Case Foundation is because, when I think that 40 percent of homicide cases have gone unsolved without a conviction—several of those cases of which I've personally worked—I feel that, as a society, we should be more demanding in our desire to put more resources toward solving these cases and bringing these perpetrators to justice on behalf of these families.

I feel that we can do more. That we must do more. That's the reason, deep down, that I created the Cold Case Foundation. The families and loved ones of these victims need us to do better. They deserve better.

And to me, that is the most haunting thing of all.

CHAPTER THREE

A TIMELESS PROCESS

The man in royal robes walked quietly into the room, each step creeping closer to his unsuspecting victim, who sat slouched in a chair sobbing. His father had just passed away, but his cries were split equally between the sadness of losing his father and the intense burden he was about to bear as a nine-year-old boy.

To be sure, the weight that pressed upon his shoulders would be a heavy cross to bear for anyone of any age. But a boy? Where would he even begin? What was he even supposed to do and, most importantly, who could he turn to for help?

In his hour of need, he was completely unaware of the squinty-eyed middle-aged man approaching slowly from behind, stalking the young royal with every deliberate step he took, taking time to ensure that his apparel fit the royal status of prime minister, a title that he had borne for so many years. His pace was that of a lion, assuring that his prey had no idea he was being hunted, all the while maintaining his status as supreme hunter.

The prime minister's breathing slow and his pace even slower, he tugged on his royal robes in between steps, making sure they were precisely even on both sides. Just a few more steps and he could make his move. He reached his arms out toward the boy from behind and placed his hands firmly on the boy's shoulders.

"Tutankhamun," he said in a soft voice, feigning a sympathetic tone, "it is a heavy weight that you bear. How are you holding up?"

The boy, who, 3,300 years later, would famously come to be known as King Tut, startled and quickly pivoted in his chair. Wiping tears from his eyes, the youngling uttered the words the prime minister had hoped to hear.

"Prime Minister Ay," he offered between sniffles, "I don't know what to do. I need help."

There it was! The hunter was luring the prey into his snare in anticipation that the Kingdom would someday be his.

"There, there," said Ay, patting the boy gently on his shoulder. "I know this is a difficult time, but you won't have to go through it alone. You have family around you of royal blood, one of whom you will take to be your wife. And your father surrounded himself with good leadership and very capable people. A sound treasurer in Maya and a powerful general in Horemheb, who will do everything to protect you and this nation."

The tears slowly began to dissipate, and Ay could see that he had the boy's attention. As he had hoped, the prime minister had the exclusive audience he had planned for with the young Tutankhamun now hanging on his every word.

"You are the pharaoh now, and that is a lot for anyone," Ay continued. "But I have faith in you. And you have my support. I will always be there for you—just as I was for your father."

Outwardly, Ay's words were true. He loyally carried out the commands of Tutankhamun's father, Akhenaten, who ruled as pharaoh for a tumultuous seventeen years before his death. During his time as king of Egypt, Akhenaten made many powerful enemies. His transfer of power was not a subtle one, to say the least. Within just a short time of taking the throne, he committed what most Egyptians saw as heresy when he declared that there was only one God and then proceeded to systematically relegate the nation's host of beloved gods to superficial status. In so doing, the pharaoh also demoted a congregation of powerful priests, who were none too happy about their power and influence summarily being stripped from them.

In a lateral move, also unpopular with the people, Akhenaten made another radical change when he relocated the capital city of Egypt from Thebes to a city he had custom-built for and named after himself, called Akhetaten. Once again, this separation from tradition rendered a bevy of influential people powerless, creating a host of enemies for the pharaoh and his family.

Privately, Prime Minister Ay disagreed vehemently with Akhenaten on many fronts. In fact, he despised the man. But his taste for power and status prevented him from ever making his opinions known to him, and instead, he lived a life of pretense reserved for those ambitious enough to patiently wait for those who stood in the way to die. And Ay would indeed do what it took so that he would be in position to be the one who would most benefit from the pharaoh's demise. When that opportunity came to return Egypt's rich heritage and beliefs to their rightful holders, Ay was determined that he would be ready.

And that day had come.

Ay now had the opportunity to effect the change so many wanted without having to get his hands dirty. There, in his midst, he had a moldable young boy in his hands that, if handled correctly, would succumb to the wishes of the prime minister and to so many former priests who once held so much power.

"And, who knows?" Ay thought to himself. "If somehow fate wills it, and the boy never has an heir to take the throne, I may one day be crowned pharaoh."

But such thoughts were so far into the future that they took the prime minister away from the task at hand. Ay was prime minister now, but the young pharaoh still had the power to choose someone else. Ay would have to be careful. He would have to entreat the boy in such a way that he would want to keep him as his entrusted advisor. And what better way to keep the boy's trust? Become a father figure to the boy. Be kind, gentle, and generous. But do not overstep. Make sure he knows he has ultimate power over every citizen in the land, including Ay himself. But, while stroking his young ego, make sure to place himself in the unique position of being the confidant, the trusted advisor he could be vulnerable with in his time of need.

What better way to start than by broaching the subject of Tutankhamun's immortality—the ultimate show of power for all pharaohs? It was one thing to be pharaoh, but Egyptian culture was so rooted in its belief in the afterlife that all that one did in life pointed to what lay in store for them after death. And, for pharaohs, their immortality would be a measure of how well they ruled their people and how much respect they showed to the gods.

As the days led up to Tutankhamun's anointing as pharaoh, Ay sought every opportunity possible to get an audience with the boy. And when he did, he never missed a chance to build the young boy's sense of power and impart some father-like advice.

"You know, the most important first act that your father initiated as pharaoh was to deploy the artisans to design his tomb," he told the young Tut. "Have you given any thought to how you want to be immortalized? To how you would want your tomb to look when you join the great ones in the afterlife?"

"I haven't thought about it much," he replied. "My father's tomb is glorious. Where did he get his inspiration for such a tomb?"

"Oh, your father was truly a visionary," Ay began. "In fact, I see a lot of you in him, but with even more potential."

"Really?" the boy responded. "I don't know if I could ever be as strong as he was."

"Strength is a trait that grows with each act you take as pharaoh," Ay counseled the soon-to-be ruler of Egypt. "But it is the attributes within a man's soul that truly make him the pharaoh he becomes. And I see so many strong qualities in you, Tutankhamun."

"What do you see?" he asked eagerly. For the first time since his father's passing, Tut felt some excitement and anticipation at the prospect of being king of Egypt.

"Oh, many things," Ay indulged. "You have a good heart, and you are open to learning the ways of our people. I see that in how you approach your studies."

"You do?"

"Oh yes," said Ay. "One of the most important duties as prime minister is to make an accounting of all of the pharaoh's most important people. And there was none more important to your father than you."

"Did he tell you that?" the boy asked.

"On many occasions," confirmed Ay. "He spoke of you fondly and he made sure that I made it a priority to ensure that you were getting the best of care. Perhaps, if you see it in your heart to find me worthy to continue on as your prime minister, I will one day watch out for your children as well."

As he finished speaking those words, Ay bowed his head in a false show of humility and deference to his new king. At the same time, he trained one eye on the boy to gauge his response.

"There is nobody else I would want in my royal circle," Tut told Ay. "You have been here for me the whole time and there is no one I trust more than you."

"Thank you, your highness," Ay said softly and with a bow of the head. "I cannot begin to express to you what that means to me to hear you say that. It is the highest honor I can think of."

With one last bow, the prime minister left the young king-in-waiting's chambers. And, for the first time, Ay allowed himself to feel confident that his plan was working to perfection. He had gotten the access to the boy he desired, and he was able to use that access to build the trust and influence he needed to have with him.

Once Tut's rule becomes official, Ay thought to himself, then we can begin the process of putting things right again. Egypt will once again be a glorious shrine to the gods.

As Ay was spending his time grooming the boy to serve his own purposes, he was also keeping company with other interested parties, namely the priests who had been put down by King Akhenaten. They met regularly enough to communicate, but not so often that they would arouse suspicion. They did not want to jeopardize their lone opportunity to reestablish their influence.

The meetings usually took place outside the capital city in an isolated location, almost always in the dark of night. Ay would update the priests on the latest developments with the incoming pharaoh and they would impatiently demand that he expedite the plan.

"The minute Tutankhamun is anointed pharaoh, changes must be made immediately," they would say. "This has gone on long enough! Why can't you just talk to him and get him to commit to moving the capital city back to Thebes and restoring the glory of the gods as they once were?"

"Gentlemen, we are talking about a whimsical young boy with the power of the gods," Ay would retort. "These things take time. They cannot be rushed."

"You say you have influence with the boy," one ex-priest would say in a tone that suggested he was challenging Ay's credibility. "He is a boy. If you are the father figure you say you are to him, then make him do as you say. You're the adult. He is the child. Surely, you can easily pressure him into doing what you say is required of him as the newly anointed pharaoh."

"Believe me when I say that I wish it were that simple, but it is not. He has the mood swings of a child and the power to dismiss me with one word. And, with the recent passing of his father, he is in a fragile state. If I don't proceed deliberately and with caution, then I risk him dismissing me. Then, what do we have? Nothing. We have no one in the pharaoh's inner circle to influence him toward our cause. I can and must be sure that he sees me as having his best interest at all times. Then, and only then, can I begin to use the power of suggestion to sway him our way."

As Ay finished making his case, one of the former head priests slowly stood and the group's murmurings quieted. This was a well-respected member of the priesthood and he had remained silent for the entire meeting until now.

"What the prime minister says is logically sound," he began. "It is true that we cannot risk our one opportunity to influence the new pharaoh. You are wise to proceed cautiously, Ay. But we need to strike a balance. He is young and is surely not fully aware of the totality of the power he wields. He is still moldable and open to suggestion. The longer you wait to assert your influence, the more he will grow into the comprehension of who he is. As time goes on, he will become less impressionable and you, Ay, will have less influence on him. Be cautious with the youngster's emotions, but also be assertive when you have the opportunity to use the power of suggestion to our advantage. Remember, he won't be a boy forever."

"I understand," Ay confirmed. "I will begin assessing the situation once he officially takes power, and I will report back to you at the soonest opportunity."

That final meeting with the former priests concluded, Ay rushed back to the palace to assist in making final preparations for the young boy's anointing.

The day came for Tutankhamun's coronation. But, as pharaoh, there was one important matter to attend to before he could officially take the throne. He was required to be married. And not only did he need to be married, but he needed to marry someone of royal blood. After some discussion among the house of royalty, it was decided that he would marry his half-sister, Ankhesenamun, who was two years his elder. At once, he became a husband and pharaoh of Egypt at the tender age of nine. The ceremony was glorious and hope filled, as a nation waited to see if its new leader would reinstitute the old ways so beloved by so many.

As the old guard hoped, one of the new pharaoh's first acts as ruler of Egypt was to officially retain Maya as national treasurer; Horemheb as general and leader over all the Egyptian armies; and, of course, Ay as prime minister.

With all the components in place, Ay sought his first opportunity to discuss some changes in policy with the new pharaoh, namely the topic of restoring the capital city of Egypt to its original home of Thebes.

But finding the best way to go about broaching the subject with the lad would be somewhat tricky. The current capital city was, after all, built and named by his father. And, although Tutankhamun and his father weren't particularly close, the boy did hold him in high regard, as most boys do their fathers regardless of their disposition or the nature of their relationship. The mere suggestion of abandoning the city of his father could cause a rift between the prime minister, who had worked ceaselessly to position himself as the boy's mentor, and the new pharaoh.

He would need to approach the boy carefully and find out just how strongly he felt tied to the city's place as capital of Egypt. On the other hand, the insecurity of childhood could be a powerful tool for Ay. The young pharaoh's need to be liked by the citizens of his kingdom might outweigh any sentimentality. During his first private meeting with Tut, the prime minister thought it best to start by asking him a series of probing questions to gauge his mindset.

Within the innermost confines of the royal palace was a room where the pharaoh conducted all of his most important business. Surrounded by a series of circumferent stone walls, it was built for both security and privacy. With only the two of them in that inner sanctuary, the prime minister could afford to be bolder with the series of questions he asked, as well as with the suggestions he made.

"Your highness," Ay began, "how are you feeling now that you are officially the ruler of Egypt?"

"Good—I guess," Tut said, shrugging his shoulders. "I don't really know what I'm supposed to do except stay inside the palace all day."

Ay smiled pleasantly at the boy.

"Yes, with all the goings on, I suppose you haven't had much instruction or direction, have you?"

"Not really."

"Well, how would you feel about going over a few things now? Would you be up for that?"

"Sure," the young pharaoh shrugged again while rubbing his hands together and squirming somewhat inattentively in his oversized chair.

"Well, then, why don't we start with your home. How do you like it here in the palace?"

"It's fine, I guess."

"You don't seem very excited about it. Is there something you would like to change?"

"Like what?" The boy perked up and, finally, the prime minister had his attention.

"Oh, there are many things that could be changed. There could be changes to various rooms in the palace or even to the palace itself. Or changes could be made to the city." Ay paused for a moment to gauge the boy's nonverbal response to that last statement, then he asked, "Did your father—or anyone for that matter—ever tell you about the city that used to serve as the capital of Egypt, the city that we came from? About Thebes?"

"Not really. What was it like? Was it like it is here in Akhetaten?"

"In some ways, it was," Ay began. Now that he had Tut's attention, he saw an opportunity to paint a glorious picture for the boy that might give him the nudge he needed to make his first big decision. "But it was much bigger. Thebes had so much more than what we have here in Akhetaten."

"Really? Like what?" the boy asked curiously.

"Well, for one, there were so many more people than we have here. So many, in fact, you could feel the energy buzzing through the city whether you were under the sun or under the moon. And, when they cheered for the pharaoh, the roar of their cheers could be heard throughout the desert!"

"Wow!" responded the boy with wonder. "That's a lot of people."

"It sure is. And that's not all. Not only are there more people, but the buildings are wondrous! There are so many pyramids, both ancient and modern, that it was a sight to behold while standing on upper floors of the palace. I have never seen a sight so grand as seeing the tombs of the ancestral greats of the past."

"That sounds amazing!"

"Oh, it is. The people of Thebes miss having the pharaoh in their midst. I will tell you, if you were ever to return to Thebes, you would be welcomed as a hero, Tutankhamun!"

"I would?"

"Oh, I am sure of it."

The boy paused, looking down at his feet. Ay sensed the young pharaoh's doubt.

"What is it, Tutankhamun? Is everything alright? Did I say something to trouble you?"

"No. It's just that, if the people of Thebes loved the pharaoh, then why did my father leave and come here?"

Ay knew he had to tread lightly with his next answer, and he took a deep breath to consider his words carefully.

"Your father was a man of great conviction," he began. "And he wanted to be his own man. He wanted to prove that he was not just another pharaoh who simply stood on the shoulders of the great leaders of the past. Your father wanted to create his own path and, by so doing, bring Egypt along with him. That is why he created a new capital city in his name. He wanted to establish his own identity. Do you understand what I'm saying?"

"I kind of do," Tut responded. "He wanted to be different than all the other pharaohs before him?"

"That's right. He was a man of great vision who was determined to do his best for the country at that time," Ay said, before pausing again. Then he knelt in front of the boy and continued, "But times have changed. The people of Egypt are looking for the new pharaoh to take them into the modern world. They need a strong leader with vision. And even though you are still young, I see that kind of strength and vision in you."

"You do?"

"Oh yes. If you were to make a bold change in your first original act as pharaoh, you would be praised all throughout Egypt! The people would no longer see you as just a boy, but as the rightful ruler you are."

"You really think so?" Tut asked wondrously. "What kind of change?"

"It would be your decision, of course, but moving the capital city back to Thebes, for example, would truly be a bold move. I believe you would be seen as one of the few men in all of Egyptian history who was strong enough to do it. And strong leaders become heroes to the people, both here and in the afterlife. Think about that, Tutankhamun. What would it be like to be a hero for the ages?"

The boy thought for a moment. Ay could tell he was pondering that last thought. Then the boy triumphantly arose from his throne and declared, "We should do it. We should move the capital back to Thebes!"

"Are you sure, your highness?" asked Ay, feigning surprise and uncertainty. "That would indeed be a bold move."

"Yes, I am sure!" Tut declared. "Make the arrangements. We shall be moving to Thebes, and I shall have my tomb built among all the great pharaohs who came before me!"

On the pharaoh's order, the arrangements were made, and, within weeks, the young king, his new bride, and his entire entourage were on their way to making history in the city of Thebes.

For Tut, it was an adventure that most boys could only dream of. Being ruler over this tiny man-made corner of Egypt was nice, but in Thebes, he would be the king among millions.

Preparations for the move were hurriedly made, mostly at the direction of Ay, but as the time quickly approached, Tut and his new bride began to feel the realities of the stark change that was about to take over their lives. So much had already happened—the death of Tutankhamun's father, their marriage, and his abrupt ascension to the throne. Now, with this sudden move away from everything that was so familiar to both he and Ankhesenamun, the uncertainty was beginning to sink in.

Maybe he was moving too fast. Maybe he should wait until some time had passed and he had some time to settle into his new role as pharaoh. Yes, that was it—make some smaller decisions first, then work his way up to the larger, more important decisions. Then he would be ready for such a bold move.

But so much had already been done to prepare for the move; how could he give the order to reverse what had already been done, especially if they were just going to do it all over again in the future? Wouldn't that make him look like a wishy-washy leader in the eyes of the people?

As Tut was beginning to reconsider, he thought it prudent to talk to his closest and most trusted advisor, Ay.

When he approached his prime minister with the idea of stalling the move, Ay was surprised, but not completely shocked. Having laid his plan, he had prepared himself for a great many scenarios that might throw the plan off track. He also prepared a number of moves that would counter any obstacles to his plan. And this was certainly one of them.

"What is it that is causing you to reconsider, your highness?" he asked the boy.

"A few things," he replied. "Ankhesenamun and I have talked about it, and we feel like this might be going a little too fast. I have only been pharaoh for a short time now and we're not sure if I am ready to make such a big move yet. I was thinking it might be better if I worked up to such a serious decision."

"Ah, so you and the queen are feeling a bit unprepared, is that it?"

The moment Tut mentioned the queen's name, Ay knew that it would be imperative to subtly drive a wedge between the boy's role as pharaoh and his new position as a husband. He hadn't been able to win the trust of Ankhesenamun as easily as he had Tut. Indeed, she even seemed a bit wary of him. That was to be somewhat expected, though. She was, after all, two years older than the boy and, having grown up in the palace as the former pharaoh's daughter, she had been around long enough to overhear rumors and chatter regarding some of the less savory goings on in the realm of royalty. Yes, she was still young, but experienced enough to be suspicious of those who might have ambitions that ran contrary to the best interests of the pharaoh.

He would need to tread carefully during this most crucial of conversations, so he listened as the boy spoke of the concerns that he and Ankhesenamun had about leaving all that was familiar to them on such relatively short notice and how they didn't feel quite ready to rule in the big city. And how maybe it was better for him to gain experience with the smaller decisions first before making such a big one.

Then, the boy said something that abruptly caught Ay's attention.

"Besides, Ankhesenamun says that the people of Thebes were angry with my father when he left and built Akhetaten up to be the capital city. She says they might be mad at us and not receive us well."

Ay knew the girl was a little more experienced than her husband, but her awareness of the goings on in the kingdom was much more than he expected. In an instant, Ay realized that he would need to keep a much closer eye on the queen than he had originally thought. But as a seasoned politician, the prime minister learned long ago how to file such things away and stay with the task at hand. So, he continued to ask questions.

"Your highness," he began, "what did your father explain to you of the situation that led up to his decision to leave Thebes?"

"Not a lot," the boy replied. "He mostly just said that it was his duty as pharaoh to do what was best for Egypt and that building the new capital city of Akhetaten would take our nation to even greater heights."

"And did he ever talk about the people of Thebes?"

"He said he had many friends there, but that he also had some enemies."

"And did he happen to say why they were his enemies?"

"Mostly because he moved the kingdom here," answered Tut. "And because he declared that Egypt would worship only one god. He said his enemies were mad at him because he relegated the traditional gods."

"That's right," Ay said, just needing the answer to one last question before he once again applied his influence as mentor and father figure to the boy. "And why do you think that made them angry?"

"Mostly because they liked having the other gods, but I think it's because they didn't get to be important priests anymore."

"You are wise beyond your years, Tutankhamun," the prime minister responded, instilling a little flattery in hopes of bringing the boy over to his way of thinking. "So, if they were angry with your father for moving the capital away from their city and for relegating the gods, how do you think they would feel about a pharaoh who returned the capital to them?"

"I would think that they would probably be pleased that it returned," the boy said with a tone of half certainty in his voice. "But what about the priests and the gods?"

"Very wise question indeed, your highness. You say you need to work your way up to more important decisions, yet you continue to demonstrate the wisdom of a seasoned king. We know how the priests feel about the gods being relegated. And I think you know that it stands to reason that they would be happy if the gods were restored. But how do you think the people of Thebes would respond to the pharaoh who returned their glorious traditions back to them?"

"If they were angry with my father for relegating them, then I should think they would be pleased with the pharaoh for bringing them back."

"I believe you are correct, your highness," Ay said, before setting the final hook. "So, if you feel that the people of Thebes would be pleased and that the pharaoh would receive a hero's welcome for returned greatness to them, then what benefit would there be in delaying the move?"

"I guess there wouldn't be any benefit," the boy said.

"Then, what says the pharaoh?" responded Ay. "Shall we halt preparations for our move, or shall we continue forward and proceed as we have been?"

At that point, there was no further discussion needed. The young pharaoh saw the logic and, even though he still felt nervous about the decision, in his mind, he knew what needed to be done. He would return to the palace and inform his bride of the decision. He suspected that she would still be unsure, but he was certain that, once he explained the rationale behind it, she would understand and come around to his way of thinking.

As they talked about the conversation Tut had with Ay, Ankhesenamun could see the logic. But she also sensed Ay's manipulation of her husband. Nevertheless, she could see the conflict within the boy she had always been fond of. He had always been kind to her in a palace that wasn't always populated with the kindest of people. Tut was different. Maybe because of his disability—a condition in his neck and spine that limited his ability to turn his head from side to side and often required him to walk with sticks in each hand for better balance—he seemed more empathetic than the others in the royal circle. He even treated the servants with more respect and more kindness than was expected from royalty.

Ankhesenamun took notice and admired that quality in him. Even before his anointing as pharaoh and before their marriage, she considered him a friend. And she certainly didn't want to cause any more unrest within him by expressing more doubts for him to consider. So, she acquiesced.

"Then it is settled," she said, smiling. "Your first significant official act as pharaoh shall be to return the capital city to Thebes."

"You really feel good about this?" Tut asked the queen, wanting one final assurance from the person who was quickly becoming his principal confidant.

"Yes," she affirmed, smiling for emphasis. "And I shall be proud to be by your side as we enter into Thebes and return to the palace in Egypt's new capital."

As Ay had hoped, there was a grand celebration as the pharaoh and queen entered the city of Thebes. For the first time in years, it seemed to the prime minister that hope was restored to the people. Yes, their new pharaoh was but a boy, but—in the eyes of the public—he had already shown the willingness to undo some of his father's most unpopular decisions. And, with that, some optimism was restored to a city and a nation that many felt had been living under a dark cloud for the better part of seventeen years.

All seemed to be going according to Ay's plan, and, for a few short years, it seemed to him that he would be able to rule from behind the scenes, a role he was starting to become more and more comfortable with. Indeed, he began to see the benefits of being a puppet master rather than being the one out in front. The office of pharaoh had its glory, but it also had its drawbacks. As king of Egypt, the pharaoh had to assume all the burden of decision-making. There was complete accountability for every move that was made and nowhere to hide if things went wrong. Additionally, there was no anonymity to be found. Every solitary move was scrutinized. And with Ay having made many dealings in the shadows shrouded in hidden places, he would not be able to reap the extra financial benefits of being the pharaoh's puppeteer. Besides, the title of prime minister carried enough weight and status that he had access to move freely throughout the country. There was virtually no place in Egypt that he wouldn't be permitted to enter.

As long as he was pulling the strings, he didn't need to rule from a throne. All he needed to do was to simply maintain his trust with both the young pharaoh and—by extension—his secret society of friends, who were mostly pleased with his progress so far. If he could maintain that delicate balance, then he would be rewarded handsomely as they gradually began to return to power.

Unfortunately for Ay, not all of his collusive acquaintances were willing to exercise the kind of patience required to restore every former priest to power. Human nature is such that, once people have had a taste of power and influence, the notion of waiting in line for their turn is out of the question for those who have once held such lofty status.

"You promised we would all be restored to power by now," those still on the outside complained. "Why have not *all* the ancient gods and sanctuaries been restored?"

"I've told you," Ay explained to them. "It takes time. The pharaoh felt it would be better to implement the old ways gradually. For whatever reason, he does not want to rush the process."

"You have enough influence on the boy to bring him back to Thebes and restore a good number of the sanctuaries, Prime Minister. Why not us? Do you not favor us as the others? Have we not been as good to you as our fellow brethren have been?"

"No, it's nothing like that," Ay explained. "The boy has grown into his adolescent years and is determined to have a mind of his own. You know how it is with young men of that age. They push back. An adolescent wants to be his own man. He is simply not as easily moldable as he was when we first arrived in Thebes."

"Then you might want to consider changing his temperament, Prime Minister. If you can't convince the young man to be reasonable soon, then we might be forced to expose some of your unsavory deeds."

"That won't be necessary. I can assure you. I have a private meeting with the pharaoh soon and I will put a little added pressure on him to expedite the process."

"See that you do. We will be in touch."

And, with that, the meeting ended ominously for Ay. Feeling pressed, he started to become desperate. He was angry with Tutankhamun and angry with himself for allowing the boy to dictate any of the terms of restoration. He should have been more aggressive in exerting his influence on Tut when he was still a mere boy. Now, the young man was aware of his place as pharaoh. Despite his physical disabilities, he had come to realize that he was the one in charge—the end-all, be-all, if you will.

Tutankhamun had even dictated the terms and size of Ay's tomb, so important in Egyptian culture for one to reach his potential in the afterlife. The prime minister had overseen the design of a sizable resting place for the boy, certainly more than most royalty got. Wasn't that enough? But, as he thought about it, Ay realized that he had allowed himself to get greedy. When he designed his own tomb, it approached the size of those generally reserved for a pharaoh. And it was certainly much more sizable than any former prime minister had ever been laid to rest in.

As he matured and became more educated, the young pharaoh took note of the difference and commanded that his own tomb design be enlarged. An afficionado of chariots, he wanted to be sure that his favorite half dozen or so designs would fit comfortably in his tomb so that he was guaranteed to be lauded for them in the afterlife. When Ay attempted to convince him that his tomb was sizable enough, Tutankhamun felt disrespected and began to see, with the guidance of his wife, that the prime minister had a penchant for manipulation.

Not uncommon for adolescents, the young man began to become more and more disagreeable to the man who had inserted himself into his life as a father figure. It was becoming more common for Tut to dismiss the prime minister's ideas and suggestions in favor of his own inspiration. Even the suggestions of others in the royal circle began to take higher priority in the eyes of the pharaoh.

Maya, the royal treasurer, and Egypt's general, Horemheb, were gaining more influence with the pharaoh. This especially caused a rift between Ay and the general, as Horemheb was not shy about confronting the prime minister on what he suspected were ulterior motives. After all, the leader of the Egyptian armies saw his primary purpose as protecting the pharaoh, no matter who held the office. He also recognized that Tutankhamun was still a young man, which added to his fierce loyalty to the pharaoh. The general was so committed to the throne and so protective of his country that he was determined to protect it from any threat—including those he suspected on the inside.

This developing trend was becoming a problem for Ay. It put him in a difficult position and now he was feeling that his place in the kingdom was jeopardized, not only in title, but in reputation, as well. The young pharaoh's insistence on becoming his own man had become a hindrance to Ay's ambitions, and now, he was being threatened with public humiliation.

He would not stand for that.

The prime minister would make one last attempt to reason with the boy, and if that did not work, he would need to take more drastic action.

"Your highness," Ay began during his private audience with the pharaoh, "it has come to my attention that—"

"Servant, I am thirsty," interrupted Tut. "Bring me some water."

Those interruptions during these encounters were becoming all too common for Ay's taste. So, too, were the expressions of disinterest on the young pharaoh's face during their private meetings—and public, for that matter—which were also becoming more infrequent. Inwardly, Ay was outraged at being so casually dismissed, but he somehow managed to keep it from showing in front of Tutankhamun. At least he thought he did. After this latest interruption, Ay attempted to politely be more blunt.

"The people are calling for all the ancient gods to be restored and for their corresponding priests to be reinserted to what they see as their rightful positions."

"Who exactly is calling for this?" queried Tut.

"The people in general, your highness," the prime minister answered.

"And who else?" the pharaoh insisted.

"The priests themselves may also have mentioned it," Ay answered, trying not to show his disdain for being interrogated by the boy, all the while attempting to show a modicum of humility.

"Is that so?" questioned the pharaoh. "If you happen to have an audience with any of these priests or any of the people who hold this opinion, please tell them that I will reinsert them when I—and I only—feel that it is the right time to do so. Are we clear?"

"Yes, your highness."

"Then, is there anything else that you think I need to be aware of?"

"No, I believe that is all."

"Then, I believe we are done here. That will be all, Ay. You are dismissed."

"Yes sir, thank you, sir."

And, with that, the meeting had reached its conclusion, and the prime minister promptly left the room. Fuming, he retired to his private chambers and groused at how he had been treated by the boy. "After all I have done for that little ingrate, how dare he treat me like this!" Ay growled to himself.

But it wasn't just Tutankhamun that bothered the prime minister. The dismissed priests, who were once inferior to him under the old regime, were now holding him hostage. After all the efforts he had made on their behalf to restore them to their positions, now they were holding his actions as leverage over his head. How dare they!

There seemed to be no hope of getting this situation resolved peacefully and Ay could only think of one way out of the precarious position he found himself in.

He would have to become pharaoh.

If the current pharaoh died unexpectedly without an heir to the throne, the prime minister could then be appointed as pharaoh. Much to his dismay, that also meant that he would have to take Ankhesenamun as his wife, but no matter. In his mind, that would just be an inconvenient formality. He could easily overpower her, and her feelings on the matter were of no importance to him.

But this would be no small task, and Ay could not afford to be caught in the act of such treachery. The consequences would be disastrous—both in this life and in the next. Were there other options? Was there any scenario where he could turn the people against King Tutankhamun and in favor of himself being anointed pharaoh? As he thought through the options, he could think of no conceivable way that would happen. After what seemed like endless days and nights of contemplation, the prime minister finally made his decision. He would have to kill the young pharaoh and take his place on the throne.

The royal couple had conceived twice, but the Queen had miscarried both times. What if it happened again, but this time successfully? There would be a natural heir to the throne and the prime minister would have no conceivable path to power. Ay could not chance a successful pregnancy. He would need to act quickly if he was going to carry out such a bold plan. He would need to end the pharaoh's life. But how?

He would have to come up with a plan so intricate and detailed that he could assassinate the young man without being detected by his security detail and without arousing suspicion.

And then there was another matter. The prime minister had always been a politician, never a warrior. Taking another's life was not something he had ever done or even contemplated. Could he really go through with it when the moment arrived?

Of course he could!

"Don't be so weak!" Ay mumbled, chastising himself for a moment of doubt. "You have worked too long and too hard for this opportunity to let it slip away simply out of fear. You have to finish the job! You have to consider this just another part of the plan, the final part."

Having calmed his fears, Ay could now turn his attention toward creating a detailed plan.

Because he knew the now nineteen-year-old pharaoh better than anyone, Ay had easy access to the most secure reaches of the palace—including Tutankhamun's private living and sleeping quarters. The prime minister also had unfettered access to the young man's schedule and to his security detail. There may have been a separation in the relationship, but Ay still had an intimate knowledge of the boy's comings and goings, his habits and his tastes.

Most important, he knew when Tut would be alone and, chillingly, when he would be most vulnerable. He knew his frailties and physical ailments. Overpowering him would be no problem.

"If I am careful, it won't be difficult," Ay calculated. Then he formulated a plan to murder the young pharaoh in cold blood.

Because the prime minister had practiced subtlety for the majority of his life, he was confident that he could be quick, quiet, and effective. He would be in and out of the pharaoh's private chambers before anyone could ever see him.

Lurking outside the inner sanctum of the palace, he watched carefully as the guards patrolled the hallways outside the pharaoh's private chambers. When the guards left the immediate vicinity, Ay moved swiftly toward Tut's sleeping quarters where he knew the boy, who was sure to be tired from the day's activities, would be resting.

Quietly, he slipped into the boy's chambers, being sure to approach the slumbering young pharaoh from behind. He quietly walked across the room, each step creeping closer to his unsuspecting victim just as he had done ten years earlier to feign comfort to the then nine-year-old, who had just lost his father, in the hopes of luring him into his snare.

At the time, the boy was completely unaware of the squinty-eyed middle-aged man approaching slowly from behind, stalking the young royal with every deliberate step he took. Now, the predator, still squinty-eyed, but now older, had a more sinister purpose. His pace was still that of a lion, assuring that his prey had no idea he was being hunted.

The man's breathing was still slow, and his pace measured. Just a few more steps and he could pounce. He reached his arms out toward the boy from behind, but this time, instead of gently placing his hands on the boy's shoulders, he wrapped his hands firmly around Tut's head and, in one swift motion, lifted the slight young man up, slid him off his bed, and slammed the back of his head on the stone floor surface beneath him.

The boy seized, but Ay quickly covered his mouth to ensure there would be no sudden noise. The boy was surprised and looked at his once father figure with dismay and pleading in his eyes. Ay returned the stare with a look that said, "You had your chance to cooperate, but you chose not to. You left me no choice."

Then, in one more violent motion, he slammed young Tutankhamun's head to the floor once more and the boy's body went limp, his breathing halted. Because of Tut's physical ailments, his body was frail and easy to move to the floor beneath. No one would be able to prove it was anything other than an accidental fall from his bed to the floor. The young man, who used sticks to walk, must have become disoriented and taken a tragic fall out of bed.

Ay checked one last time to see if Tut was breathing. There were no evident breaths, but he smothered the boy's mouth and nose with his hands to be sure. After a few moments of absolute stillness, the prime minister was certain of the young man's death.

The deed complete, the prime minister moved toward the doorway leading to the halls. The guards were still making their rounds and no one else was in the area. He had just enough time to leave the scene undetected. Ay tugged on his royal robes, making sure they were precisely even on both sides, and exited the pharaoh's private quarters, making sure he was seen by no one.

No one would ever know what happened. And, even if they suspected, no one would ever be able to offer proof of his homicidal act. Most important to Ay, once he was crowned king of Egypt, no one would dare try.

Days later, prime minister Ay was indeed crowned king and his ambitions fulfilled.

It wouldn't be until 1922, when Howard Carter and Lord Carnarvon famously found King Tut's tomb, that there would be a legitimate opportunity to investigate King Tutankhamun's suspicious death. Since that time, there has been a plethora of speculation as to what happened to the young pharaoh. Why did he die so young? What happened to him? What do we know about his history that could give us clues to what would answer these and a host of other questions about this young man who died so young and so mysteriously?

Of course, the depiction described in the opening pages of this chapter is less about proclaiming what actually happened to King Tut and more about the investigative process as it relates to the behavioral aspects of this 3,300-year-old case. I was asked by the Atlantic Production Company to investigate King Tut's case for a Discovery Channel documentary special that eventually aired back in 2002.

I accepted their invitation and asked a colleague of mine, Mike King, to join me on this adventure of a lifetime. Unbeknownst to us at the time, we were fortunate enough to be selected from among several candidates who had extensive detective and investigative experience in law enforcement.

In so doing, we were teamed with renowned experts on the subject from around the world, including Dr. Joann Fletcher, a remarkable Egyptologist from Great Britain; Harold Burstein, MD, who was codirector of the Harvard Medical School Program in Psychiatry and the Law; and a host of other subject and forensic experts who contributed their time, talents, energy, and information that helped guide us to the clues that we needed to put together a behavioral profile of this case.

Working on this case was a reminder that, no matter what the physical clues, investigating cold cases starts with the victims and those closest to them (not necessarily as suspects, but as people who know the victim best and can provide you with the most thorough information about who that person is and what might have contributed to them being targeted by their respective perpetrators).

Cold cases are also primarily about human behavior. And no matter how old the case—whether the crime happened today or 3,300 years ago—human behavior has remained constant throughout the ages.

That said, even though we just provided a dramatic fictional account of what might or might not have happened between King Tut and Prime Minister Ay, the fact is, we don't know exactly what happened. Besides the pharaoh's body, we weren't able to collect any physical evidence at the crime scene—as we would during a typical homicide investigation—and we don't even know for sure where the crime scene was located. From a physical evidence perspective, all we really have is a body and the place where the body was deposited. And even those two important pieces of physical evidence were compromised when King Tut's tomb was discovered in 1922.

Fortunately, thanks to modern forensic science—such as X-ray and CT technology—we were able to extract some clues from the body itself that at least determined that there were some physical signs of a potential attack on the young pharaoh. But, aside from that, we didn't have much to work with, so we were left to find signs that could point us to the young man's life and the lives of those who were closest to him, as well as their behaviors leading up to and around the time of King Tut's death.

Additionally, we do have some historical archives that point us to important behavioral evidence that can help us narrow things down, and because of the circumstances surrounding the victim, we were able to narrow them down substantially.

All that said, you may be wondering why we would include this case in a book about The Cold Case Foundation.

Well, we included it because it gives us the starkest example of how the principles of victimology and human behavior serve as core foundations for any homicide case. That's why we highlighted the behavioral aspects of the principal people we featured in the first part of this chapter.

You may have noticed that we underscored human traits in these people such as ambition, naivete, the need for control, the need for love, thirst for power and status, and even desperation. From a behavioral perspective, this gave us a starting point as we began the process of putting the pieces together in this suspicious death investigation.

All of this begs the questions, what did we find that led us to these conclusions and, just as important, how do these investigative principles apply to the work we do at the Cold Case Foundation? And when we look at modern cold cases on behalf of the families of the victims—and on behalf of the police agencies in need of additional resources to solve these cases— what exactly are we looking for?

The answer is that we start with any physical evidence we have.

In the King Tut case, for example, we started with very limited physical evidence. We forwarded X-ray evidence of King Tut's body to Dr. Todd Gray, the chief medical examiner of the Salt Lake County Coroner's Office. As he studied the X-rays, he noticed some bone fragments that had been chipped off and separated from the back of the skull. This confirmed that there had been some type of trauma to the back of Tutankhamun's head.

What exactly caused that trauma? We couldn't say, but we had to consider all possibilities. The skull fracture could have been the result of an intentional blow to the head, and therefore, would lead us into a homicide investigation. But we also had to consider the possibility that the young man's death was accidental.

Either way, that meant that we would need to put most of our focus on the behaviors and circumstances around the young pharaoh himself and work from there.

And, like the cases we look into at the Cold Case Foundation, we would start by gathering every bit of information available to us about him and those around him. We would focus on the behavioral evidence and then rule out suspects as that evidence dictated.

That is truly the foundation of our approach to any homicide or missing person investigation. In this chapter, we highlighted our approach to the King Tut case to illustrate the core pillars that we work from to investigate modern cold cases, namely:

- communication
- coordination
- collaboration
- cooperation

Each of these four pillars is critical in gathering both physical and behavioral evidence and in developing leads that narrow the search for the assailant. For example, how do we communicate and coordinate with families and loved ones, as well as the public, in a way that will help us find the most probable suspects in the most effective way possible?

In subsequent chapters, we will go into greater depth and detail of just how we develop strategies for homicide and missing person cases of any age by adhering to these four principles in real-life situations.

But in a case as old as that of King Tut's, one might think that utilizing these pillars would prove to be a difficult task. With any potential witnesses, family members, or suspects having been deceased for over 3,300 years, how could we possibly collaborate, cooperate, coordinate, or communicate with anyone from that time period?

The answer was simple.

Since we couldn't talk directly to them, we let them talk to us. Because it was of utmost importance for royalty to keep records of their time in power, we were fortunate enough to have well-preserved art renderings on the walls of the royal tombs, as well as historical records and other historical items left behind from King Tut's reign. And we were also lucky enough to have experts in the field who could interpret those communications based on their extensive knowledge of Egyptian culture and history during the time period that we were investigating.

So, when looking at our four pillars of communication, coordination, collaboration, and cooperation, we can see that all four of those principles were just as essential in investigating this case as they are in working any modern case that we would be looking into today.

For example, when we look at the communication aspect of this case, we can see that the communication came directly from ancient scribes and artists. We were able to determine who the people were who had the easiest access to the young pharaoh and what the circumstances were surrounding them. Those were key elements in this investigation.

And, just as important as those communicative aspects were to the case, were the coordination, collaboration, and cooperation with key people who were able to permit us access to the tomb. Additionally, there were others who were so crucial in interpreting that communication for us so that we could have the pieces of this investigation to put together in the first place.

We never would have had an investigation at all if it hadn't been for the cooperation of the Egyptian government. And, because of the Discovery Channel spearheading this documentary special, we were introduced to incredible experts who gave us crucial information about the records that we came across, as well as the physical evidence.

For example, the reason we were able to narrow the search to four key people of interest was because some of the world's most renowned Egyptologists shared the inner workings of the pharaoh's immense security with us. Because of that information, we knew that there was an extremely high probability that any assassination had to be an inside job. With security upon security and guards watching over the young pharaoh everywhere, the likelihood of anyone sneaking into the palace was almost zero. And assassinating the pharaoh outside the walls of the capital with his royal guard present while going completely undetected? Forget about it. That was not happening. Because of this insight, the probability of the murder occurring inside the confines of the palace was extremely high.

That also meant that the probability of the killer being in Tut's close circle was also extremely high. So, when we did narrow down our list of potential suspects to the four closest people to the young pharaoh—Tut's wife, Ankhesenamun; Egypt's royal treasurer, Maya; military chief General Horemheb; and Prime Minister Ay—the experts we collaborated with were able to share the role that each of these people played in Tutankhamun's life, which was critical to the behavioral aspects of our investigation.

For instance, we were able to look at the circumstances surrounding Tut's wife Ankhesenamun—both during their marriage and after the young pharaoh's death. Because she was closest to him, we wanted to know if there were any records or renderings depicting their marriage. And there were plenty. Compared to artist renderings of other royal couples, the depiction of Tutankhamun and Ankhesenamun showed an affection not common among paintings of other royal couples of that period in history. We also found physical evidence that the young couple was trying to start a family. Mummified fetuses were found in King Tut's tomb. It appeared that Ankhesenamun had miscarried twice.

As we continued looking into records of Ankhesenamun after her husband's death, we found something that caused us to raise an eyebrow, to say the least. Ancient records showed that, within days of Tut's passing, she hurriedly attempted to remarry—not to a man she previously knew, but to an enemy of Egypt, a Hittite. A record of her sending a secret letter to the king of the Hittites, proposing that the kingdoms merge through the marriage of her and a Hittite prince, was discovered. The king accepted Ankhesenamun's proposal, but unfortunately for him, the chosen prince was murdered while traveling to Thebes. Through our collaboration with our team of experts, it became a key piece of behavioral evidence in that it shed light on why the young Queen would send such a letter to Egypt's enemies. Under ancient Egyptian custom and law, Ankhesenamun was set to marry the next in line for the throne, none other than Prime Minister Ay. What this meant to us is that, for some compelling reason, she felt it better to marry an enemy of the state rather than marry the man who had served as her late husband's prime minister.

But before we turned our attention to Prime Minister Ay, we wanted to vet out the other two people of interest in this case—Treasurer Maya and General Horemheb.

As we looked into Maya, we were able to quickly rule out the Treasurer because of his behavior before and after the pharaoh's death. During King Tut's reign, the records indicate no history of financial indiscretion or irresponsibility on Maya's part. And, after the young pharaoh's passing, artist renderings showed that Maya was especially sensitive in caring for Tutankhamun's tomb and body during a burial process that was suspiciously rushed.

Our expert friends were also able to show us that the records and artist renderings of Tut's tomb indicated that Horemheb was a loyal general, who saw it as his primary duty to guard the country—and the throne—passionately. Whether he agreed or disagreed with whichever pharaoh he was charged with protecting, he did so with equal levels of commitment and passion. We also discovered one additional element to this case: After Ay's rule as pharaoh came to an end, Horemheb ascended to the throne. His first act as pharaoh was a strict command to have the royal artisans remove the mouth and eyes of the royal renderings of Ay's depiction as pharaoh. Through our work with historical experts, we came to learn that this was a sign of utter disrespect and disgust for the previous pharaoh. In other words, in the eyes of Horemheb, Ay committed an act so atrocious, the former general found him worthy of disgracing his memory.

Having investigated the behavioral evidence of these three people of interest, we then turned our attention to Prime Minister Ay, the man who took it upon himself to be young Tutankhamun's father figure and mentor.

We wondered why. Why would a distinguished prime minister be so quick to mentor a child he barely knew and the child of a pharaoh he did not agree with or like?

In an attempt to answer those questions, we decided to home in on Tut's father, who had preceded him as pharaoh. Because Tutankhamun was so young at the time of his father's death, it was important for us to vet out anyone who might have had a motive to harm the boy. So, we looked into what possible motives Ay might have.

Looking at the situation, we had a nine-year-old boy who was, all of a sudden, the ruler of one of the most powerful nations in the world. That made him extremely vulnerable to anyone who would want to usurp his power. But it couldn't be just anybody. It had to be somebody who had close access to the boy. Someone who held the status of Ay.

We also had to ask, who were the enemies of King Tut's father, King Akhenaten? Who would have the strongest motives and the most to gain by eliminating the boy? Most important, the question of access came up. Who had the kind of access to the pharaoh that would allow someone to commit murder of the highest degree and go undetected?

In terms of Akhenaten's enemies, our experts were unanimous in their opinion that the former priests of the multiple gods of ancient Egypt were the clear choices. They were the ones who had carried so much power and influence previous to Akhenaten's reign. And the prime minister was sympathetic to them. Ay wanted them back in power as we discovered once he took the throne, having almost immediately restored the priests and their gods to power and prominence.

From a motivational perspective, it was just as clear that Ay sought a path to the throne. Or at least to influence. Shortly into the young pharaoh's reign, Ay convinced Tut to move the capital city back to Thebes. And, by degrees, he convinced the boy to undo his father's work by gradually restoring the old gods and their priests to their previous posts.

But, when the boy became an adolescent and developed his own opinions, he came to realize the power he wielded. And that was in direct conflict to the prime minister's ambitions. But was that enough behavioral evidence for us to surmise that Ay was the most likely suspect in Tut's murder?

In and of itself, the answer is no. But, when we looked at Ay's behavior after the young pharaoh's death, we had the evidence we needed. As our team of historical and cultural experts taught us about ancient Egypt's customs and beliefs, we came to learn that one of the strongest held beliefs in that ancient culture was the belief of preparing for the afterlife. It was custom that people spent their entire lives preparing for a glorious afterlife. That preparation not only entailed one's activities during this life, but just as importantly, it also involved the preparation of one's tomb. This was especially true for a pharaoh.

We discovered that, after King Tut's death, Ay made the bold decision to trade his allotted resting place for Tut's, which was much larger and grander, befitting an Egyptian king. Essentially, according to ancient Egyptian culture, Ay desecrated and stole Tut's grave. Not only that, but he also ordered a rushed burial, an act that was unheard of for a deceased pharaoh. This was very suspicious behavior indeed, but we had one more question to address, that of access to King Tutankhamun.

Because the palace was a heavily guarded fortress and the pharaoh was watched over around the clock, it was nearly impossible that even an assassin of the highest skill would be able to penetrate the fortress, access the innermost chamber of the palace, slip by Tutankhamun's guards, kill the young pharaoh, and then skip out of the fortress unnoticed. It had to be someone who had unfettered access and would not arouse the suspicion of the guards by being seen in the innermost sanctum of the palace.

Could Ay have been the one that had enough access that he physically could have put himself in a place where he could commit the murder of a pharaoh and flee undetected? The answer was unequivocally, yes. Of all the people we had on record as being closest to the young King Tutankhamun, it was Ay. He had the access, and his behavior—from the beginning—was consistent of someone willing and able to kill to serve his ambitions.

If this were a criminal case in today's world, we would at the very least bring Ay in for questioning and we probably would be able to find enough physical evidence to make an arrest. And it would be because so many people—the Egyptian community that we found to be so cooperative and our team of fine experts—worked together in a way that promoted communication, coordination, collaboration, and cooperation.

Our hope is that, as you continue reading, you will see how so many in our communities throughout the country—and around the world—can contribute so much to the investigations of the tragic homicide and missing person cases that we see all too often.

Finding closure to these heartbreaking cases is not just about the police "doing their jobs." It requires all of us to come together in a collaborative and cooperative effort. We believe we have a foundational model for bringing the police, victims' families, and the communities around them together in an organized way that will help solve these cases and bring some semblance of closure to those families and friends who think about their lost loved ones every single day.

CHAPTER FOUR

THE FOUR Cs

Erik Rault gazed out the large front room window from his living room chair, reflecting on his life and marveling at how fast the time had passed. Spring was nearing, but a smattering of snow still covered the ground and the bright sun shining through the family room window belied the thirty-degree temperatures that sometimes put a chill in the air on a spring day in Boise, Idaho. In a room nearby, his daughter Kristal Rault, who was now helping to care for her father in the home they shared, was tidying up.

They would soon receive a call from the Yellowstone County Sheriff's Office, anticipating that they would get some news that might bring some measure of finality to a family tragedy that had occurred decades ago. Erik's oldest daughter, Lisa, and her husband, Carl Bennett, had been brutally murdered in their home one November night in 1973, and despite their best efforts, detectives had been unable to find their killer. Now, this phone call might be the one that they had been waiting to get for forty-five years.

Erik had turned ninety-nine a few months prior and was in pretty good health for a man his age. In almost a century of life, he had experienced so much. He had seen more advances than any generation before him had ever experienced in the history of the world. The automobile, the airplane, motion pictures, TV, VCRs, the microwave oven, personal computers, the internet, satellite TV, cell phones, and social media had all either been invented or come into prominence during his lifetime. Born just twelve years after the Wright Brothers were first in flight, Erik was forty-nine when Neil Armstrong walked on the moon.

And in his personal life, he had seen and experienced more suffering in one lifetime than most people do ten lifetimes over. Extreme hunger and poverty that came with the Great Depression and multiple wars—including his service in Europe during World War II.

Sometimes, as he would think about the events of the war, his eye would turn toward a medal displayed on a nearby shelf. It had only been a few weeks since he had been awarded the prestigious Legion of Honor by the French government for his active duty at Omaha Beach in Normandy and at the Battle of the Bulge in the Ardennes region of Europe.

It was a marvelous day.

The ceremony was conducted at the Capitol Rotunda in Boise and attended by current and past service members, legislators, family, and friends. Erik was proud of his military service and grateful to have been recognized for his part in helping to liberate the allies during World War II. During that ceremonious event, he considered it an honor, not just for himself, but for all those who fought to maintain freedom for the United States and the allied nations.

"There were so many who were deserving of this honor," he would say quietly, his head bowed in remembrance of so many who had lost so much, including those who had paid the ultimate price in giving their lives for the cause. "I wish they all could have been there with me."

Sometimes he would reflect on the several weeks that he spent fighting German troops in late 1944 and into early 1945, trying to keep them from breaking through the border into Belgium. It started on December 16, on a day when Erik—just a month shy of his twenty-fifth birthday—and his fellow troops were working hard to fortify the Belgian border.

The work in the Ardennes Forest was exhausting, and temperatures freezing, but American and Allied troops felt they had plenty of time to prepare for any attempted Nazi invasion. Freezing temperatures and limited German resources would make a Nazi victory nearly impossible. Surely, they believed, if German troops were planning an invasion of any kind, it would have to wait until the spring.

So, the decision was made to send mostly new, inexperienced troops, as well as battle-weary soldiers, to the Belgian region to reinforce the barrier. This would help the newer troops gain much needed training and experience. And, for the more experienced soldiers, it would give them a much-needed break from the rigors of battle.

Erik was among those who had seen more than his share of action on the battlefields of Europe. Familiar with multiple dialects of the German language from having grown up in Wishek, North Dakota, a small town settled by German immigrants, he was assigned to serve in areas where US and Allied forces were battling German troops so that he could be utilized as an interpreter. Often, that meant that Erik would be where the fighting was at its most fierce.

Just a few months earlier in the summer of 1944, he was among those assigned to battle in Normandy, France, where American forces suffered more than a hundred thousand casualties. He didn't think he would ever experience anything so brutal again and, though the work was exhausting, Erik was glad to be doing the labor he had originally signed up for when he joined the Civilian Conservation Corps and enlisted in the Army.

He welcomed hard labor over the alternative of artillery fire and the death and carnage that came with it. He had always enjoyed working with his hands and building things. And even though the conditions were harsh, he was getting a chance to do that here.

He sometimes thought back to those days, and he reflected on how he and his fellow soldiers talked about home while they worked to erect fortifications along the regional parallel. With it being so close to Christmas, they talked about their hometowns, about family traditions, and, of course, about the cute girls who would be waiting for them when the war was over and they were back on American soil.

"I've got a cute one waiting for me back home," he remembered one of the newer soldiers bragging while sporting a crooked grin. The young man, barely eighteen, used any excuse he could find to show off the photo of his girl. "Yeah, she's a looker, ain't she?"

"She sure is," another nearby soldier could be heard chuckling at the young soldier's enthusiastic naivete. "Now, let's get back to work, lover boy."

The good-natured razzing continued among the troops working in his area, until, seemingly out of nowhere, German artillery began raining down on them. In just minutes, Nazi tanks and armed vehicles came rolling toward the forest and a ferocious battle began that would last for weeks.

Sitting in the comfort of his living room chair in Boise, Idaho, nearly seventy-five years later, Erik shook his head at the contrast. Had it really been seventy-five years since that horrific day?

Soldiers scrambled to hurriedly find cover. Battle-tested soldiers beckoned to the newer, inexperienced soldiers, who were just supposed to be getting their feet wet, to line up and form a wall of defense to hold back the invaders. Artillery fire seemed to be coming from every direction and the veteran soldiers were trying to keep some semblance of calm among their inexperienced comrades. They knew that panic would be their worst enemy in this situation, so they tried to create some degree of focus for their younger counterparts.

"We can't let them get through!" they could be heard yelling to their fellow troops. "Just follow my lead and stay low!"

"Fall back and start digging!" others directed.

The Allied troops somehow managed to hold off the immediate assault just long enough for reinforcements to arrive, but while there was success in doing so, Erik's memory would sometimes conjure up the senseless deaths of so many. In all, American troops suffered an estimated eighty-one thousand casualties during the Battle of the Bulge. It was terrible to see so many young lives lost.

One minute, an exuberant young man was showing off photographs of his girlfriend. The next minute, he was gone. Along with him, any dreams he ever had of returning to her had also vanished. Nobody saw it coming. No one thought the Nazis would be so brazen—and foolish—as to launch an all-out assault in that area of Europe—especially in such severe weather. Surely, they had to have known that their troops and resources were too scarce to sustain the kind of assault needed to break through.

Didn't they?

As it turned out, this would be an order that Adolf Hitler gave directly, despite the misgivings of some of his top generals. It was an act of desperation, and it would ultimately fail. While allied reinforcements arrived quickly enough to prevent German troops from breaking through the western border, the Nazis eventually ran out of resources. Within a few weeks, German troops were either captured or had retreated, and the war would come to an end just a few months later.

Having survived that assault—and so much more—Erik, who turned twenty-five on January 19, 1945, during the height of the weeks-long battle, returned home after the war. He could only shake his head as he thought about the senseless loss of young life.

Unlike so many of his fellow soldiers—many of them good friends lost to the war—he was able to feel the embrace of family and breathe the familiar air of his hometown in North Dakota. He knew he was fortunate to survive what he did and make it back home. After all, not many soldiers could say that they battled in both Normandy and in the Battle of the Bulge. Far fewer could say they survived both. He was fortunate. He knew he was fortunate. And he was determined to make the most of his life while living out the rest of his days in peace.

It wasn't long after he returned when he met his sweetheart, Joan Carter. She was the most beautiful girl he had ever laid eyes on. More important, as he got to know her, he knew she would be his better half in so many ways and inspire him to be the man he wanted to become. They fell in love, married, and eventually settled in Billings, Montana.

Erik would go on to find a career that suited his talents, becoming a roofer before eventually taking on a career as a general contractor. He would get to spend the rest of his professional life building homes, something he had always wanted to do.

Not long after he and Joan married, Erik became the family man he had always wanted to be. Growing up in the open spaces of North Dakota in a family of fourteen children, he had hoped to one day have a family of his own and provide his children with the wonderful childhood he had experienced. A childhood filled with days running through the fields and playing with friends in open prairies and pastures, spending their days fishing in nearby creeks and lakes.

Montana reminded him of his North Dakota roots and he and Joan were thrilled at the prospect of their children getting to grow up in a quality, safe environment in the open spaces of nature. After all the trouble and turmoil that he had survived overseas, it seemed that he would settle into a calm, peaceful life that would carry him through the rest of his days.

It certainly began that way.

Over the course of the next few years, Joan and Erik would welcome four children—two boys and two girls, alternating one after another starting with a girl, Lisa. She reminded him of his sweet wife. The day Lisa was born, Erik was instantly smitten, and it didn't take long for her to become daddy's little girl.

She followed in his footsteps in so many ways. She was kind and giving, and she loved the outdoors. And, like her father, she also loved to work with her hands, building and drawing whenever she could.

Lisa had a great childhood, and as kids tend to do, she grew up fast.

Before Erik and Joan knew it, their little girl had quickly become a young lady and soon became interested in the boy she would eventually marry, Carl Bennett. What started as puppy love at the age of twelve eventually blossomed into becoming high school sweethearts. Like most dads, Erik initially wasn't fond of the idea of boys hanging around his daughter, but he quickly took a liking to this young man. Carl was a hard worker, polite, and most important, he treated his daughter well and made her happy.

Then came a twist. The Vietnam War.

Like Erik, Carl was sent overseas to fight for his country. Within two years of graduating high school, he proposed to Lisa, and on June 7, 1969, the young couple married. Eighteen days later, Carl would begin his military service in the Vietnam War.

He was deployed to Vietnam and then Cambodia where he would serve with the First Calvary Division. He went willingly and served faithfully, but it was hard for Erik to see his daughter fearful and constantly worried. He tried to give her reason to be optimistic about her husband's safe return.

"Don't watch all that doom and gloom on the news," Erik would tell her. "If he follows his training, he will make it back all right. Carl is a smart young man. He will do just fine, and he will be back before you know it."

On the surface, those words were meant to reassure Lisa, but in reality, Erik wasn't sure who he was trying to convince more—his worried daughter or himself. He knew full well what war was like. And he knew that all anyone could really do was pray for Carl and hope for the best. But, around his daughter, he kept a stiff upper lip. He wasn't about to let her see any concern on his face. Why give her any reason to worry until there was indeed a reason to worry?

The weeks and months passed, and, finally, in the spring of 1971, there was some news. Carl had been wounded in action, but he was in stable condition. He would be home soon. And not only would he be coming home, but he would be arriving a hero, having been awarded both a Bronze Star and a Purple Heart. Most important, Carl was home, and his daughter was happy.

Erik was happy, too. Partly, he was glad to see his son-in-law safe and sound, and the other part was simply being relieved that he wouldn't have to see Lisa suffer. So many families had to feel the anguish of learning that their loved ones had been killed or had gone missing in action.

Not long after Carl returned, the stout young man got a job laying concrete. It wouldn't be long before the young couple moved into a home of their own. They were determined to make a good life together. They both had full-time jobs—Carl in concrete and Lisa as a billing and accounting clerk with a wholesale grocery company.

As a third means of income, they would clean offices together at night for a small cleaning business that Erik had started.

With the money they had saved, they soon moved into a house approximately one hundred feet away and kitty corner from Lisa's parents. It was a great starter home—two bedrooms, including a beautiful master bedroom and guest room. The young couple was thrilled.

Knowing that their daughter and son-in-law would be living so close to them also made Erik and Joan happy.

"Our little girl will be staying close to home and even closer to us," Joan would often say to Erik after they got news about where the house would be built. "And that means grandchildren might not be too far behind!"

Erik would just smile. He was excited too, but he was always most happy when something made his wife giddy.

As Carl and Lisa moved into their new home there were still a few things that needed to be done—finishing touches like drapes, décor, carpet, and such—but Carl and Lisa were at least able to move into their home and finish those things little by little as they saved enough money to complete each phase.

It was an exciting time for them and for their extended families.

Erik and Joan felt like they were living out the dream they envisioned when they first started their young family. After all the hard times and all the sacrifices, the life they built was good, and it seemed that it would carry over to their children and grandchildren, as well.

During the tough moments overseas in World War II, Erik would remind himself that he wasn't just fighting for his generation. He was fighting for the well-being of generations to come. That thought got him through so many hard times and, during those reflective moments later in life, he found his soul filled with heart-felt joy that it all seemed to have come together the way he had hoped it would.

Then came the morning of November 7, 1973.

The uncontrollable sobbing of his wife still echoed in his ears nearly forty-six years later. The crushed look on her face, that ever-optimistic beautiful face that he fell in love with, was transformed by the discovery of an act of violence so heinous that it trumped any horror he had seen fighting overseas.

Erik and Joan's beautiful daughter had been brutally assaulted and killed the night before. Along with her, the son-in-law they adored had also been horrifically strangled to death. What made it even more tragic for Erik was how they were discovered.

Carl and Lisa hadn't shown up for their family's annual celebratory end-of-elk-hunt dinner the night before, nor had they gone to the office they had been scheduled to clean. Initially, that morning, Joan called Lisa at work but was told that Lisa did not come in, which was uncharacteristic of her. Joan, worried that Erik hadn't been able to reach the kids by phone the night before, decided to make a quick trip to the young couple's home. Maybe one or both of them might have gotten sick? After all, she was still Mom, and it was in her nature to help. Besides, wasn't that one of the benefits of them living so close to their parents?

As she approached the front door, she immediately noticed something odd.

The couples' vehicle was parked in the driveway, and the windows of the house were partially open, which was very unusual for a November day in Montana, especially since the temperature had dropped down to six degrees that night. They wouldn't have forgotten to close the windows if they were still at home, especially if they were under the weather. Would they?

Joan knocked on the door. No answer. She knocked again. Still no answer. She turned the doorknob, but the door was locked. Not sure what to do, she walked back home and called a family member to get their opinion.

"Do you think I should knock again?" she asked. "I'm getting worried, but I don't want to bother them if they're not feeling well or sleeping. What do you think I should do?"

"That's not like them," one of the family members responded. "The house is new so I'm worried it might be an issue with the gas. Are the windows open wide enough that you could crawl in that way?"

"No, they aren't open enough that I could manage that," she replied.

"If it's a gas issue, I think you need to find a way in," the family member advised. "Even if you have to break a window to get in, it would be best if you checked on them. A window can always be replaced."

"You're probably right," Joan agreed. "I'll head back over and try again."

Upon arriving at the house, she tried knocking one more time, as loud as possible. But still no answer. So, she broke the window closest to the door and reached around to unlock it from the inside.

Joan opened the door slightly. Wanting to respect the young couple's privacy, she called out, "Hello! Are you home? Lisa? Carl?"

When she didn't get an answer, she proceeded to take a few steps into the front room. She called again.

"Hello? Are you kids home? I just wanted to check on you and make sure you are okay."

She took a few more steps toward the kitchen, sniffing to see if she could detect a gas odor. But she didn't smell anything.

At this point, Joan's concern began to increase, and she decided to take a more thorough look around. She went into the kitchen and saw Lisa's leftover hamburger casserole sitting out on the dining room table.

Now, she was growing more and more uneasy. Leaving leftover food out overnight was not something Lisa ever did. "What is going on?" she asked herself. "Something is not right here."

Slowly, she walked down the hall toward the bedroom.

"Lisa?" she called one more time, this time her voice a little shaky. "Carl? Is anybody home?"

When she reached the door of one of the spare rooms, she nervously gave one more knock.

"Hello? If you're in here, I'm just going to come in to make sure you're okay. Is that all right?"

Tentatively, she took another step and peeked into the room.

"Oh my! Lisa!!!" she shrieked.

Seeing her daughter face down on the spare bedroom floor, she ran to Lisa's side.

"Lisa! Lisa!" she hollered. "Please! This can't be happening! Please wake up!"

In an effort to wake her daughter, she gave her a slight shake. Then another.

"Lisa, please wake up!" she cried. "Please tell me you're okay. Please tell me this isn't happening."

But reality started to set in, and her mind began to process that this horrifying scene was indeed real. Somebody had bound her daughter and strangled her to death.

Joan could only collapse on the floor next to her daughter's lifeless body and sob.

She had lost her baby girl. And at such a young age, just as her life was getting started. As she sat on the floor next to her daughter, so many questions flooded her mind.

What happened? Who would have done such a sadistic thing to her little girl? And why?

As tears streamed down her cheeks and her mind continued racing, Joan suddenly realized that she needed to call someone for help. She needed to call the police. And Erik. And Carl.

"Oh my, how can I tell them what happened? This is going to break their hearts. This is going to crush them," she said to herself.

But before she could call them, she would have to call the police and get help. She remembered that there was a telephone in another room that she could use. She walked to the adjacent bedroom, unaware of what she was about to encounter.

There lay her son-in-law's body, also face down, blood visible from a gash on his head.

Joan fell to her knees in the doorway of the bedroom and cried uncontrollably. The sight was too much to bear. She knelt, paralyzed and sobbing for several minutes. How could this have happened? How will her family deal with this? And what about Carl's family? How could she possibly get the words out to tell them? So many questions raced through her mind. It was all so overwhelming; she wasn't sure that she would be able to even move again—or even breathe.

Finally, she took a deep breath and summoned the strength to get back to her feet. Her mind was slowly coming to terms with what had happened.

Then the strength of a mother of four took over.

She saw that the telephone on the side table was off the hook. She would have to walk around Carl to get to the phone, so she took another

THE FOUR Cs   91

deep breath and tried to gather herself before walking over to the phone to call the police.

Suddenly, she realized that strangers would be in the house and that they would see her daughter's unclothed body.

She didn't want that, and she knew Lisa wouldn't want that.

This was a terrible thing that had happened, and she understood that the authorities had a job to do, but her daughter deserved to maintain her dignity.

Before she called the authorities, Joan composed herself again, hung up the phone, and reentered the bedroom where Lisa was. Seeing a pair of Lisa's purple flowered pants laying nearby, Joan gently and reverently laid the pants over her daughter's body, making sure to cover as much of her as possible.

Before leaving the room, she took one last longing look at her daughter, knowing that this would most likely be the last private moment she would have with Lisa before detectives started investigating and the authorities removed her from the house.

She went into where the telephone was and made the call to the police.

The dispatcher instructed Joan to stay at the house and advised her that sheriff's deputies would be there in a few minutes. While she waited, her motherly instincts again kicked in.

"Lisa wouldn't want anyone to see the house cluttered," she told herself. "I'd better at least pick up a little before anyone gets here."

In the few minutes she had, Joan put some things away and began to clear the dishes from the dining room table, but before she could finish, sheriff's deputies had already arrived.

"Hello," called one of the deputies, knocking on the front door. "Is anybody home?"

"Yes," answered Joan, walking to the door to greet them. Seeing sheriff's deputies inside her daughter's house brought with it another wave of reality for the grief-stricken mother and the tears once again flowed as the detectives entered the home.

"It's horrible in there!" she blurted out to them. "My daughter and son-in-law are dead. Somebody murdered them!"

"We know it's difficult," one of the deputies replied in an even-toned voice. He had been with the department for several years and had learned that the calmer he spoke, the better chance he could help people stay as calm as possible. "Can you show us where they are?"

Joan pointed the way before taking a few steps down the hall toward the bedrooms. Then, abruptly, she stopped.

"I can't," her words choking. "I can't bear to see them that way again."

The deputies looked at one another before a sheriff's detective motioned for them to head to the room to start securing the crime scene.

The detective was a veteran of the Yellowstone County Sheriff's Office and had seen his share of crime scenes. But never anything like this. Still, he knew how important it was to put people—especially family members—at ease as much as possible.

"I understand," he told Joan. "Why don't we go out to the living room and sit down. Would you like some water?"

Staring blankly, she nodded her head.

He motioned to one of the deputies standing nearby, who dutifully left the room to fetch Joan a glass of water.

"I know this is overwhelming," the detective said to Joan. "But I have to ask you a few questions and then we can let you go home. Do you think you'd be up to that?"

"Yes, I suppose so," Joan agreed.

The detective made sure Joan had a chance to take a few sips of her water before he asked her any questions. He wanted her to be able to gather her thoughts. When she indicated that she was ready, he had her take him through the last few days and particularly through the past twenty-four hours. He asked questions around when she last saw the couple or last spoke to her daughter. What brought her over to the house that morning? Had she noticed anything unusual going on with Lisa and Carl recently? And had she been aware of any threats directed toward the couple?

She hadn't.

"When did you first start to worry there might be something wrong?" he asked.

"Last night," she responded. "We called them to see how they were. We had a special family dinner that we have every year at the end of hunting season and Lisa called to tell us they wouldn't be able to make it. After dinner, my husband called again to see how they were doing. We wanted to see if they were okay."

"Did you get a chance to talk to them?" the detective asked. "And, if so, what was their demeanor? What did they say?"

"No, we weren't able to talk to them," she said slowly, before remembering a peculiar detail. "I think Lisa answered the phone, but my husband said she didn't sound like herself. He said her voice was gargled. Then, we lost the connection. I'm not sure what happened."

"Did that worry you?"

"A little," she responded. "But sometimes calls get disconnected out here, so we didn't panic over it. But then I found out that Lisa didn't show up to work this morning. That's why I came over to check on them. When we hadn't heard from them, I thought Lisa, or even both of them, might be a little under the weather."

Then came the hard part of the interview.

The detective asked Joan to take him through that morning's events. Trying to choke back tears, Joan retraced her steps and talked investigators through what she had seen in as much detail as she could muster.

It was heart-wrenching, but she got through it. When the interview was finally over, Joan asked if she could call her husband.

"Of course," the detective replied.

Tears were now rolling down Erik's cheeks as he sat in his Boise home that day in 2019, thinking about that fateful telephone call. It had been decades, but to him, it was as if it was happening right in the moment. He remembered that he took the call at work and how his sweet wife sobbed immediately upon hearing her husband's voice.

"What's the matter, Joan?" he asked, startled to hear her so panicked. He had never heard so much agony in her voice and he was immediately unsettled by it.

"Something terrible has happened!" she exclaimed. "Lisa and Carl! They're gone!"

"What do you mean they're gone?" he asked, suspecting that he already knew the answer to his own question. "Joan, what happened?"

"Someone murdered Lisa and Carl!" she sobbed, barely able to get the words out. "Somebody killed our baby girl! Somebody killed Carl! It's so awful, Erik. They did terrible things to our daughter!"

Stunned, all Erik could get out was, "Where are you now? I will be right there."

She was still at Carl and Lisa's house, and Erik rushed over right away to be at his wife's side. As he drove to the house, all he could think about was the pain in his sweetheart's voice. He had trouble processing that they had lost their beautiful daughter and son-in-law.

That just couldn't be possible. Not here.

On occasion, Erik would think back to the moment he arrived at the house and first saw the agonized look on Joan's face. He knew that shell-shocked look from his time at war overseas. He had seen it all too often and he had experienced it more times than he could count. That feeling that felt as if someone had reached in and ripped the very soul from your body.

But this was different. This was his sweetheart.

He looked at Joan and immediately wished it would have been him. He would have given anything to protect her from having to experience that horrific scene.

"I would have fought the Battle of the Bulge a thousand times over if it meant sparing her from walking into that house," he would quietly say to himself. "There are some things you just can't un-see."

Any time that decades-old memory of Joan's expression crossed his mind, he experienced that startling hurt all over again. And it never felt like an old memory, only a fresh wound opened again by a harsh reality that played over and over again in his mind.

That day, he would take Joan home and they would cry together. He held her for hours to try and console her, knowing that there was really nothing he would be able to do to take the pain away. There was also the realization that they would have to tell the rest of the family. Their sons, Lance and Terry, would be devastated. They were so close to Lisa.

They also had a sixteen-year-old daughter still at home, Lisa's sister, Kristal. This news was going to hit her hard. In Erik's mind, she was still so young and innocent. They would have to find a way to help her work her way through all this senselessness.

But how? How would they help her when they weren't even sure how they would work through it themselves?

"We will just have to work through it together," he remembered Joan telling him during one of their many conversations. Looking back, he was struck by her composed tone and resolved demeanor. He was never short on reasons to marvel at his wife, and this experience was yet another one.

He was the one with all the hard life experience. Wasn't he supposed to be the one comforting her?

Yet here she was, consoling him. Another reason he was so grateful to be married to her. So much wisdom that held their family together for so many years. They would eventually get through it like they did so many things—one day at a time.

The next several weeks would be trying for both them and the Bennett family. While Erik and Joan were working through the tragic death of their daughter, Carl's parents, Lawrence and Emma, were doing the same for their son.

They were good people. The families got along well, and both were especially glad that Carl and Lisa had become a couple and married.

In his later years, Erik thought about them often. Emma passed away in 2000 and Lawrence in 2003.

The families had so many things in common—a love of the outdoors, of hunting, and of woodworking. And, like Erik, Lawrence had served in World War II. He had been a tank mechanic in England and in Northern Africa. Every once in a while, they would get together and would sometimes spend hours talking about the things they loved to do. Unfortunately, they also had the horrific loss of their children in common, along with all the difficult experiences that come with losing children in such a tragic way.

Over the next several months, the grieving families would answer a lot of questions posed by the police, searching for leads and trying to identify suspects. There would also be media inquiries and questions from reporters. So many things thrown at them at once. All this while trying to plan and coordinate funeral services for their children that no parents should ever have to plan.

They made it through the funerals and the weeks that followed. So many well-wishers—both close friends and casual acquaintances—offered their sympathies, offered to help in any way possible. It was a difficult time, but the families held out hope that their children's brutal killer would be discovered and brought to justice.

As the weeks turned into months and months into years, answers were fleeting.

Detectives had painstakingly gone through the house and had collected every shred of evidence available. They ran tests for fingerprints, interviewed people of interest, and tried to narrow down potential suspects. There were times they thought they were close, but to the families' disappointment, the leads came up empty. It felt like each time the authorities were close to solving the case, there was just not enough evidence to justify an arrest. The families never gave up hope, but eventually it became clear that they would be better off if they didn't obsess over the investigation.

"Lisa and Carl wouldn't want us to stop living our lives," Joan told Erik. "Maybe it's just best if we let the authorities do their jobs and we move on with our lives. Don't you think that's what Lisa and Carl would tell us if they were here?"

As was seemingly always the case, Erik knew that Joan was right.

As tempting as it was to second-guess the sheriff's detectives' every move, he knew in his heart of hearts that the authorities were doing their best. They wanted to find the killer. He knew that they felt the pain of this loss, too. The whole community did. It might not have been as intimate as the family's pain, but their pain was real, and it still hurt.

And the hurt was a lot to feel and a lot to see.

Everything around them seemed to remind them of what happened to Lisa and Carl, so Erik and Joan eventually decided to move and get a fresh start. Their travels took them to some great communities where they met some wonderful people. First to Carson City, Nevada, then to Portland, Oregon, before finally retiring to Boise, Idaho, in 1993.

As Erik reflected on his life in his later years, his thoughts would inevitably turn to the many people he had gotten to know over almost a century of life.

"Most of them were good people," he would often say.

Yes, he had also seen the worst this world had to offer, but looking back, his life experience taught him that most people just want to do some good with their lives.

He lamented that his daughter and son-in-law had to cross paths with one of the truly evil ones, but he didn't want to let that experience control his perspective on life. He would live to honor the noble wishes of those who had gone before him. He would live to rise above the horror.

Often, as he aged into his eighties and even into his nineties, whenever people would ask him what the key to his longevity was, he would reply, "Be happy."

Despite all he had been through and despite more than four decades of not getting answers to who killed his daughter and son-in-law, Erik Rault was determined to live his life the happiest he could.

That spring day in 2019, Kristal had been contemplating some things of her own.

She was sixteen when Lisa and Carl were murdered. Navigating adolescence is hard enough. But to try and work through the emotions of such a senseless act of violence against the sister she adored, how was she able to do that?

Her sister and brother-in-law's deaths paralyzed her existence.

Not only had she lost them, but she also had the difficult task of watching the rest of her family try to cope with such a devastating loss. How could she lessen the sadness of others when she could not find a way to comfort herself? And how was she going to blend this tragedy into her life?

Even at the tender age of sixteen, as she watched the people around her grapple with their own grief, she began to realize that they did not know any more than she did how to navigate those uncharted waters.

"We were all drifting," Kristal thought, "unaware of the mornings or the night times when we slept."

She had come to the conclusion that people compartmentalized their memories—the darkness, the anger, the grief. A staggering of emotions that do not fit together but live in the same place. There was a time when Kristal wondered how long the grief would last and if she would ever be happy. As she thought back on her own life, she remembered a day when she felt a speckle of sunshine and knew that she would find a way to navigate her life. In thinking back, Kristal also knew that each of her siblings and her parents had discovered their own path, though it was never easy. Such contemplation seemed to come whenever there was the prospect of news on the horizon. Just then, her thoughts were interrupted by the ringing of the telephone.

A representative from the Yellowstone County Sheriff's Office was on the phone and wanted to talk to her. It was Monty Wallis, who was the civilian supervisor over the Yellowstone County Sheriff's Volunteer Cold Case Unit.

In 2010, Monty, a former television news reporter and reserve deputy of twenty-nine years, had been tasked by the sheriff's office to recruit and assemble a group of retired detectives and a list of solvable cold cases.

He started by calling around to other law enforcement communities across the country who had organized similar volunteer units. Having learned their best practices, Monty and his team eventually narrowed down the list of cases to nine, Carl and Lisa's included.

Monty told Kristal that he was calling with some big news.

"Well, what update do you have for us?" Kristal asked. "You must have something pretty important to share with us."

As she uttered those very words, Kristal tried to repress any hope that they might be calling with news of an arrest. She had hoped for years that, before her father passed away, there would be an actual conclusion to the mystery surrounding Lisa and Carl's murders. In a way, it was also kind of scary to get that news. What if it was someone who knew the family? Or even worse, someone who had been a close friend of the family?

Not wanting to let her imagination get too far ahead of her or to get her hopes up too high, Kristal thought it best to simply reserve judgment and listen to what Monty had to say. And this time something seemed different. Even the tone of Monty's voice on the other end of the line was different from anything she had heard before.

"Kristal, we have what we think is very good news," Monty responded.

Then he paused, almost unable to get the words out.

"We've found him," he said. "We know who the man is who is responsible for murdering Lisa and Carl."

Kristal was stunned. For so long, the family had stopped believing that they would hear those words uttered aloud. Was this really happening?

Kristal paused, seemingly hesitant to ask the inevitable question the entire family had spent decades wanting to know the answer to but had also been somewhat afraid to hear.

She sat down and paused for a second before she was finally able to speak.

"Who?" she asked in a somewhat cautious tone of voice. "Who did this to Lisa and Carl?"

"We have some pretty strong scientific evidence that we didn't have available to us back then that it's a man named Cecil Caldwell," Monty replied. "He more commonly went by his middle name of Stan. Does his name sound familiar?"

"Not really," Kristal replied, relieved that it wasn't a close family acquaintance. "But it's been such a long time. Did you arrest him? Is he in jail?"

"Unfortunately, we were not able to arrest him. He passed away several years ago, in 2003," Monty explained. "But once we were able to identify him through the use of advanced DNA technology, the county attorney said that would be enough compelling evidence to charge him if he was alive. Because he isn't alive to stand trial, the case is now considered closed. We wanted you to be the first to know. After all these years, we thought you and your father deserved to be the first people we notified."

In that moment, Kristal wasn't sure exactly how to feel.

On one hand, she was glad that they finally found the man who had made her sister suffer so much before brutally cutting her life short—and that they did so with such strong evidence. On the other hand, it brought so many difficult memories back to the surface. Still, she was grateful, and she knew her father would feel the same way.

"Thank you, Monty," she replied. "Thank you to you and everyone at the sheriff's office for never giving up on Lisa and Carl's case. That means a lot to us."

"Well, we're glad we were able to find the identity of the person who did this and that your father is still around to get the news. We really wanted to solve this for you and for him."

After she finished her conversation with Monty, Kristal took a deep breath before going into the living room where Erik was sitting. This was indeed going to be some big news to deliver to her father.

"Dad," she said, pulling a nearby chair over to him. "I've got something to tell you. Are you up to talking?"

"Yes," he answered with a slow nod of the head. "What do you want to talk about?"

"Well," Kristal started, "I just got off the phone with Monty from the sheriff's office in Montana. He just gave me some pretty big news about Lisa and Carl."

Kristal took her father's hand and held it for a minute or two, trying to gauge the best way to tell him.

"What is it?" he asked, his head still bowed somewhat. "What did they tell you?"

"They found out who did those horrible things to Lisa and Carl, Dad," she said. "They know who is responsible for their deaths."

Erik lifted his head and looked directly at his daughter; his eyes widened.

"Who?" he asked. "Who did this to Lisa and Carl?"

"Monty said it was a man named Cecil Caldwell," Kristal answered. "He said he went by the name of Stan. Have you ever heard of him?"

Erik thought for a moment, then answered, "No. I've never heard that name before, at least not that I can remember. Have you?"

"No, Dad," she said. "I didn't know that name either."

"Did they arrest him?" Erik asked.

"No, they didn't," Kristal replied. "They said he passed away in 2003. But they know he did it because of some new DNA tests they did. So, at least we know now. Monty said he wanted us to be the first to know and that they worked really hard to solve it for you. They respect you a lot, Dad."

"I appreciate that," he said, turning his gaze back toward the window.

Erik sat quietly for several minutes while Kristal sat with him and held his hand. Nothing more needed to be said. Father and daughter had a mutual understanding of what this meant.

Kristal's thoughts turned to her brothers, Lance and Terry, and to her mother—all of whom had passed away years earlier. She wondered how they would have reacted to the news.

There was a sense of melancholy as she wished that this advancement in DNA technology would have been available years ago so they could have been a part of it, so that Kristal and her father could have shared this moment with them. Not that it would have changed the outcome.

In fact, in some ways, getting this news meant having to relive the pain all over again. But at least it was a chapter in this family's history that could now finally be closed. No more unresolved questions. No more wondering what happened. They could at least move on from that part of this terrible event in their family's history.

On one hand, Kristal thought her brothers especially might have appreciated knowing that Lisa's killer had finally been identified.

Lance and Lisa were very close, and her death was extremely hard for him to take. But both brothers had stayed in touch with the sheriff's office throughout the years and she thought there would have been a part of them, at least, that would have been pleased with the outcome of the investigation.

On the other hand, Kristal thought, there might have been a sense of disappointment among the family that this horrible human being's crimes weren't discovered while he was still alive to face justice. Kristal felt that the family probably would have liked to have seen Cecil Caldwell answer for his crimes. As a father, a mother, and as siblings, they most likely would have wanted to have confronted him in open court, to tell this man just who he had taken from the world—from their family; from the Bennett family; and from the entire world as a whole.

Then Kristal thought about her mother, Joan. What would she have said if she had still been around to get this call? She most likely would have wanted to confront him, but in the end, Joan probably would have viewed the situation with the wisdom she seemingly approached every life situation.

"No matter," Joan might have said. "A depraved individual like that wouldn't have blinked twice over anything we had to say. He didn't care about my daughter's life then and he probably wouldn't care now."

Overall, Kristal was grateful—grateful that the authorities had never quit on her sister and brother-in-law's case and grateful that she and Erik were around to find out about it. She was especially happy that her father had lived long enough to see the outcome. Forty-five years is a long time to wait, and whether it was good genetics or sheer determination, he lived long enough to know the ending.

As Kristal pondered on these things, her thoughts were suddenly interrupted.

"How?" Erik asked, breaking the silence. "After all these years. How did they finally find the man who did this to our family?"

Kristal would have to talk to the sheriff's investigators to get more details, which meant she would have to save that conversation for another time.

But the question was a valid one. How indeed?

That has been the age-old question since crime-solving began.

How do we, as officers of the law, prove beyond a reasonable doubt that a specific individual actually committed a crime as serious as murder? And, more especially, how do we do so after so much time has gone by?

After decades, how did detectives in 2019 finally solve a case that the Yellowstone County Sheriff's Office had been working on since 1973?

The answer is not a simple one because there is a lot that goes into solving cold cases. So much training, inspection, and attention to detail are required to find and appropriately collect evidence at the scene of a crime, especially a crime so violent as sexual assault and murder. Detectives spend years honing their investigative skills, learning how to effectively collect and maintain evidence and how to interview and interrogate suspects so that they can ask the right questions and get answers from those who might be hiding the truth.

But most important, solving cold cases requires a wide variety of people who are willing to stick with a case for the long haul and follow the core foundational principles that we referenced in the last chapter, "The 4 Cs":

- communication
- coordination
- collaboration
- cooperation

In my opinion, as far as cold cases go, the Bennett case is a great example of how good things can happen when agencies, families, volunteers, and the general public come together and adhere to these principles. There were so many people involved in finding answers for these families and trying to get justice for Carl and Lisa Bennett—not just law enforcement, but citizens, too.

During that forty-five-year period, hundreds of people assisted with this case in one form or another, including twenty-one law enforcement agencies spanning twelve states. Credit also needs to go to private companies, citizens, and people who donated their time, resources, and expertise in cooperatively working with authorities during their hours of interviews and evidence collection.

In the course of this decades-long investigation, 894 people were contacted, most of whom willingly talked to sheriff's investigators in the hopes that they could provide some piece of information that would lead to this case being solved. As for our part, in 2016, the Cold Case Foundation was asked to assist in the investigation from a criminal behavioral analysis standpoint. To his credit, Captain Vince Wallis, who supervised the detective unit for the Yellowstone County Sheriff's Office at the time, assigned the Bennett case to himself in 2016 and immediately enlisted as much help from as many sources as possible.

It was a case that had haunted the Billings community for decades and, now that the sheriff's office had a cold case unit, Vince thought it would be a good time to give it a fresh start.

He enlisted the help of his father, Monty Wallis, who had actually created the unit in 2012, and Scott Goodwin, a reserve deputy who donated his time and expertise to help investigate the case.

"From day one, we made this a brand new case," Scott told us when we talked to him about the case a few years after it was solved. "We wanted to look at it with a fresh perspective and investigate it as if it was a new case. We didn't want to overlook anything or leave any stone unturned."

Once Vince took the case, one of his first items of business was to take an unconventional approach to the case. He told us that was one of the main reasons he brought Scott in on the case.

"Scott's one of those guys that kind of has a photographic memory," Vince said. "While most of us have to go through our notes to recall details or evidence, Scott can call it out right off the top of his head. The guy's amazing that way." With all the moving parts involved in this case, Scott's ability to recall details was invaluable to the investigation.

Vince's unconventional approach was also key to solving the case. His strategy included bringing in family members of both Carl and Lisa to brainstorm some possibilities of people they thought detectives should talk to or re-interview.

"I told them that this is a new group," Vince recalled. "We're going to do this together. It's going to be a group effort. So, I handed everyone a notebook and a pencil, and I asked, 'Who might this be?' Then, as we went through the case, everyone took notes, offered suggestions of people we should interview, and then we moved forward from there."

Not long after that meeting, Vince decided he wanted a behavioral analysis done on the offender, so he reached out to John Douglas's publisher, got John's email, and sent him a note asking if he could help with the case.

Since John was the chairman of the board of the Cold Case Foundation at the time, he introduced Vince to me, and we got to work on the case.

This was the first case that the foundation assisted with as an organization, and it was an honor to be invited to help. At the time, we had just a few investigators on the team, which included John and myself. John and I were asked to create a criminal profile including the probable relationship between the offender and the victims, Carl and Lisa Bennett, based on the perpetrator's behavior at the crime scene.

It was no small task.

We had to be very methodical as we developed the profile of the offender. A violent crime of this nature, taking place in a small community, is an unusual occurrence in and of itself, and our work had to be painstakingly detailed.

Add to it that, because the crime had occurred almost forty-five years prior, we were being tasked to do a thorough study of twenty-four-year-old victims who would both be in their seventies if they were alive today. Additionally, the circumstances surrounding the crime scene had undergone so many changes over the past five decades.

We really had our work cut out for us.

Still, the process we use is always the same. As is our protocol when we develop a criminal profile on any case, we started with the victims and worked outward from there. So, our first order of business was to study the overall lifestyles of Carl and Lisa Bennett to determine their risk levels.

What we discovered was a very low-risk young married couple.

"Both of these individuals were responsible, hard workers," I told John, as we began our study of the victims' lives.

Carl served in the Vietnam War and had returned two years earlier a decorated veteran, awarded both a Bronze Star and a Purple Heart. He worked full-time at Quality Concrete company and Lisa worked as a billing and accounting clerk at a Ryan's Wholesale Grocery during the day. At night, they worked together cleaning offices to earn the extra money they needed to put the finishing touches on the home they had recently built.

Based on their background information, we were quickly able to determine that they weren't prone to the types of activities that would typically put someone at a high risk for this kind of violent crime (things like illegal drug use, criminal activity, etc.). They were both good students in school and responsible, hard-working people as adults.

That being the case, why were they targeted?

"The question we need to answer is: How would someone be able to perpetrate this kind of a crime on this young couple living a low-risk life in a quiet, rural neighborhood so close to her parents?" When we took into account Carl's combat experience—along with the demanding physical nature of his concrete job and his large, rugged build at 210 pounds—it seemed quite improbable that the perpetrator overpowered him and forced his way into the house.

"Also, we need to ask ourselves, how would the offender have been able to subdue this strong young man to the point that he was able to impose his will on both him and his wife?" I queried. The circumstances of the victims and their activities around the time of the murders suggested that someone would have had to manipulate them into a situation where they were abruptly thrust into a high-risk situation. We needed to put the pieces together to try and determine how that might have happened.

At the time of the murders, Lisa and Carl were in their home, which was located kitty corner from Lisa's parents. Since they were still in the finishing stages of completing their home, neither drapes nor curtains had been installed on any of the windows.

"This would indicate that the offender had to feel a high level of confidence being in the home," I said, "as if he was invited into the house, which he probably was on some level, possibly to come in and do some work for them. It's quite possible that he showed up while the couple was eating dinner."

My opinion was based on evidence detectives found when they arrived at the house the next morning.

They discovered leftover hamburger casserole on the dining room table and what appeared to be remnants of at least two place settings, maybe three. It's hard to know if there were more than two place settings because Lisa's mother, as mothers often do, began to clean up before the sheriff's deputies arrived. So, there was a chance that the man who would eventually perpetrate this crime had shown up to the home while the couple was in the middle of eating their meal and was invited inside. It was cold outside, so if the perpetrator did show up to the house, there's a good chance that the young couple would have at least let him into the house to get out of the cold.

Additionally, detectives found candles and cigarette ashes at the dining table. Keeping in mind that this was just a normal Tuesday evening, we asked ourselves why then were there candles on the table? Was it possible that it was the offender living out his fantasy with Lisa before he eventually killed her?

Either way, when the victimology was taken into account, the circumstances surrounding this case definitely raised some eyebrows.

With that information in hand, John and I did what we typically do when we profile a case. We began building the criminal profile by making what we call threshold diagnoses, which are initial observations based on the basic information of the case. From there, we typically continue to communicate with the investigating law enforcement agency to gather more details about the case so that we can then further develop the profile.

And we always consider a criminal profile a living document. It takes a lot of collaboration for this process to work effectively so that the profile develops over time as additional information about the case continues to come in. So, this is not an overnight process. It takes time and, in this case, it took several months to create a working profile of the offender.

As we dove further into the victimology, we made some foundational observations about the Bennetts' possible relationship to the offender.

"One or both of them had to have known the perpetrator," I observed.

"Or, at the very least, they were familiar and comfortable enough to invite him into their home," John added.

We needed more details about the circumstances of their lives to find out what was going on around the time this crime was committed. And we needed to find out who would have been associated with one or both of them in a way in which the offender would have been invited to enter their house. We immediately got to work and found that some key things happened the day of the murders that were out of the ordinary.

First, because it was snowing, the concrete company that Carl worked for had to send him and the rest of the crew home earlier than usual from work, as the inclement weather delayed the concrete project he was working on. So, he spent most of the day with a friend/co-worker until being dropped off at home around 4:30 p.m.

Second, Carl had called Lisa at work and asked her to stop at the bank on her way home to transfer a large amount of their savings—$690—to their checking account, which she did. This was notable because Carl told his friend that they had a carpet layer scheduled to come over to finish the staircase later that evening. "The deposit she made would have definitely been sufficient to cover that kind of work," John said. Evidently, they had already paid one payment and the $690 could have been toward the second.

The third key occurrence from that day was that Lisa called her mom to tell her that they would not be able to attend the annual family dinner scheduled for that evening. That dinner was a big event for the Rault family because it typically signaled the end of the hunting season and was an annual family tradition. So, it wasn't a small dinner to miss. But, based on the conversation that Carl had with his friend that day, they may have had to stay in and wait for a subcontractor before heading out to their office-cleaning job later that night.

As we began to piece these events together, we narrowed the criminal profile down to people whom one or both of the victims had known or had been somewhat familiar with on a consistent basis, meaning he was not a person whom they had just recently met, nor was he a stranger.

"The offender was probably either someone Lisa worked with or someone who worked for the couple, such as one of the subcontractors on their home," I said. "Whatever the relationship was, they did not feel initially that the offender posed a threat to them."

"I agree," John responded. "And it's clear by the behavior at the crime scene that the offender was fixated on the wife. She was definitely the primary target."

"And if the offender was one of Lisa's coworkers, even if he worked in separate areas of the warehouse, he could have orchestrated reasons to be in proximity to her," I said. "Even if it was just at a distance, but within sight of her, he would want to feed his fantasy. The offender's behavior suggests that, even if he didn't interact daily with Lisa, he was obsessed with keeping his fantasy alive."

"Absolutely," John agreed. "And it appears that his obsessive feelings of romance for her would not have been reciprocated."

Next, we turned our attention to the crime itself.

As we analyzed the perpetrator's behavior, we were vicariously understanding the motivations of the offender's actions during the commission of the crime. Based on what we saw, the offender had spent a lot of time fantasizing both about Lisa and about the level of power and control he would use in fulfilling his sexual fantasy.

We were looking for both modus operandi and, if present, signature behavior.

Typically, when we deal with a violent sexual assault and murder—especially one that takes place in the victim's home—we can usually gauge the offender's experience and comfort level based on how much time he spends at the crime scene during and after the commission of the crime. In this case, all indications were that he spent several hours at the home that night, which is a considerable amount of time for an offender to spend at the scene of a double homicide and sexual assault—especially when you consider that there were no window coverings.

Finally, going through the perpetrator's behavior at the crime scene also helps us to determine what he might have possibly done in the days, weeks, months, and years after he killed this young couple. Would he have picked up and moved on with his life out of state or even out of the country? Or would he have been the type of person to actually stay in the small community where he committed such an atrocious crime? As we began to dig into the crime scene, we immediately took note of some specific behaviors that provided some key answers.

One, there were no signs of forced entry.

"And there weren't any signs of a physical struggle," John observed. "No broken lamps, no pictures fallen off the wall, not even scratches on the walls."

This was especially notable because the couple had only lived in the newly painted home for a few weeks.

The lack of any apparent damage inside the home suggested to John and me that Lisa and Carl went to the respective rooms where their bodies were discovered without putting up a physical fight. There were no defense wounds on either of the victims.

"This suggests that the offender had some form of leverage," I said, "either through some kind of guise or through a combination of threats, intimidation, and/or promises in order to commandeer them into separate rooms without using physical force."

"And, as we discussed earlier, it's highly unlikely that he would have been able to overpower the husband," John opined. "We're talking about a strong young man who laid concrete for a living and had seen combat in Vietnam. Without some form of leverage or guise, and under this set of circumstances, the offender would have been no match for him."

This was an important point, because it was consistent with a theory that sheriff's detectives had developed earlier in the investigation. Evidently Carl liked to demonstrate a newly installed ceiling fan in the room where his body was located. Surmising that Carl did show the ceiling fan to the offender, detectives think he would have been in a vulnerable position when he entered the guest room closet where the switch was located. They believed that if Carl went into the closet to turn on the switch, with his back turned, the offender could have struck him in the back of the head. That was definitely a possibility.

As we visualized how the events of the crime might have played out, we thought it was also possible that the offender could have surprised the young couple by pulling a gun on them while specifically threatening Lisa so that Carl would be compliant with his demands. Because they were at least somewhat familiar with him, they would be surprised by his behavior and caught off guard by the unpredictability of his actions.

In this instance, the perpetrator could have ordered them to one of the bedrooms and had one of them tie the other up by both the wrists and ankles.

Either way, at some point, the offender followed Carl into the room where he struck him on the back of the head with some type of blunt instrument, incapacitating the young husband just long enough to strangle him to death with a leather boot lace.

Then he entered the room where Lisa was bound, at which point he sexually assaulted her repeatedly over the next several hours. When he was done, he coldly strangled her to death in the same manner that he strangled her husband.

Before leaving the home, the killer did some post-crime things that gave us some additional clues about his overall mindset.

First, he turned down the thermostat to forty-five degrees, the lowest possible setting, then opened several windows throughout the house. A November night in Montana gets very cold. On that November night in 1973, the recorded temperature had dropped to six degrees.

"It looks like the offender wanted to keep the bodies as cold as possible," I said. "It's highly probable that his intent was to manipulate the time of death and give himself an alibi in case detectives came knocking at his door."

This was also a telling behavior in regard to the likelihood that the offender may have been a resident who lived in the area.

"If he was going to commit a crime of this nature in a community this small," John added, "then the offender wouldn't want to arouse suspicion by picking up and abruptly moving so soon after the murder. And, to your point, he would also need a reasonable alibi."

In this case, we believed that the offender wanted to manipulate the decomposition process so that he would have an alibi that would keep him covered. This way, he could stick to his day-to-day routine without arousing suspicion.

By so doing, the assailant could literally have been hiding in plain sight.

The second thing the offender did was one of his most bizarre post-crime behaviors. He stole every pair of undergarments belonging to Lisa, including any that were left in the dirty clothes hamper downstairs.

"He took the time to search the house for every bra and set of underwear that he could find," I noted. "That is significant because it is indicative of the intensity of his fantasies about her."

Once the offender collected every undergarment he could find, he opted to steal a large suitcase from the couple so he could transport and conceal them. Often in these types of crimes offenders may take personal possessions belonging to the victim. We refer to such items as trophies or souvenirs taken by the offender for the purpose of reliving the crime over and over again. This behavior is categorized as a "signature" aspect of the crime. It symbolically represents for the offender an intimate and personal connection to the victim while reminding the offender of the crime and enabling him to repeat the acting out of his fantasy with the victim.

The way in which the victims were discovered at the crime scene emphasizes that Lisa was the primary target and the offender's sexual motivation for the crime. Unfortunately, Carl was collateral damage in that he represented an obstacle that the offender had to remove in order to achieve his ultimate fantasy.

Finally, the perpetrator did one peculiar thing that had police detectives scratching their heads.

He left one item behind—red lingerie that belonged to Lisa Bennett. Not only had the assailant left it behind, but he displayed it by draping it over a chair in the bedroom. I was asked about that after we submitted our report to the Yellowstone County Sheriffs Cold Case Unit.

Why would the perpetrator go to all the effort to search the house for every single piece of undergarment she owned, but leave behind the sexy lingerie?

The answer: His obsession was Lisa. He wanted to possess her. In his mind, the undergarments symbolized an intimate representation of Lisa and facilitated his sexual fantasies with her.

But the lingerie? The lingerie represented intimacy between Lisa and her husband Carl. The offender couldn't act out his fantasies using the lingerie without thinking about her husband having been intimate with her. The husband basically spoiled the fantasy for the perpetrator, so he most likely placed it in the guest bedroom with Carl because it was of no use to him. He associated it with Lisa and Carl's intimate relationship. And he wanted no part of that. Whatever his association was with Lisa, his fixation was solely on her.

"I am convinced that there were at least occasional, but intentional interactions that the offender had with Lisa," I said. "Whether he worked with her or whatever the association was, it's highly likely that he would have sought out opportunities to be in proximity to her often enough that he could at least watch her and allow his fantasies to play out in his mind." I was certain that this was the case because deviant fantasies include the element of focused concentration over time, which enables the offender to summon the courage needed to actually carry those fantasies out.

When the analysis was completed, we submitted it to the detectives from the Yellowstone County Sheriff's Cold Case Unit.

In our report we identified the types of characteristics of people who would be valid people of interest, specifically the following:

- knew the Bennetts
- was obsessed with Lisa
- most likely worked with Lisa and was aware of her, or could have been some sort of subcontractor
- would be a high school graduate
- would have a blue-collar manual labor job
- would have an interest in pornography
- has above-average intelligence
- was not a stranger walking through the neighborhood and would have had a legitimate reason to be there, such as a subcontractor at a job site
- is an organized offender, and these characteristics would be manifest in his personal life and controlled environment
- has above-average level of both forensic and criminal knowledge

We also provided some investigative recommendations to follow up on based on our behavioral analysis. These were the suggestions we made to help focus the investigation:

- The Bennetts would have been at least casually aware of the offender.
- The offender would be within five years (before or after) the age of the victim (as it turned out, Caldwell was twenty-eight and Lisa was twenty-four at the time of the murder).
- The offender would have kept the suitcase full of Lisa's underwear and someone who was close to the offender may have seen the items and questioned him about them.
- Check the funeral guest list. He may have attended Lisa's funeral and possibly Carl's as well.
- Lisa was the primary victim and the object of the offender's obsession.
- Look into the employees she worked with and subcontractors.

Over the next couple of years, sheriff's investigators did an outstanding job of following up on these investigative leads and the case began to gain momentum. As detectives re-interviewed people, they began to see that many of them remembered details that they hadn't previously articulated. That's why it's important to stay in touch with and circle back to people who have already been interviewed. Time has a way of changing perspective, memory, and relationships. Over the years, details may be shared with law enforcement that for various reasons were not previously disclosed.

Technological advances also play a key role in solving cold cases. And, in this case, technological advances in DNA would ultimately play a huge part in solving the Bennett murders.

Of course, DNA evidence has played a role in solving cases long before 2019. And, because the Yellowstone County Sheriff's Office continued to work the case, they had tried applying DNA evidence as far back as the 1990s. Once DNA evidence became a realistic option, eighty-three persons of interest were asked for DNA samples, and only three refused to provide samples, which led to eighty of them quickly being ruled out as suspects.

But the problem is that, when it comes to using DNA for the purposes of criminal investigations, the evidence you have is only as good as the DNA matches that we have in the CODIS system, a federal database that helps law enforcement agencies link crime-scene evidence to other cases or to persons already convicted or arrested for specific crimes. Unfortunately, there were no matches because Cecil Caldwell had never been arrested for anything, nor had he ever provided a DNA sample. So, DNA that authorities were able to recover from the crime scene never returned any matches, which is why it took another couple of decades before the DNA evidence that was collected finally returned results.

That's where Parabon Labs entered the picture.

In 2019, not long after we developed the offender's behavioral profile, there was a physical break in the case. Parabon Labs—a citizen-led DNA database analysis company—provided much-needed answers from a scientific perspective. If that organization sounds familiar, it is because the face of Parabon is CeCe Moore, who is famously known as "The Genealogy Detective" for her work in linking DNA typically gathered for family history purposes to cold cases such as this one that didn't have DNA technology when the crimes were originally committed. We are extremely grateful for their work on this case because it ultimately provided the incontrovertible evidence needed to solve this case.

From a physical evidence perspective, it's also important to call out the stellar work that the original police investigators did at the crime scene back on that November day in 1973. Obviously, DNA evidence was not even a concept back then. But detectives still demonstrated the professionalism to carefully collect and store any and all evidence they found at the house. Because of their exemplary work, some key evidence ended up providing workable DNA samples that were key to solving the case.

One of those items was a group of five cigarette butts left unflushed in the toilet of the master bathroom. Because of the careful handling of that evidence, the lab was able to extract DNA from two of the cigarettes left in the bathroom.

The final key piece of physical evidence we attribute to a mother's love. Normally, when a crime scene is disturbed in any way, it can be a detriment to an investigation. But, when Joan Rault covered her daughter's body with the nearby purple flower pants she found in the bedroom, the result was a DNA transfer to those pants that ended up being a key piece of physical evidence.

Applying modern DNA science to that evidence, Parabon Labs was able to provide a high confidence lead identifying two brothers—one living and one deceased. After looking into the living brother, police quickly ruled him out, as he had never been to Montana. He cooperated with police and donated a DNA sample of his own, which came back as a sibling match to the DNA found at the crime scene. That meant that the deceased brother, Cecil Stan Caldwell, was the owner of the DNA obtained from the evidence and ultimately confirmed as the perpetrator of the terrible crimes committed that November night in 1973.

From a criminal behavioral perspective, Vince would later tell us that the behavioral profile we developed, along with the investigative recommendations we shared, helped point their cold case team in a more specific direction.

"It really helped us home in on a narrower group," Vince said. "I remember Greg telling us, 'Your guy is close. He's a neighbor, a friend, or a coworker.' And the part that really stood out to me was that we would be looking for a blue-collar worker. That's one of the things that really helped us narrow it down."

As it turned out, many of the behaviors we called out were confirmed. For example, as detectives continued to work the case, they discovered that Caldwell had signed the guest book for the funerals of both Carl and Lisa Bennett. He attended his victims' funerals, which killers sometimes do.

Another interesting discovery was that, decades later, when investigators spoke with Caldwell's ex-wife, who was married to him at the time of the murders, she said that she had not attended their funerals, nor did her husband mention that he had attended them either. During that same interview, the police corroborated that she remembered finding a suitcase full of women's panties and bras while she was married to Caldwell. She said he passed it off as an old college prank that he and friends would play on female co-eds. He had just "forgotten" about the old suitcase.

Finally, detectives also discovered that Caldwell laid carpet on the side and was probably the carpet layer hired to do the Bennetts' home. More than forty years into the investigation, detectives from the Yellowstone County Sheriff's Cold Case Unit decided to interview anyone who had worked on the Bennett home. They did not have records showing who laid the carpet, but they did find who did the tile work in the house and interviewed him. When asked if he remembered anything unusual, he mentioned that one day after the couple had moved in, he had gone to the downstairs bathroom to finish installing some tile. As he was walking down the stairs, he passed by the carpet layer and noticed a pair of light green panties sitting near the man's belongings. He entered the bathroom and finished his work on the tile, which only took about five minutes. He told investigators that, when he exited the bathroom, both the carpet layer and the panties were gone.

Finally, from the perspective of the relationship of the offender to the victims, as it turned out, Caldwell worked with Lisa at Ryan's Warehouse Grocery, a local grocery store warehouse. He had been promoted to the second-shift foreman and the meat manager for Ryan's. Additionally, we discovered that Caldwell and Lisa actually lived close to one another when they were younger.

Looking at company records, Caldwell worked in Lisa's department for a couple of years and spent quite a bit of time around her, confirming that the perpetrator did have consistent interactions with her. People who worked with them told investigators that he did interact with her every day at work and would go out of his way to repeatedly visit and talk with her. In a sick twist, after Lisa's murder, Caldwell would continue to work at Ryan's Warehouse Grocery for another two and a half years before taking a job with the city of Billings. He remained in Billings until the age of fifty-nine when he passed away in 2003—thirty years after the Bennetts' murder.

As we put the pieces together, we found it highly probable that Caldwell was the carpet layer for the Bennetts' new home and that he was the one that Carl and Lisa were expecting to come lay carpet on the stairs the night of the murders.

Vince Wallis's father, Monty Wallis, put it best when he said that the Bennetts' killer was "hiding in plain sight." That was exactly what Caldwell did. He blended into the community and kept a low profile to reduce the likelihood that anyone would point the finger at him. Eventually, though, because of the work of the Yellowstone County Cold Case Unit, Caldwell was discovered.

When looking at this cold case from an investigative perspective, we see that our guiding principles of communicating, cooperating, coordinating, and collaborating were displayed by so many different groups of people close to the case.

The Cold Case Unit in Yellowstone County was formed in 2012 under the jurisdiction of the Yellowstone County Sheriff's Office Detective Division, in the hopes of solving several cold cases in the area, including the Bennetts' case, which at the time was thirty-nine years old. The unit is comprised of Yellowstone County Sheriff's Office detectives, volunteers including retired investigators, reserve deputies, a crime analyst, and forensic experts. They are all sworn in as special service officers and supervised by sheriff's detectives. This means that, essentially, most everyone in this unit is volunteering their time and expertise to their mission, which is to speak for those who cannot speak for themselves by seeking answers and justice for victims and their families.

I can't stress how crucial it is for both law enforcement officials and the citizens in any given community to work in a way that brings harmony to an investigation. The Bennett case is a shining example of the good that can happen when all involved follow these principles. In addition to the great work done by the cold case unit's investigators, it was private members of the community who also made key contributions, donating in excess of $20,000 to pay for the DNA technology and analysis that Parabon Labs provided in this case. What a tremendous and generous contribution by the community to help solve the case on behalf of the families who had been waiting for answers all these years. Without it, there could not have been the level of DNA testing needed and it's unlikely that the case ever would have been solved.

In the end, it was so satisfying to see the Yellowstone County, Montana Cold Case Unit's success in solving this case because I believe the publicity around their work will lead to other law enforcement communities creating cold case units just like this. These units will bring in much-needed resources to help solve these cases, and most important, send a message to the families of these victims that their loved ones have not been forgotten. That we, as law enforcement, will go to whatever lengths we possibly can to bring their perpetrators to justice.

As for Erik Rault, two months after receiving the news that spring day, he passed away peacefully in his sleep on July 7, 2019. This man and his family had been through so much in their lifetimes. But, through it all, they had also accomplished much. That's why it brought such a sense of fulfillment for all those who had been involved in working this case over the nearly five decades to be able to tell this family that the case had finally been solved. That their loved ones hadn't been given up on and that they were remembered. That we, as investigating authorities, don't forget and that we want to get justice on behalf of those who are victimized by the individuals who commit these heinous crimes.

CHAPTER FIVE

COORDINATION

The More People Looking, the Better

It was a warm summer night in 1996 as Kathy sat in her car outside a roadside bar in a small town in southern Oregon. As she watched the comings and goings of bar patrons entering and exiting the establishment, her thoughts took her back to a similar place in 1959. It was almost as if she could see the five-year-old version of herself dancing and singing on a bar room table while her father held out his checker-plaid hat, asking for money, food, beer, or whatever they could give.

Mostly, though, he asked for beer. If they gave his daughter some food, then so be it. After all, she was really more of a means to an end. Back in those days, adults were allowed to bring their kids into bars, or beer houses, as they were called.

Kathy was all too familiar with the smell of beer and the wispiness of alcohol-laced breath. As a small child, that smell offered her a semblance of security and hope.

Why? Because it's what kept her father around. The prospect of another drink sometimes seemed to be the only thing that made him smile, that made it so he actually wanted her around. Beer is what provided the rare occasions when he would talk to her nicely—like fathers were supposed to talk to their daughters.

"You just get on up on them tables and dance," he would tell her, flashing a rare smile.

Smiling wasn't something Leo Thomas had done much of since he had lost his arm in an accident a few years earlier while playing "chicken" with a freight train in Oklahoma.

After the accident, he and his wife, Jessie, fought constantly and the stress of a man in his condition trying to provide for their three children put additional pressure on the marriage.

Even at the age of forty-two, as Kathy thought back to her childhood, she wondered if it was her fault that their parents' marriage fell apart. Maybe if she had behaved better, there wouldn't have been as much stress. No matter, Kathy thought. Whatever the reasons were that her parents split up, all she remembered was that he chose to take her with him from Oklahoma to the Oregon coast. Kathy's thoughts soon returned to that time when it was just her and her dad.

"Sing your little heart out, you hear? You've got a beautiful little voice that folks here take to real quick like. You see how all them folks light right up when you dance and sing?"

"Yes, daddy," the five-year-old would dutifully answer.

Truth be told, Kathy did love to sing and dance. It was one of her favorite things to do. Even though the barroom tables she danced on were often cold or wet, sometimes even splintery, Kathy didn't mind. She loved the applause, and she enjoyed putting smiles on people's faces. It was a powerful feeling, the ability to make people respond the way she wanted them to.

Mostly, though, she loved the escape. The diversion from the somber reality of her life was worth the price of cold, blistery feet.

She remembered how folks would shout, "Sing another one!"

All the while, Leo would be passing the hat and receiving a pat on the back or two for bringing the entertainment.

"You sure got yourself a talented little girl there!" they would tell him.

"Yes sir, I do!" he would exclaim before guzzling another beer. "That little girl of mine is one of a kind!"

Then they would give him another drink and clamor for more. Most nights father and daughter would be out well past midnight. She would sometimes grow tired and want to stop, but she didn't dare ever say anything. The drinks kept her father happy, and it was important to keep him that way. The alternative was too painful.

Back in Oklahoma, Kathy's mother struggled too. Unable to make their marriage work, Jessie often turned to alcohol to escape the unending pressure of a contentious marriage and all that goes with raising three children in that environment. The fights with her husband were constant, and she often looked to alcohol as her way out.

Kathy had two older sisters. One was two and half years older than her and the other just a year older. In the end, the girls proved to be too much for Kathy's mother. Maybe she felt like they were stealing her youth, or perhaps they had simply interrupted her freedom. Whatever the case, Jessie liked to go bar hopping, and that couldn't happen—at least not as freely as she would have liked—while tied down to three little kids and a husband she didn't love anymore. So, the couple divorced, and they decided to put the two older girls up for adoption.

Just like that, they weren't a family anymore.

The state wasn't able to find homes for all three of the girls, so the decision was made to send the two older girls to separate homes. With nowhere for Kathy to go, her father decided to take her with him as he made his way west.

Over the next few years, Leo had the little girl dancing and singing from Oklahoma, across Colorado and Idaho, and into Oregon, where they would put roots down for a time. They eventually settled into a small makeshift one-bedroom apartment on the top floor of an old farmhouse. It wasn't much, but at least it was a place to call home.

Over the next four years, most nights saw them head to the beer houses and repeat the routine Kathy had become so accustomed to. Wearing the same tattered dress, she would dance and sing and make the beer house patrons smile. And her daddy would drink.

As a little girl, she thought that if she could just make him happy, then maybe he wouldn't give her away to someone else like he and her mother did her sisters. But, one day, Leo decided it was time for him to go.

He had taken his now nine-year-old daughter to almost every beer house in the area and the donations became fewer and fewer. Leo had heard about a train station job about a hundred miles north. It was a rough area, no place for a little girl, so he thought it best to leave Kathy behind.

Leo had seen her over at the landlord's house on several occasions, asking for food. The landlord's wife was kind enough to feed his daughter on those occasions, so Leo knew she would be taken care of.

No one would let her starve.

"I'm going away for a while," she remembered him telling her. "But I'll be back in a few weeks. You just be sure and mind yourself. Don't cause any trouble, you hear?"

"Yes, daddy," she remembered replying. "But why do you have to go?"

"There's work a few towns over. If I can make enough money for rent, we can stay here a while longer. Maybe even get a decent place."

"But doesn't my singing make us enough money?" she asked.

"No, it don't," he answered bluntly. "All your singing and dancing does is buy us a little food and a few drinks. It don't give us nothing more."

With that, she watched as her father left their tiny farmhouse apartment and started making his way to where the work was. Kathy was dejected, but she tried to do what she was told. Like most children, she didn't want to displease her father. But a few days turned into a few weeks, and eventually she caught the attention of the property owners, Aileen and Orlin Buxton. The couple owned a few rental properties in town—including the one Kathy and her father were staying in.

"Where is your father?" Aileen asked the little girl one day.

"He went to find work up the road," Kathy replied. "Just a few towns over."

The rent was overdue, and the couple had come to collect. But, when they saw the little girl's condition, they didn't have the heart to send her away—especially Aileen, who had always wanted a daughter. Unable to have children of their own, Aileen and Orlin had adopted a baby boy a few years prior. The boy was about the same age as Kathy, and it didn't take long for Aileen to develop a soft spot for the little girl.

"When did your daddy leave?" she asked.

Kathy could only shrug her shoulders. Time wasn't something she had been taught to measure. But she didn't need to answer. The sight of the shoeless, unkempt little girl standing in front of her told Aileen all she needed to know about how Kathy had been treated.

"Oh, I see," Aileen said, trying to keep her emotions from showing. It was clear that the little girl hadn't eaten much. "Well, are you hungry?"

"Yes, ma'am," she answered.

"Would you like to come over to our house and eat dinner with us?" Aileen asked. "Maybe you could even stay with us until your father gets back. It's getting kind of cold and Orlin needs to fix the windows so that you don't catch a chill. What do you say?"

"I don't know," Kathy responded. "What if my daddy comes back and I'm not here?"

"Well, I'll tell you what," Aileen said, now kneeling next to the little girl. "How about we leave a note for your father and then he'll know where to come get you?"

"I guess that'll be okay," Kathy answered.

"Well, then it's settled," said Aileen. "You'll come have dinner and stay with us. Our house is just a few blocks away. Why don't you go get your shoes and we'll walk on over there?"

Kathy stood there for a minute, not quite knowing how to answer. Then she said, "I don't have any shoes."

Aileen was stunned.

Having grown up during the Great Depression, she had seen poverty before, but she had never seen a child neglected to this degree. Fighting to hold back her tears, she took a moment to compose herself and said, "Well, I guess you'll have to take a ride with us in our car. Then we'll see about getting you some shoes. How does that sound?"

The little girl agreed, and they were off to the couple's home.

A few weeks went by, and the couple finally heard from Kathy's father. Leo was living several towns away and never bothered to send word to anyone about his daughter.

Then one day, the telephone rang. Leo was calling to ask if they had seen his daughter. She confirmed that they had and that Kathy was staying with them until he came back to get her.

"When do you think you will be coming back this way?" Aileen asked Leo.

What Kathy's father said next made Aileen's heart sink.

"Y'all can just give her to the state," he said. "They'll know what to do with her. That's what we did with her sisters."

Aileen was shocked. She couldn't believe what she was hearing. How could he just walk away from his own daughter?

It was immediately clear to her what she had to do. Aileen would adopt Kathy and raise her as her own.

"What if you just let us adopt her?" she asked, thinking that he would surely agree.

But once Leo realized that he had something Aileen wanted, the conversation shifted, and he began to negotiate with Aileen.

"Well, I don't know," he responded, thinking that Aileen and her husband probably made a pretty good living off their rental properties. "How much are y'all willing to offer? If you aren't going to pay me for her, I'd just as soon turn her over to the state."

Aileen was angry. How could he barter with his own daughter like that? It was almost as if he was selling livestock. How dare he, she thought.

But Aileen didn't want to hurt Kathy's chances of having a good home, so she kept calm and agreed to meet Leo's asking price of $5,000 for the right to adopt her, an enormous amount of money at the time. To Aileen, though, the price was worth it.

It was plain to see that this little girl had already been through so much and Aileen was determined to give her some stability. Kathy had finally found a place to call home, but despite Aileen's love, it was hard for her to trust that she wouldn't soon be discarded.

After all, that's all she had ever known, so why would things be different now?

Aileen took the little girl under her wing and began to make some progress with her when Orlin suddenly passed away of heart disease. Aileen was now a widow raising two children on her own.

But she was determined to make it work.

She did everything she could to make Kathy feel that she was truly part of the family. Over the next few years, she mentored her as the young lady grew into a teenager. Kathy was finally beginning to feel a sense of security and belonging when more tragedy struck.

Aileen was diagnosed with terminal cancer, and the doctors told her she had only a short time to live.

Kathy, now about sixteen, was devastated and decided to head out on her own. She figured that if she had done it before, then she could do it again. So she headed out and found work cleaning motel rooms in a town nearby. Soon, she would meet the young man who would become her first husband.

Kathy was convinced that he was the love of her life and within a few months, they were married. Not long after, Kathy was pregnant with their first child. But it didn't take long before the marriage soured, and the couple divorced when she was seventeen.

Wanting nothing to do with her ex-husband, Kathy set off on her own again, this time with a young baby in tow. Now a young single mom, she took whatever work she could find, but providing for a child on her own was much harder than she imagined it would be.

Struggling to make ends meet, Kathy began to lose hope. That was when another man, Jeff Edwards, entered her life and a relationship developed. As they dated, Jeff offered the prospect of a stable family life. Soon, Kathy entered into her second marriage and the couple settled down in a small logging community in rural Oregon.

"This marriage will be different," she thought.

But it wasn't. The next few years brought constant fighting and, even though they tried to make it work, the never-ending arguments proved to be too much for the couple. Despite having two children together, they parted ways after a contentious divorce.

Kathy was on her own again. Two toxic relationships left her reeling, and caring for three little ones was a lot to handle.

With nowhere to go and no one to turn to, Kathy thought she might find help in the place where it all started. She hoped that maybe she could make a change. So, she packed up her children and moved to Oklahoma City, not far from where she was born. Maybe a homecoming of sorts would bring her some peace. Or, at the very least, maybe some luck.

Unfortunately for Kathy, she was unable to find the relief she was looking for. Struggling to make life work for herself and her children, she had no idea how to move on or what to do next.

She took a job waitressing at a small café, but the long shifts sapped her energy and she had very little left for her three small children. To find an escape, Kathy turned to the party lifestyle her mother had turned to for refuge years before.

Most nights, she would head to the bar after her shift at the café, leaving her children to fend for themselves.

It wasn't long before neighbors noticed Kathy leaving home early in the day and not returning until late at night. They noticed her kids running loose, unsupervised, and someone finally called the authorities.

Kathy wanted to be a good mom, but in the end, she felt like she was fighting a losing battle. She didn't know how to be a mom. In her heart Kathy knew it, and she felt as if the whole world knew it. There was no sense in putting her kids through it anymore, so she agreed to let the state take her kids and put them in foster care where they at least had a chance to be adopted into a good home environment.

"Maybe you'll find them a good home," she told the case worker. "Anything's got to be better than what I can give them."

The images of watching her kids cry as the case workers drove away with them was too much for Kathy to bear. Needing a change of scenery, Kathy packed up and headed back to the Pacific Northwest.

"This time, though," she thought, "my life will be different. All I need is a fresh start." Kathy wanted to find a place to hide, somewhere she could just blend in.

A big city like Portland, Oregon, seemed to be just the place. There would be so many people, nobody would even notice her. So, she headed for a big city, got a waitressing job, and settled in.

That's when she met Brian Clifton. He approached her at a bar in the city, and soon they began dating. A few months later they got married and eventually moved to a more secluded area near Salem, Oregon. This time around, there would be no children. But there would be problems. Abuse became the norm for Kathy, but at least he stayed. At least she was wanted by someone, and Kathy couldn't bear the thought of being discarded yet again.

The only person in her life who hadn't actively discarded her was Aileen. But when her adopted mother passed away, Kathy still felt left behind. So, she endured the pain her husband put her through. No matter how bad it got, this was the first time somebody chose to stay with her. Kathy was determined to stick it out and make the best of this relationship. As turbulent as it was, at least she had something she could count on for once.

As the years rolled on, the fights became more frequent, more physical, and more intense. She began to fight back more and there were times she even instigated a few fights.

But Clifton grew weary of the contentious relationship with his wife and, unbeknownst to Kathy, began a long-distance affair with another woman. Eventually, the woman made arrangements to come out to Oregon from her home on the East Coast, and Clifton decided it was time to be rid of Kathy once and for all.

On a summer night in 1996, Clifton waited for Kathy to fall asleep, then quietly removed a hunting knife he had kept in the drawer by his side of the bed and plunged the knife into the back of Kathy's neck, repeatedly stabbing her until she died.

Once he was sure she was dead, Brian grabbed a tarp and tied it around Kathy's body, securing the tarp at both ends. He then buried her in the backyard. But after a few days, he began to worry that someone would suspect something and might begin searching.

So, in the dark of night, he dug up the grave in the backyard and carried the body, still wrapped in the tarp, to his car. He drove out to a secluded area of the forest—one that he was very familiar with—and dragged Kathy's body down a hill where he left her remains under a row of small trees.

Then, fearing that someone would become suspicious because of the stains on his clothes, he undressed, put his clothes in a bag, and hurled them down the hill near where he dumped his wife's body.

That summer night would be the last anyone would see of Kathy Thomas until two hunters came across a human skull while searching for game deep in the forest several weeks later. They called the authorities, and detectives from the Polk County Sheriff's Office arrived at the scene soon after.

As they searched the area, they found other parts of the skeletal remains scattered hundreds of feet in either direction.

"This is a bad one," said one of the sheriff's deputies. "How long do you think the body's been here?"

"Not sure," said Burney Krauger, the lead detective on site at the time. "I've been doing this for a lot of years, and I've never seen anything like this. But just comparing the length of the grass around her to the length of it under her, I'd say not more than a few weeks."

After forty-two years, Kathy Thomas, the woman who had known so much hardship in her life, was reduced to this. The little girl, who once danced and sang on beer house tabletops to stay in her father's good graces, was now an unidentified skeleton wrapped in a tarp and left in a wooded area to be devoured by wild animals. She was now officially labeled "Jane Doe."

Sadly, no one had any idea who she was. There had been no recent calls to local authorities to report a missing person and DNA tracking was still in its infancy when Kathy's remains were discovered.

But that didn't stop investigators from the Polk County Sheriff's Office from trying.

Shortly after the body was found, an examination was performed. Based on the density, shape, and condition of the bones, the medical examiner was able to determine that the remains belonged to a woman in her forties. She would have stood about five feet, three inches tall and, based on the width of the pelvic bones, her build would have been somewhat stout. So, she likely would not have been a frail woman.

One other important discovery that came from the autopsy was that, at some point in her life, the victim had given birth to at least one child. To all involved in trying to solve this case, this meant that there could possibly be a child—or children—who had been wondering what happened to their mother.

Beyond that, there was nothing more that science could provide at that time to help detectives find out who she was. The sheriff's office could only utilize the media to ask anyone who might know this person's identity to come forward.

Unfortunately, no one did.

Like the other forty thousand unidentified bodies found throughout the United States, Kathy Thomas's identity was unknown. It would be more than twenty years before technology would reach a point where law enforcement could use more sophisticated scientific methods to search for her identity.

In the spring of 2018, Dean and I were providing Cold Case Training for the Oregon Peace Officers Association. Following the training, Detective John Williams asked us if we could meet with the Polk County Sherriff's Cold Case Unit Office to review the 1996 Jane Doe case as well as two others. John was particularly eager to solve this case. He had been assigned to it in 2011 and wasn't able to get very far with it. He was only a few short years from retirement, so his sense of urgency to solve it was very high. In talking to John about his background, we soon learned that he had a perspective that was unique to most law enforcement professionals we meet. This was probably because John took a more circuitous route to his law enforcement career than most.

Shortly after graduating from high school, John took a job with his father's building supply company. He would work in one of the supply house stores as a credit manager for nineteen years before the family-owned business was acquired by a larger company. During most of that time, John had been a reserve officer for the Polk County Sheriff's Office but hadn't given much consideration to becoming a full-time deputy. But when it became clear that the new company had plans for the business that didn't include the family, John, who was already in his late thirties, submitted his application when a full-time position opened with the sheriff's office. He was hired to work patrol a few weeks later.

It didn't take long for John to show that he had the natural talent, people skills, and sense of teamwork to become a detective. During his four years in patrol, John solved a large casino counterfeit case that led to his appointment as a full-time detective with the Polk County Sheriff's Office. During his first few years as a detective, he specialized in child sex abuse cases and was quite successful in solving them. And he was just as effective with his work in this unidentified body case from 1996.

Upon meeting John, we immediately got the sense that he and the other members of the Cold Case Unit were victim-centric in every sense of the word. They were determined to identify the victim in this case and make things right for her. And they were very receptive to our thoughts, observations, and recommendations.

We met with the detectives in a conference room at the historic Polk County Courthouse. Built in 1899, it was a beautiful building constructed of local sandstone and surrounded by pine trees common to the area. Entering the building, it almost felt as if we were going back in time to consult with the detectives, which, in a way, made it the perfect setting to discuss this particular cold case. Because, when we review cold cases, that is essentially what we are doing. We are going back in time.

As John and his team presented their "Jane Doe" case to us, our primary goals were threefold. One: provide a working criminal behavioral assessment of the offender. Two: recommend investigative strategies. And three: point them to resources that could help them identify the victim and, potentially, her killer.

We started with the victim herself. There wasn't a lot of information, so the victimology was limited, but knowing her size, approximate age, and that she had given birth at some point in her life told us something about her.

"She had lived into her forties and was a mother, which was significant in that no one had reported her missing," I said to the group gathered to study the case. "So, she had a family of some kind and that begs the question, why wasn't she reported missing?"

Then we looked closely at the physical evidence in the area where the body had been discovered. The first thing that stood out to us was the level of effort that the offender made to dispose of the body in a remote logging area of the forest. There were several logging roads in that area that led deep into the forest, crisscrossing one another in some locations. It was a location that would be easy to get lost in if you didn't know your way around.

"A killer looking to hide a body in this type of remote location and likely under the cloak of darkness," I told the investigators, "suggests that the offender was familiar with the area, had been there before, and probably lived or worked in that area or at least in a neighboring area at the time of the murder."

The second thing we noticed was the layout and rugged terrain of the area around where the body was left. It was a heavily wooded area with a lot of shrubbery and thick wild grass all throughout. Soon after the hunters showed authorities the small clearing where they had found the human skull, sheriff's detectives began searching the area and found that there were additional bones scattered throughout the scene. Just a couple hundred feet away from where the skull had been discovered was a tarp with more skeletal remains wrapped inside.

It appeared that, between the time the victim's body had been dumped and the time it was discovered, wild animals had gotten to the body and had pulled most of it out of the tarp to feed on. That was an important piece of information because it again spoke to the level of experience with this type of area that the offender had to have had in order to secretly move the body to this location. Additionally, from the roadside to where the tarp was discovered, someone had to have dragged the body down a fairly steep hillside and through a heavily wooded terrain to the eventual deposit site.

"That tells us something about the offender's physical abilities," I observed. "He would have to have been physically strong enough and had enough endurance to be able to move an adult human body several hundred feet through that kind of rough terrain."

The deposit site also gave us another clue about the offender. To be able to drive her to that specific logging road in a sophisticated network of roads, then take the time to drag the victim's body down a rough, steep terrain, and then be able to leave the scene undetected in the dark of night would mean that the perpetrator would have to have been very familiar with this specific location.

"This wasn't someone just driving around in the general area looking for a place to dump the body," I told the group. "There is a high probability that he preplanned this location and took her directly to this specific site. He is trying to keep from being detected, from being seen, so he has to be as efficient and precise as possible in disposing the body."

As the detectives continued to present the evidence to us, they showed us photos of the bag of clothes that sheriff's investigators had discovered while searching the area. They found the bag under one of the bushes near the tarp where the body had been deposited. Among the items in the bag were men's pants, underwear, shoes, and a shirt. It appeared that the killer decided to change clothes before leaving the scene.

"It's possible he was trying to hide evidence," John told us. "Whatever the reason, we were able to get some important physical evidence from the clothes."

That evidence included the size of the pants—thirty-four-inch waist and thirty-four-inch length. That length is typical of someone around six feet tall or more. And the waist would indicate someone who is slender enough to be in pretty decent physical shape.

If those were indeed the offender's pants, that would confirm that he was a larger man in the kind of physical condition that would give him the ability to move a body through the forest as quickly as he would have needed to in order to avoid detection.

In addition to the pants, detectives also found two key pieces of evidence that they were hoping would lead to DNA identification of the offender.

First, the underwear found in the bag of clothing contained semen stains on it. There was a chance that the sample could be enough to enter into the national database and hopefully find a match. Leaving his clothing with semen at the scene suggested that a potentially intimate and personal relationship occurred between the victim and the offender.

The second piece of evidence was a chunk of hair and skin from the scalp that had been found on a tree branch just above where the tarp had been found.

"We believe that it's possible that, while the perpetrator was laying the body on the ground," John explained, "he may have hit his head on the tree branch as he stood up."

Both samples had been sent for testing multiple times over the years, but unfortunately no matches in the federal database system turned up. Beyond finding a match for the offender's DNA, there just weren't many investigative possibilities for the detectives to follow up on.

While our criminal behavioral analysis and investigative recommendations were helpful insights, we knew that the investigation would not be able to go much further until the person's remains were identified. So, we talked to them about the possibility of using genealogical DNA methodology and introduced the Polk County detectives to Francine Bardole, who works with our foundation as our foremost forensics expert, specializing in DNA evidence.

Having founded her own organization, Cold Case Solutions & Resources, which is based in Utah, Francine has had a distinguished thirty-year career in the Salt Lake City area, working primarily in the field of crime scene investigation and specializing in the fields of forensic serology and DNA. We are fortunate to have her working with our foundation. She is a renowned expert in DNA extraction and identification, having developed a groundbreaking method for extracting touch DNA from spent shell casings as well as other smaller items of evidence such as jewelry, fingernails, hair ties, and firearm components. The method, fittingly called the Bardole Method, has been used to solve numerous homicide cases across the country.

In talking to the detectives, Francine pointed them toward the types of DNA technologies she felt would be good starting points for skeletonized remains cases, including genealogical DNA technology.

"But there is a challenge with genealogical DNA testing," she told them. "It is expensive, so you will probably need to find some funding."

Undeterred, John and his team began to look into where they might be able to raise the funds for the genealogical testing, which can quickly climb to a cost of around $20,000 and beyond, much more than most agencies have the resources to cover.

As fate would have it, their search for funding didn't take long. Within a year of our meeting, John got a call from Dr. Nicci Vance, the Oregon State Forensic Anthropologist with the state medical examiner's office in Portland, Oregon. She had just gotten off the phone with Yolanda McClary, a former CSI, who was looking to feature an unidentified body case for a true crime television special that would air on the Oxygen channel. She explained that the premise of the show was to follow the unidentified body investigation and provide the resources necessary to do whatever testing was needed in order to identify the body and, hopefully, solve the case.

It was exactly what John and his team needed. John met with Yolanda, a retired CSI with the Las Vegas Metropolitan Police Department, and agreed to do the show. Their collaboration on the case formed the basis of a true crime television special called *The Jane Doe Murders*, which aired on the Oxygen channel in January 2021. Although the show is about ninety minutes long, the work they put in to identify the remains and solve the crime actually took more than two years.

The Polk County Sheriff's Office cold case unit is a stellar example of what can happen when authorities work to coordinate with as many people and organizations necessary to get the job done. And the television special is a fascinating tale of how all the coordinated efforts from everyone involved came together to solve this case.

Their journey started in the medical examiner's office with the victim. The skeletal remains had been stored in the Oregon State Forensics lab for nearly twenty-five years. There was no sign of bullet wounds, knife wounds, or blunt-force trauma damage to any of the bone tissue.

Even though the bones had been exposed to the elements for several weeks and had been sitting in storage at the lab for more than two decades, the skeletal remains had been preserved well enough that there was still an opportunity to extract usable DNA from the bone. So, the cold case unit, Yolanda, and the Oxygen network contracted with DNA Solutions labs in Oklahoma to see if their advanced technology could pull enough DNA out of the bone to establish a profile that would test and compare with public open-source databases.

"We've been extracting DNA from bones for quite a few years now," explained Dr. James Anstead, director of DNA Solutions, to the producers of the show. "But what's changed is the technology to actually recover the DNA and apply this to forensic genealogy. It's definitely a really new field."

Injecting a needle to the inner core of the femur, DNA specialists extracted two samples and sent them to the lab for testing, which typically takes several months. When we met with John at their offices in 2018, he said that the last time they had tried DNA technology was in 2014. They had been able to obtain samples that were viable enough to run through CODIS, a national database that records and tracks DNA from convicted offenders. Unfortunately, those tests came back without a match to anyone in the national database.

But in April 2019, the Polk County Sheriff's Office got some good news. The test results from DNA Solutions showed that there was enough DNA in the sample to produce a DNA profile for the then-unknown victim. Five years after the disappointing results of the 2014 tests, Polk County detectives now had the means to run the DNA through open sources and compare their DNA profile to multiple family trees. They were that much closer to identifying their Jane Doe than they ever had been.

At that point, genealogists could now trace the DNA to family trees from public forum databases such as court, land, probate, military, tax, and genealogy service forums. While that sounds easy, it can be a long, arduous process depending on how many relatives have submitted DNA samples and how closely related they are.

"The more DNA you share with somebody, the closer the relationship," explained Charles McGee, one of the genealogical researchers tasked with identifying the victim. "So, a paternal line and a maternal line coming together, beneath there, somewhere, is going to be our Jane Doe, hopefully."

The probability that a team of genealogists was going to find DNA matches for distant relatives was hopeful—and that's exactly what happened. But the results were less than ideal. "Our Jane Doe matches were so distantly related that she likely never even knew them during her life," Charles said. "That makes the research pretty difficult."

Despite the challenge ahead of them, Yolanda and the team of genealogists took the top ten closest matches and began checking their vast database of public records to begin narrowing down the field. Essentially, they were creating multiple family trees for each of the ten matches, looking for specific crossover relationships that would lead to Jane Doe's direct DNA.

"We're looking for the crossover when one person in this tree marries somebody in that tree," explained Jean Grier, a forensic genealogist on the team. The process took months of arduous public records searches and phone calls, trying to track down someone who might be able to point them to a close living relative.

"It was common for me to get a call from one of the genealogists," John told us recently while talking to us about the outcome of the case. "I made dozens of phone calls to people we thought might be family members of our Jane Doe. At that point, we were just seeing if anyone could tell us about a missing family member or someone they hadn't seen since 1996. It was a long process."

After all the calls and records searches, the team finally found the family tree crossover they were looking for: the grandparents of the Polk County Sheriff's Jane Doe. The only challenge was that those grandparents had seven children—six boys and a girl—so identifying which of those seven was the actual parent would take some leg work. In searching through public records, the team found that all but one of the seven had passed away, and none were officially listed as having any daughters. The only surviving member of the group of siblings was eighty-five-year-old Billy Thomas, who lived in Oklahoma.

So, John called Billy and asked him to elaborate on his family's history.

"I've got five brothers," he told John. "I'm the sixth boy. Leo (the second oldest of the children) and his wife, they were the only ones to have girls. They had three daughters—Sandra, Linda, and Kathy."

Finally, John and his team had their Jane Doe narrowed down to three possibilities. As he continued his investigation, John discovered that the two oldest girls were adopted out to families in Oklahoma in 1959 while Leo took the youngest, Kathy, out west to Oregon.

There was a high probability that Jane Doe was Kathy Thomas, but they had to be sure. After talking to Billy, John was able to locate Linda and she agreed to give him a DNA sample to compare with the person they had found in 1996. Within a week, authorities got the results from the lab: the sample was a sibling match. At long last, the Polk County Sheriff's Office had confirmed the identity of the victim whose body had been left in the woods nearly twenty-five years prior.

"I've said to people I was working with, 'For twenty-three years, there's somebody out there asking where is my mom? Where is my sister?'" John said. "And that's who I want to get the answers for."

While finding that answer was gratifying, it also came with an emotional cost for the family members left behind.

"I always wanted a family when I was young, so bad," Linda told Yolanda and John shortly after they had broken the news to her. "But, now I have it, and she's gone. And I'll never have my sister back."

As difficult as it was to get the news of Kathy's passing, there was still the hope that this development could start the process of healing for Linda and other loved ones.

In terms of the investigation, the discovery of Kathy's identity meant that detectives could now move forward with the investigative strategies that come from studying the life of the victim and the circumstances that surrounded her—the victimology. They also had a relative who could give them some information that could point them in a direction that might help solve the case.

As it turned out, Kathy's uncle Billy had remembered hearing that Leo had adopted her out to a family in Oregon. He had remembered that the family's last name was Buxton, but he didn't have any more information than that. No location or even knowledge of whether there were still living family members around. And if there were, would they even still be in Oregon?

Still, the name was enough for John to move forward. He began by looking a little more closely at Leo's life. That's when he found an old newspaper article about Leo from 1966.

A few years after having given Kathy up for adoption, Leo and an associate were found dead in a car that had gotten stuck in the mud one night. They had apparently been unable to get the car out of the mud and, due to the cold weather, they decided to leave the car running and turn on the heater. Sometime during the night, they died of asphyxiation.

As John looked through the article, he noticed that Leo was mentioned as living in Oakland, Oregon, a small town not far from where the sheriff's office was located. So, John did a property search for any owners by the name of Buxton. He called an older couple out there, but to his disappointment, it wasn't them. Then, a last-minute thought occurred to the man he was talking to.

"I was just about to hang up," John recalled. "But then the man said, 'You know, for years, people asked me if I was related to Richard Buxton.' So, I looked Richard up and called him, and he immediately asked, 'Is this about my adopted sister Kathy?'"

Within a few days, John and Yolanda headed out to visit Richard to find out what he knew. Kathy's adopted brother had a lot of valuable information for the investigators. He provided photos, shared memories of the few years he had of growing up with Kathy, and discussed what he knew about her life. That's when detectives learned that Richard's mother, Aileen, had rented out a room in an old house to Leo and Kathy. It's also when they learned about Kathy's early childhood in Oregon. They were told about Leo taking five-year-old Kathy to dance for money in beer halls; about her wandering over to their house to ask for something to eat; and about Leo leaving the little girl behind with no food to eat and not much to wear.

"We had a heck of a time getting her to wear shoes," Richard remembered. "Because she had never worn shoes before."

He also remembered the day that his parents decided to adopt Kathy.

"He (Leo) got in contact with my mom and, he was up against it. And my mom sent him $5,000, which was a lot of money in 1960. And he signed the adoption papers."

At that point, detectives were able to track Kathy's life. They found marriage licenses to her first husband, an eighteen-year-old whom she married at the age of sixteen before divorcing him a few months later. Shortly after the divorce, she delivered her first child, just three months before Aileen passed away.

Detectives then found a marriage license to her second husband, James Edwards, with whom she would have two more children. That was confirmed by Kathy's sister, Linda. In 1977, shortly after welcoming her third child, Kathy went to Oklahoma and reunited briefly with Linda. Kathy told her that she was married and showed her pictures of her three children. It was a brief visit and, unfortunately, the two never saw each other again.

Detectives discovered that, shortly after her return home, the couple divorced, and Kathy took the kids to live in Oklahoma City where she tried to raise the children on her own. But it proved to be too much for her, and the state ended up removing the children, then ages five to seven years old, citing negligence.

She moved back to Oregon, this time opting for a bigger city in Portland.

There, she met Brian Clifton, and in 1984, they were married. Not much is known about their marriage except that it officially ended with her death in 1996. Once they learned of Kathy's marriage to Clifton, detectives set to work on finding him. They were curious as to why a husband wouldn't call in a missing person's report.

"To me, this lines up with someone who doesn't want anyone looking into Kathy's background," John told the producers of the show. "It's a huge red flag."

Yes, it was a red flag, but John also knew that the team needed evidence that would hold up in court, so he started by contacting Clifton's closest relatives, one of whom—his sister—agreed to provide a DNA sample. The sample was a 99 percent sibling match to the DNA evidence they found in the underwear left at the crime scene and the clump of hair found on the tree branch near the tarp.

Detectives had two things left to do: find Brian Clifton and interview him to see what he could tell them about Kathy's disappearance. Locating him took several months, but finally, in late summer of 2020, they found Clifton and saw him on surveillance video outside a local store in, of all places, Oklahoma. After gathering more intel and evidence, John and a member of his team, Detective Jeff Williams, went out to Oklahoma to visit Clifton in December of that same year. During their first interview, which lasted several hours, Clifton denied any involvement with Kathy's disappearance or knowledge of her body's disposal.

"He was a talker," John told us when we asked him about his first interview with Clifton. "But he would only talk about anything that didn't involve Kathy. For example, he would go on and on about a truck he had twenty years ago, but when we asked him about Kathy, just one-word answers. He wouldn't say anything about her."

Despite the lack of a confession or any relevant statements about Kathy, the detectives did learn two key things about their suspect: One, while he was a little cooler in his interactions with John, he seemed to develop a bit of a rapport with Jeff. Two, they got the sense that, if Jeff could develop a relationship with Clifton, there was a good chance that he would confess if they confronted him with key facts about the case.

And that's exactly what happened.

In the spring of 2021, three interviews later, Jeff confronted Clifton with the DNA evidence found in his underwear and on the tree branch where Kathy's body was found. Jeff also showed Clifton a picture they had found from their last Christmas together. In that picture, Clifton was wearing the exact shirt that was one of the items found in the bag of clothing near Kathy's body.

With no feasible lie to concoct, Clifton confessed to Kathy's murder and was arrested before being extradited to Oregon to await trial. In his confession, he told detectives that he had plunged the hunting knife he kept in his bedside table drawer into the back of Kathy's neck, stabbing her ten times while she slept. He even drew a map of exactly where on her neck he stabbed her and admitted that he had planned out the body's disposal after he killed her, which included tying her up in a tarp and leaving her at the disposal site where the hunters eventually found her body.

Clifton was convicted of first-degree murder, and, on October 20, 2022, was sentenced to life in prison.

One of the more troubling aspects to this case is that Kathy never should have crossed paths with Brian Clifton in the first place. In 1974, he was convicted of first-degree murder and sentenced to life in prison for strangling a female motel clerk with a vacuum cleaner cord. But he served only seven years in prison and was released on parole in 1981. He would meet and marry Kathy just three years later.

Just a couple of weeks after the authorities arrested Clifton, I got a nice note from John to let me know how the case had unfolded. With his permission, I share this message because I believe the Polk County Sheriff's Office, their Cold Case Unit, and Detective John Williams to be shining examples of the good that can happen when we, as law enforcement officials, put our egos aside and coordinate with as many people as necessary to get justice on behalf of the victims and their families.

John's note reads:

Hi Greg,

In July 2018, you came out to Oregon and taught at a conference and you met with our cold case team about some of our cold cases and you gave some great advice and direction for those cases. One of our cases was from 1996 where unidentified remains were found in the woods and we were still attempting to identify her when we met with you.

We got help from Yolanda McClary in early 2019 with genealogical DNA, and in September 2019 we finally identified our lady. Her last husband immediately became a person of interest and finally, after two more years, we made an arrest in this case. Yep, it was the husband. It is quite a story, but I was on the team that went to Oklahoma where he was living and after interviewing him in December 2020, July 2021, and finally in August 2021, he confessed to her killing. He is now in our jail after being extradited to Oregon and is awaiting trial. Yolanda made a documentary which I was part of called The Jane Doe Murders on Oxygen and it aired in January 2021, and it documents the ID process as well as finding her children and sister, who did not know she was dead.

I thought you would be interested in how we finally got this case to an arrest.

Thanks,
John

As an organization, when we see people in an agency like the Polk County Sheriff's Office go to all the work and effort they did to solve a case that lasted for so many years, it is extremely gratifying. And they did this not only with Kathy Thomas's case, but in other cases, as well.

When we initially met with them, the Polk County Sheriff's Office asked us to consult on three unsolved cases, another of which was solved using sophisticated FBI database technology that was developed by a former colleague of mine at the FBI, Butch Rabiega, who worked for me as an analyst in ViCAP, the FBI's violent crimes database system, and he now donates his time and expertise to our foundation. Because the victim in the second case turned out to be a suicide, we won't go into too much detail due to the sensitive nature of the case and the family's right to privacy. But suffice to say that while we were meeting with the sheriff's office, we called Butch in the middle of the meeting, and he shared his method of changing search patterns for missing persons.

Using that method, which widened the parameters for the database search, detectives were able to identify the body and conduct an investigation that led to a determination of the cause of death. It was obviously a difficult time for the family, but we were told later that they were grateful to know what happened and to have been able to give their loved one a proper burial and memorial service.

In terms of coordination, the principle for the suicide case the detectives solved is the same as it was for Kathy Thomas's case. In coordinating with everyone they possibly could, the Polk County Sheriff's Office demonstrated that they were willing to do everything humanly possible to make sure that neither of these people were ever forgotten or given up on.

"There used to be a culture in law enforcement that, 'This is my case,'" John told us as we talked to him about his experience with these cases. "But we just can't afford to do that anymore, and I think, as law enforcement, we're starting to realize that it's better when we can bring professionals with varying degrees of experience and expertise to the table to look at cases with a fresh set of eyes and a fresh perspective. It certainly helped in our situation."

It helped so much that the Oregon Peace Officers Association now has set up the Cold Case Investigative Association in which law enforcement authorities—both active and retired—come together to discuss cold cases from across the state. It's the kind of thing that we feel needs to be replicated across the country and even internationally.

In Kathy Thomas's case, when we list out the number of organizations that they coordinated with to identify her and find her killer, the number approaches a hundred people and organizations that they ultimately had to contact to get the job done. And the list includes much more than just law enforcement-related organizations. It includes family, community members, private companies, organizations, and media, just to name a few. If it hadn't been for John and his team persistently reaching out to all these people, this case wouldn't have been solved. There wouldn't have been enough funding and resources to contract with the private companies that were so vital to solving this case.

That's one of the reasons networks who produce true crime specials, like the Oxygen Channel, are so important. They are kind enough to provide the thousands of dollars it costs to use sophisticated DNA technology that is so essential to solving these cases. And, in this case, there was so much good that came out of this work that goes far beyond simply solving Kathy Thomas's case.

They were actually able to help reconnect a family that had been separated for decades.

During the course of the investigation, John and Yolanda located Kathy's children—now adults—in 2019. In talking to them about their stories, they discovered that the three were adopted out. Imagine that. Two generations of children from the same family adopted out and then coming back together decades later. The oldest of the three, Tina, remembered that final day as a child with her mother.

"I have this vision and flashes of her face," Tina told producers of the show. "I remember crying. I was holding this little bag, and I was crying, 'I want to go with you, mommy. I want to go.'"

To hear this story is heartbreaking, but it underscores the importance of every unidentified victim deserving to get their identities back and having their stories told. When that happens, there is potential for families and loved ones to get the full picture of their own story. That's important in the healing process because, sometimes, the greatest pain for the loved ones left behind are the broken pieces of a life's story, the unexplained and the unanswered, that only that loved one can provide.

"I just wanted to ask her why," said Candice, the youngest of Kathy's three children. "My mom was young. She had a rough life and she needed support. It's very understandable that my mom would make mistakes. And then it finally dawned on me that my mom was the victim and not the perpetrator in this crime. And so it changes things quite a bit."

In the end, Yolanda and John were able to bring family members together who probably wouldn't have ever met otherwise. The two daughters, Tina and Candice, were reunited with their aunt Linda, who had also been separated from her parents as a child. It was an amazing moment to see these three come together and create a bond that might not have existed otherwise.

"That's all I ever wanted," Linda said to her nieces as they engaged in an emotional embrace. "It's amazing. We're kin. We're really kin, blood kin. I never thought I'd have this, but now we do. We really need to keep in touch, please."

They now have the family they had been missing for decades. They stay in touch with each other, and it is a beautiful thing to have been able to witness. It's also gratifying for those who worked on the case. A friendship between the family and the members of the cold case unit also developed.

After Clifton was convicted in 2022, authorities were then able to turn Kathy's remains over to the family so she could have a proper funeral and burial. John had retired from the Polk County Sheriff's Office a few months before, but the family still reached out and invited John and his wife to the graveside service.

"That meant so much to us," John said. "To be able to be there was such a wonderful experience and it was such an honor to be invited to see Kathy finally laid to rest by her family."

During my career in law enforcement, some of the most difficult calls I ever received involved the discovery of bodies or partial remains dumped in a variety of different places. I believe that most of us in law enforcement have a hard time with these types of discoveries for the same reasons I do: We know that these remains represent far more than physical evidence. These were people who once had lives, who once had dreams and aspirations. But, due to some unfortunate circumstance, those hopes and dreams were cut short.

And there are far too many. In the United States alone, there are more than forty thousand unidentified bodies or remains still lying in medical examiners' offices across the country. That also means there are thousands of families and loved ones wondering what happened to them.

One of the benefits I have always hoped would come from the formation of the Cold Case Foundation is the coordination of a multifaceted network of agencies and private citizens coming together, not only to solve violent crimes, but also to identify the people whose bodies are found during the course of those investigations. The good news is that, over the past few years, progress has been made in this area. Law enforcement agencies are reaching out to people and resources that extend far beyond their jurisdictions and that bridge the gap between the public and private sectors. And we are starting to see the results.

Kathy Thomas's case is just one example of how things are coming together. As a foundation, we want to see more organizations and individuals participating in these efforts. The more experts that join the cause, the better the chance we have at reducing that number from forty thousand to zero.

As Yolanda said at the outset of her Oxygen Channel special, we have to do this one case at a time, and as we see how much time, effort, and coordination goes into solving just one case, we also see the need for more resources and expertise. With so many law enforcement agencies having limited funding, it will take help from the private sector—both private organizations and citizens alike—to provide the means necessary to solve the thousands of cold cases that remain and give the families a chance to start healing. That is one of the reasons we began this chapter with a description of how we imagined Kathy's life had played out up to the point she was murdered.

And, while the way we visualized her life could only be based on records, evidence discovered, and the few memories her existing family shared, we wanted to humanize her so that her story would resonate with you as it did with us when John first presented it.

When we receive a case—especially one like Kathy's—it goes beyond evidence, reports, and crime scene photos for me. I've done this for decades and, in every case I review, I can't look at evidence without picturing the victim from childhood to adulthood. It's hard not to look at skeletal remains in a wooded clearing and wonder, what was this person like? Where did she come from? If I could meet this person, what would it be like to talk to her and have her tell me her story?

Tina said it best toward the end of the Oxygen Channel show.

"My mother's case, it's not just another Jane Doe," she told the producers. "She's a person with a story. She had family that cared about her."

In many ways, Kathy's life story is difficult to hear. But it is also a lesson for us to remember that there is a story behind every victim. And, like all life stories, there are always families involved. As I've thought about this former Jane Doe's story, I have reflected on her life and everything that it encompassed. I thought about all that she went through, all that her family went through. And I thought about the many people involved in making sure that her death didn't remain anonymous.

That's why we encourage any who are able to assist in whatever way possible with the coordination of time, people, and resources to reduce the number of unsolved cold cases and, thus, the amount of heartache that the families of these victims are suffering through.

CHAPTER SIX

COOPERATION

The Team Approach

A s the SUV approached the old house in Lubbock, Texas, Liz Flatt's hands began to tremble ever so slightly.

It was a summer afternoon in 2017, and this was the first time she had been to her sister's old home since the night of August 24, 1975. That was the last night she saw her older sister, Debbie Sue Williamson, alive. On this day in 2017, Liz was returning to Debbie's old home with Dean and me, as well as with producers of a Netflix series called *The Confession Killer*. Liz was only eight years old at the time, and after all these years, she was hoping that taking part in the series would generate renewed interest—and possibly some new leads—in her sister's decades-old murder case.

As the SUV weaved through the streets of that old Lubbock neighborhood, Liz spoke reverently of the older sister she idolized as a child. Debbie, then eighteen, had just gotten married two months prior to that August night in 1975. Liz had spent most of the summer with Debbie, often spending the night at her house while Debbie's husband, Doug, worked the late shift at the Pizza Inn, the same local pizza parlor at which the family would hold many of their family celebrations. It was an exciting time for the family with so much going on and so much to celebrate.

Even though Liz was only eight years old at the time of Debbie's murder, she remembered so many details about that night. She recalled how the family dropped Debbie off at home that night after celebrating their father's birthday at the Pizza Inn. Now, more than forty years later, Liz found herself staring intently out the back seat window at the streets of the once familiar neighborhood. She began to recognize some of the landmarks that were, at one time, commonplace, but she was somewhat surprised by how much the area still looked the same to her.

After four decades, Liz had expected that there would be more change.

She thought that maybe more of the houses would be remodeled, that there might be a new subdivision or two and maybe even some new retail development in that area of town. Maybe it would look different through her now-adult eyes than it did through the eyes of her childhood.

But, to her surprise, not much was different from the pictures she had carried in her mind since the age of eight. In some ways, that made her even more apprehensive about returning to Debbie's old home.

"This is the first time I've been back since that night," she said as the SUV made its final turn before pulling over and parking on the street next to the now infamous driveway.

As Liz exited the vehicle, she took a few steps down the carport driveway toward the home's side entrance before hesitating. Her knees buckled somewhat as the reality of what had occurred so long ago washed over her.

That warm August evening in 1975, shortly after the family had dropped her off at home, Debbie went inside to watch a little TV. It was around 8:30 p.m. and Debbie had planned to return a little later to the Pizza Inn to wait for her husband while he finished up his shift. That was a fairly routine thing for her to do, as she would usually sit and wait with a puzzle book while her husband finished cleaning up, typically finishing his shift a little after midnight. Then, they would drive home together.

That was the plan, anyway.

After Debbie was done watching her show, the eighteen-year-old new-lywed gathered a few things to take with her and headed out the side door to the carport.

Puzzle book and car keys in hand, Debbie approached the driver's side door of her car when someone emerged out of the darkness and ambushed her with a knife. The attacker savagely stabbed Debbie fifteen times in the torso then dragged her body to the side entrance step of the house, leaving a streak of blood that stretched twenty-eight feet from the car to the side entrance step of the house.

Debbie's assailant then tore the clothing off her body and left her face-down in a pool of blood.

The attack was so savage that it left Debbie with punctures to both her left and right lungs, and the left atrium of her heart was completely severed. It wasn't until about 1 a.m. that Debbie's body was discovered.

When Debbie didn't show up at the usual time to pick up her husband, Doug, from work, he called her but got no answer. Thinking that she must have fallen asleep, he got a ride home from a coworker and found her body in the driveway.

Soon, police were at the scene, and Debbie's family was alerted to what had happened.

Now, more than forty years later, Liz was standing in that very same driveway, overcome with emotion. She lifted her hands to her cheeks as the tears began to flow. Seeing the house, the driveway, and that side doorstep brought it all back; the difficulty of it all was overwhelming.

But she wanted to confront it. If she was going to go through with what she had started—or, in this case, restarted—she knew that she needed to face the past head-on. Having lived with the pain and uncertainty for so long, Liz slowly took a few more determined steps toward the side door of the house and reverently sat down on that side entrance porch step.

"I've never been this close," she said, sniffling through her tears. "I just need to do this."

Then, in a motion that paid homage to the older sister she had spent the early part of her childhood with, she leaned over and tenderly patted the decades-old concrete driveway in front of her. It was as if Liz were gently patting her sister on the back to comfort her, to show deep love and concern for what her departed big sister had gone through.

Such a moment might have been emblematic of a sister's need to re-claim some semblance of what she had lost. Or maybe she just needed to feel close to her sister's presence in that moment. Whatever the emotion was, she just felt the need to be there, to have that moment, because so many of life's shared moments had been snatched from her in the most brutal way imaginable.

Someone had taken Debbie, and along with her, all the experiences that sisters are meant to share together over decades of life. The pain of not having her around for some of life's most cherished moments—grad-uations, weddings, vacations, holidays, children and even grandchildren—came pouring out in that instant. All those things over the years that she would love to have sat around the table talking to Debbie about were no longer possible because they were snatched from Liz by the hands of a brutal killer.

For us at the Cold Case Foundation, these are the moments that we sometimes have the privilege to be a part of. They can be painful, but these are the times that remind us how short life can be and just how important it is to cherish every moment with our loved ones. They remind us why it is important to do what we do. Experiences like these serve as reminders of how important it is for us as criminal investigators to do whatever it takes to get the investigation right, to make sure that we bring the right person to justice—the person who truly committed the crime. And getting it right often requires us to strictly adhere to the principles of cooperation.

Whether it's cooperation within our own investigative agencies, with prosecutors, with other departments, the general public, or, of course, the families themselves, cooperation is an essential element of any investigation if we expect to solve a crime as heart-wrenching and complex as a homicide. And it has to go beyond just closing the case. The families of the victims expect that we will do everything necessary to get justice for the victim and for them. Not only do they expect it, but they deserve it. When we fall short of doing all we should from an investigative and cooperative standpoint, the negative consequences reverberate throughout the victims' families and throughout the communities affected. Sometimes, even further.

Unfortunately, in Debbie Sue Williamson's case, the breakdown in cooperation happened on several fronts and its consequences were devastating for the entire family. As it would turn out, they would also reverberate throughout so many communities across the country.

When we met with Liz and Joyce Lemons, Debbie's mother, they told us their story and shared their family's journey through this whole process.

"My dad died of a heart attack in his sleep," Liz told us. "He would have done anything humanly possible to find who killed her."

Like most everyone, Liz's father, Bob Lemons, thought the authorities had found Debbie's killer. The whole family did.

"We never gave up hope that Debbie's killer would be caught," said Joyce. "Nine years went by with no leads. We were getting pretty low."

Then, in 1984, investigators in Lubbock were contacted by the Texas Rangers and told that they might have Debbie's killer in custody. In 1984, the Rangers informed detectives from the Lubbock Police Department that infamous self-proclaimed serial killer Henry Lee Lucas told them that he had committed the murder that night in Lubbock, Texas. Authorities were willing to bring him to Lubbock so that detectives could interview him and corroborate his confession.

By 1984, Lucas had already confessed to more than two hundred murders across the United States, and they thought Debbie's murder might have been another one that the notorious serial killer had committed. Lubbock Police agreed, and a meeting with Lucas in Lubbock was arranged.

He met with local authorities, who drove him to the house and had him walk them through the crime scene. As Lucas walked police around the area where the crime was committed, he detailed how he had attacked Debbie, entered the home, then fled out the back to avoid detection. He confessed to the murder and, just like that, the case was closed.

Like so many police agencies throughout the country, detectives from the Lubbock Police Department thought they had their man. Lucas signed the confession, and the department officially declared the investigation complete.

"When we got the call from the police and they said they had a confession," Joyce recalled, "we didn't know who, but it didn't matter to us. We were just so happy."

"There's a lot of emotions with that," Liz added. "Getting that news and thinking it's over."

Unfortunately, also like so many agencies across the country, Lubbock authorities would be forced to face a new truth just a few short years later.

The infamous "confession killer" had falsely confessed to Debbie's murder.

"And that's where nightmare number two began," said Liz. "Henry Lee Lucas came into our lives."

As it turned out, Lucas was nowhere near Lubbock, Texas, the night of Debbie's murder. He was in Maryland—more than 1,500 miles away—too far away to have realistically been able to travel all the way to Debbie and Doug Williamson's house to commit the murder that night. Additionally, his description of what happened was consistent with neither the crime scene nor the evidence. As he had done with so many other police agencies, Lucas had lied to the Lubbock P.D.

But Debbie's family knew almost immediately after hearing the confession.

Upon reading the details of Lucas's account of events from that night, Bob and Joyce Lemons suspected that something was off. There were too many important details amiss in the serial killer's confession for him to have truly been the one to have committed the crime.

"They handed us this confession," Joyce told producers of the Netflix series. "He [Lucas] said that he went in through the glass door."

But Joyce said that Lucas couldn't possibly have entered the house through those doors.

"There was a big curio cabinet in front of that patio door," she described. "He could not have gone through it."

She went on to describe other details that also explained why it was unlikely that Lucas had been there the night of the murder.

"'Went down the hall, into the bedroom and went out the back door,'" she read from the written confession. "None of that happened."

With that information in hand, the family approached Lubbock authorities and presented them with the details they felt had been missed, asking them to reopen the case and take a closer look at the evidence.

"We told the detectives we did not believe this," Joyce said. "He could not have done this. How can you even accept this?"

Convinced that they did indeed have enough evidence to corroborate Lucas's confession, the DA refused to reopen the investigation.

"We were mad," she recalled. "We went straight to the media."

Disappointed, and feeling that they were out of legal options, Debbie's family launched a public crusade to reopen the case in the hopes of finding the real killer.

"We had no help, no support," Joyce explained. "So, we decided to do our own investigation."

They appeared on many of that era's major national television news shows, hoping to apply enough public pressure that authorities would have no choice but to reopen the investigation.

"There was absolutely nothing in the confession that indicated to us that he knew anything about it," Bob Lemons said of Lucas's statements to police during an interview with *60 Minutes* in 1985. "He [the Lubbock district attorney] was absolutely amazed because we didn't buy what he was trying to sell us."

"He was very upset because we found something wrong with the tape," Joyce added during the interview.

Bob and Joyce traveled the country, retracing Lucas's steps around the time of Debbie's murder to try and find evidence that could disprove his involvement in Debbie's murder.

"They wanted her case reopened," Liz said of her parents. "And that was the only way to prove either Henry did it or he didn't. They spent month after month after month investigating and finding these people and getting actual factual documentation to prove where Henry was."

At one point during the family's investigation, Bob worked with famous investigative journalist Hugh Aynesworth—author of two books about serial killer Ted Bundy and eventually one about Henry Lee Lucas—to retrace Lucas's steps. The goal was to try and find enough evidence to disprove the self-proclaimed serial killer's confession so that police would reopen Debbie's case.

They traveled to Maryland where they made an important discovery.

"We found Betty Crawford, who had been married to Henry Lucas," Aynesworth told producers of *The Confession Killer*. "We got a certificate showing that they were married on the same day that Lucas had already confessed to killing someone in Pennsylvania."

They also found documentation that Lucas had been released from prison in Michigan on August 22, 1975, just two days before Debbie's murder. From there, he traveled to Perryville, Maryland, where he called his half-sister and asked her to come pick him up from the bus depot and bring him to her house. Bob Lemons and Aynesworth met with Lucas's half-sister, and she confirmed that he was with her in Maryland around the time of the murder.

"In that process of discovering who he was and where he was," Liz said, "there was no way he could have been in Texas at the time Debbie was killed."

"He was living there with his half-sister at the time Debbie was murdered," Joyce added.

The family's public appearances began to gain traction, prompting law enforcement agencies around the country to look into several more murder cases that Lucas had confessed to. As investigators from various agencies throughout the United States began to uncover evidence that disproved Lucas's confessions, many of the hundreds of cases that Lucas confessed to were reopened and investigations began anew. Still, other agencies declined to reopen those cases, citing the lack of compelling evidence, resources, or manpower.

Finally, a few years after Lucas's confession, Lubbock County District Attorney Jim Bob Darnell publicly went on record and dismissed the confession.

"In looking at the evidence available to us now," he said in a press conference, "we have determined that Henry Lee Lucas's confession is indeed invalid." It seemed that Debbie's family had finally gotten what they had hoped for—a new investigation.

Unfortunately, that's not what happened. Despite the confession being dismissed, authorities chose not to reopen the investigation at that time. The family was left to forge ahead on their own, with them leading the investigation themselves. They were told that there was not enough new compelling evidence or manpower to initiate a renewed investigation. Unless such evidence came to light, the investigation would remain inactive.

Frustrated, the family pursued other avenues to try and find what the department needed to reopen Debbie's case, even making more public pleas through the media.

"I don't know who it was," the visibly frustrated stepfather said during a press conference with Joyce at his side. "I have never known who it was and never had any idea who it was. All we have ever asked for, all we ever wanted, was for them [legal authorities] to reconsider, to take another look, to do their job. That's all we ever wanted."

Unfortunately, just a few short years into their quest for a new investigation, Bob Lemons passed away with the case still unresolved and the family still in limbo. Things would remain that way until 2017 when Liz decided it was time to try again.

"For so many years, the Lubbock P.D. have not actively worked the case, so I decided that I was going to start the journey again," she told producers while discussing her interest in taking part in *The Confession Killer* series. She told them that she had met with the authorities at the department but had not gotten the answer she had hoped for.

"They just told me that they don't have the manpower," she said. "So, I took that to heart and told them that I would find them the help."

It was then that she sought out that assistance and, before long, she came in contact with us through the production of *The Confession Killer* series.

"That's when I found the Cold Case Foundation," she related. "And they agreed to take Debbie's case."

When we met with Liz, she told us about her close relationship with Debbie and how she had spent that summer in 1975 with her, how they had spent many nights together waiting for Doug to get off work.

"I was a flower girl in her wedding," Liz said. "I was so nervous I was going to mess up. And I wanted to do it so right for her."

Liz also shared her recollections of the last night she saw Debbie.

"I was supposed to stay the night with her," she recalled. "And for whatever reason, when we pulled into the driveway, mother had decided that I was not. I almost felt like if I was there, I could have made a difference."

Liz had kept all the police reports that the family had obtained years earlier. After years of conflict with the Lemons family, prosecutors had finally grown frustrated enough to give Bob all the files pertaining to the case and let the family try and come up with answers on their own.

Liz also had the documentation that her parents had discovered during the course of their own investigation. She shared those files with us, and we used the reports and crime scene photos to begin looking into Debbie's case.

Despite Lucas being ruled out by Lubbock authorities years earlier, we wanted to vet him ourselves, so our first order of business was to look at Lucas and determine the likelihood of him having murdered Debbie the night of August 24, 1975.

Ruling out Lucas as Debbie's killer didn't take long.

As Bob Lemons and Hugh Aynesworth had discovered, evidence placed him in Maryland—nearly 1,500 miles away from Lubbock—the night before Debbie was murdered. The probability of him even making the trip to Lubbock in that amount of time was unlikely, much less him happening to be at the exact location at the exact time that she was murdered. Technically, it was possible, but it was highly unlikely. Our findings lined up with what the Lemons family and other investigators over the years had determined.

Lucas was not the man who killed Debbie Williamson.

As an added request, the producers of the show asked us to compare the crimes Lucas had claimed to commit to the typical patterns and profiles of serial killers. When we canvased Lucas's trail of confessions, we looked at several of the murders that he had confessed to while purportedly crisscrossing the country. During the case analysis with our team I explained that Lucus had confessed to murders that varied in range of the victim's age, sex, type of weapon, geography, crime classification, and motivation.

"There are certain characteristics between many serial killers that are consistent, but there are also some very unique characteristics that are tailored to that individual."

Notorious serial killer Ted Bundy, for example, selected mostly the young co-ed type. There was a consistency in victimology. Gary Ridgway, known as the Green River killer, left a pattern of victims up and down a main thoroughfare in Washington state.

"That's not to say that a guy can't commit a crime in Florida and then also go to California," I continued. "But we're looking for clusters."

As we moved into the specifics of the murders Lucas confessed to, Dean presented the distinction between the purported Lucas victims and the patterns of victims we typically see from serial killers.

"Now we take a look at Lucas," Dean said. "We see all types of victims: hitchhikers, children, burglary victims, stranded motorists. He was continuing, supposedly, to kill all over the country."

"There's no consistency," I added. "The only pattern that exists here is that there is no pattern—at any level."

Before our meeting concluded, we turned our attention to the means with which Lucas claimed to have killed his victims.

In all he claimed to have used about forty different types of weapons to carry out the homicides: tire tools, forks, electrical cords, a scarf, a nylon cord, his feet, pantyhose, his own vehicle, a mop handle, knives, bricks, and guns, among many others.

"We've never come across a serial killer that uses all of those," I told the group. "That's not to say it's not possible. But, from a probability perspective, it's fictional."

With Lucas vetted and ultimately eliminated as a viable suspect in Debbie Sue Williamson's case, we dug into all the evidence we had and began to develop a criminal profile of her killer. As we looked through the evidence and studied the details of the crime-scene photos, the thing that most jumped out at us was the signature behavior.

"This is a classic case of overkill," I told the group. "That's to say, that the offender did far more than what was necessary to kill his victim. That's the primary signature behavior in this case."

"She was stabbed fifteen to seventeen times," Dean pointed out. "Then she was dragged approximately twenty-eight feet to the back porch area of the carport. But there was no sign of sexual assault."

That the victim was stabbed so many times, then dragged toward the house and stripped of her clothing without a sexual assault being committed were important elements of the case. So was the posing of her body.

"See how the offender poses the body?" I asked the group. "That's a message," I said. "In this case the posing, overkill, the victimology, and the crime scene tells us something about the relationship between the victim and the offender. It suggests that the offender knew the victim, and she certainly knew her attacker."

Why would we come to that conclusion?

In studying Debbie's victimology, she was not someone who led a high-risk lifestyle. She had recently been married, shortly after graduating from high school, and she had never been in any kind of legal trouble. She lived near her family, and, on most nights, she would go to the pizza parlor where her husband worked to wait for him while he finished his shift.

"Debbie was an exceptional daughter," her mother, Joyce, said of Debbie during filming of *The Confession Killer*. "She was kind. She was friendly. She was very helpful to anybody."

As we studied the victimology further, we discovered that Debbie's social interactions were centered around her husband, family, and a small circle of known friends. She was also a very cautious person. Debbie preferred not to be alone due to a break-in at the couple's first home while they were on their honeymoon, as well as media coverage of a recent homicide of a young female classmate. Even in looking at the last twenty-four hours of her life, Debbie was celebrating her stepfather's birthday and, after being dropped off at home, simply watched a television show to pass the time before she was going to return to the Pizza Inn to wait for her husband to finish work.

Basically, she led a very low-risk, routine-oriented life. This suggested to us that the killer was someone whom she knew and probably knew well. It certainly wasn't someone she suddenly crossed paths with or who happened to just show up at her house. The offender was more than likely someone with an agenda, someone who had some kind of vendetta against Debbie.

The overkill aspect of the crime told us that this was someone who had a great amount of anger and hostility toward her. That overwhelming rage acted out against her was indicative of someone who had known Debbie and had known her for some time. Such a high level of rage and anger against a person usually takes time to develop.

"The way he displays her," I added, "that's personal. For whatever reason—real or perceived—the offender is someone who has a deep-seated hatred toward her."

In addition to the way the killer posed Debbie's body, we noted the place he left her, specifically the bottom of the doorstep leading into the kitchen area. "The limited light coming through the backdoor windows allowed for partial illumination of the victim for the offender to complete the posing of the body," I pointed out. "This location also provided partial concealment from the street and privacy for the offender to complete the commission of this heinous crime."

Also, the amount of time required to commit this crime—including the posing and staging aspects—were noteworthy aspects of the crime. "This suggests to us that the offender was familiar and comfortable with the crime scene," I said. "Furthermore, the amount of time required to complete all the crime scene activity indicates to us that the assailant was not concerned about being interrupted. For us, that underscores the killer's familiarity with the crime scene location and environment."

Finally, there was additional staging of what appears to be a burglary at the crime scene. The back door was found ajar. The kitchen window screen was removed, and the window was broken out with glass fragments lying on concrete, on top of dry blood evidence, and inside the kitchen sink. Finally, bloody keys were strewn at the scene just above the victim's right arm.

"This evidence," I continued, "combined with investigative police reports, all suggest that there was no evidence to support that the offender entered the residence. However, the lack of evidence doesn't prove that he didn't enter the residence."

As we developed the profile, we homed in on an offender who would possess the following characteristics:

- High probability that the killer was someone Debbie had known and who certainly knew her.
- Someone who would fixate on her for a long enough period of time that a deep-seated hatred could develop.

- Someone who knew where she lived and was familiar with the surroundings and environment.
- Someone who was familiar enough with her schedule and/or routine that they knew that she would be there alone that night and around that time. It's possible the killer was watching her through a window before the attack.
- Finally, someone who had some experience with using a knife. Her wounds were deep enough to puncture both lungs and sever the aorta. They were not superficial. This was not the work of someone who was unfamiliar with handling a knife in that way.

As we rounded out the profile of Debbie's killer, we looked at the people in her life. We wanted to create a list of individuals who would be people of interest to interview—or interview again if investigators had spoken with them already during the course of the original investigation. We recommended some individuals to follow up with, most of whom were close with both Debbie and her family. That can be a difficult thing for the family to face—that it might be someone close to them who committed the murder.

We narrowed the list down to a few people within the close circle of associates that was consistent with the behavioral analysis and probable offender characteristics. Because the case was still being investigated at the time of this book's writing, we aren't at liberty to disclose those people by name because we don't want to compromise the integrity of the investigation. However, what we can share is that, when we review people of interest in a homicide case, we typically examine critical factors associated with each person and then ask ourselves the following types of questions surrounding those factors, both pre- and post-offense:

1. The relationship that specific person of interest had with the victim
   - What was the nature of that person's relationship to the victim?
   - What was the nature of the relationship that individual had with others who were close to the victim and how did that relationship change after the murder?
   - If the crime scene was a location familiar to the victim, then how familiar with that location is the person of interest?

2. Behavioral characteristics
   • What were typical behaviors of that individual before the crime? Did those behaviors abruptly change after the crime?
   • If so, what was the nature of those changes?
   • What was a typical emotional pattern for this individual pre-crime and did those change post-crime? Also, it's important for us to examine what emotions this person exhibited immediately after the crime and how those emotions changed as time went on.
   • How did this individual react to the victim in certain situations before the crime? For example, was there ever any anger or hostility directed toward the victim?
3. Life and lifestyle changes
   • What life changes were made post-crime? For example, did this person suddenly move out of town or even out of state? If so, what prompted the individual to do so?
   • Did the person's routine change? If so, how soon after the crime was the change made and how abrupt was that change?

It's important to note that the observations and questions we are sharing here are just some of the examples of the types of things we look at as we develop profiles of the various people of interest. There is much more, but we just wanted to highlight some core samples of what we focus on. And these were the kinds of things we focused on in reviewing Debbie's case.

After we created behavioral profiles around these people of interest, we also included a list of investigative recommendations for the Lubbock Police Department to follow up on. Since that time—especially over the past two or three years—law enforcement officials have assigned a detective to specifically work the case and have made some progress in moving the case forward. In May 2023, the family worked cooperatively with Lubbock authorities to have Debbie's body exhumed, hoping to find DNA samples that might identify her killer.

"I really appreciate Sgt. Justin Anderson's work on my sister's case," Liz told us when we talked to her about the status of Debbie's case. "He's been so good to me and to our family. I realize that the police can't reveal certain details, but he has been so good to communicate with us and keep us up on any developments. It's almost like we're partners and that's the way I feel it should be between law enforcement and the family."

Having graduated from the police academy in 2011, Sgt. Anderson quickly ascended the ranks from patrol officer to sergeant and has demonstrated a remarkable ability to work cooperatively with Liz and her family in a way that productively moved Debbie's case forward. And, in working cooperatively with Liz, what had been years of conflict between the Lemons family and the Lubbock Police Department has become a cooperative effort to help solve Debbie's case.

"It took a lot of hard work to get to this point," Liz told members of the Lubbock media upon announcing that the family and the department had agreed to exhume Debbie's body to do the DNA testing. "I cannot thank [the Lubbock Police Department] enough."

As an organization, we at the Cold Case Foundation have been privileged to be able to help in this regard, donating resources to help pay for advanced DNA testing that we hope will produce leads in identifying Debbie's killer.

We are grateful for the many people who have been so generous to donate to the foundation. It's this type of generosity that makes these activities possible on behalf of the victims' families and the law enforcement agencies that investigate these homicides. These donations have been extremely helpful in building a cooperative bridge between investigators and the families. None of this would be possible without the kind donations and cooperation of those who give to help solve these crimes.

Because of these donations, there are other ways that we are set up to help, as well. For example, police agencies in smaller communities have limited resources when it comes to investigating cold cases. Our partnership with these agencies enables us to leverage the vast amount of multidisciplinary resources from the criminal justice community and facilitate the synergistic effect of these combined resources for these law enforcement agencies at no cost.

During the filming of *The Confession Killer* series, for instance, we were introduced to the family member of the victim of another so-called Henry Lee Lucas case that we were asked to look at. Jean Abla, a single mother living in San Jon, New Mexico, mysteriously disappeared one night in 1982. "My mom went to a bar and she left sometime that evening," her daughter,

Samantha Thompson, told us as we talked to her about her mother's case. "But we don't know where she went. It was as if she had just fallen off the end of the Earth, and we didn't know where to look."

Nearly seven months went by without any information or sign of her. Authorities had no leads, and the family didn't know what to do. Then, Jean's remains were found in the desert, buried in a shallow grave. "Not long after that," Samantha told us, "I got news that Henry Lee Lucas had killed her."

Police detectives in San Jon had gotten a missing person report on Jean and followed up on her last known whereabouts. Dennis Smart, a Sheriff's deputy for the San Jon Police Department at the time—and now retired—remembered the case and gave us background on the original investigation.

"We got a report that she'd been seen in a bar that night and was drinking with a man in there that fit Henry Lee Lucas's description," he told us. "The sheriff and I went to Texas together to talk to Henry Lee Lucas, and of course, people were in line to talk to him, you know. People from agencies all over the United States had come to talk to him. And, so, they gave us twenty minutes to talk to him. They had so many people waiting to get in, we got twenty minutes for the interview."

Twenty minutes later, the sheriff and his deputy walked out of the Georgetown Williamson County Jail—headquarters of the Henry Lee Lucas Taskforce—with a signed confession in hand.

"He [Lucas] admitted it," Dennis told us. "He said to Sheriff Garnett, 'Yeah, I did that one.' And, of course, he was having a good day. He was a superstar. You know, he was a movie star. He was something special."

As we continued to talk to Dennis about the details that Lucas shared with them about Jean's case, he told us that Lucas went into graphic detail, which left them little doubt about the validity of his confession.

"It was kind of morbid because he said that he liked to behead them," Dennis recalled. "He said it was because he didn't like to have sex with a woman with a head, so he'd take the head off and have sex with the head gone. He said he does all his victims that way."

As we looked into the case, one of the things that raised a red flag for us was how quickly they got the confession from Lucas. Twenty minutes is light speed in terms of the amount of time it typically takes to get a confession from a suspect—even among the most cooperative of suspects. "It generally takes on average, several hours to get a confession from an individual that has committed a heinous crime and who is going to suffer the consequences of that," I told producers of *The Confession Killer* series. That thought prompted us to ask Dennis if they had looked at any other suspects during the time of the initial investigation.

"There wasn't anybody else that we knew of who was a suspect," Dennis said. "We both had the same feeling on it, that we were about 80 percent sure we thought he'd [Lucas] done it."

As we dug further into Jean Abla's case, we were once again able to rule Lucas out as a suspect. Similar to the situation with Debbie Williamson's case, Lucas was nowhere near the location of the crime the night Jean disappeared. The investigation revealed that Lucas had made a collect phone call from another state on the date of her disappearance.

We found that Jean's victimology placed her in a medium-risk lifestyle that at times could be elevated due to circumstances and situations.

In talking to Samantha, we learned that Jean had recently been in a toxic relationship with an abusive boyfriend. It's also notable that she was last seen leaving a bar. It would be important to know who she crossed paths with during her visit to the establishment. The lack of those particular details left Samantha and her family feeling frustrated with the original investigation. "[The police] should have gotten more answers from interviewing witnesses," Samantha said. "Questioning her boyfriend that she'd just broken up with, who had tried to strangle her."

Unfortunately, we can't go back in time and interview all the patrons who were at the bar that night. But we can identify the people Jean was closely associated with and work outwardly from there, beginning with the boyfriend that Samantha referenced.

Sheriff Russell Shafer worked cooperatively with us as much as possible; however, there were some circumstances that made this cold case more difficult to investigate, namely the lack of collected evidence and original police reports. "From what I understand, there was a flood in the basement [of the sheriff's office]," he told us. "And it wiped out some records."

When we run into challenges like this, we have to rely on information from the families and close associates of the victim. Even though some reports had gone missing, family and friends can provide investigators with solid leads to follow up on. Samantha, Jean's daughter, is a great example of how family members can provide relevant information that can help detectives follow up on the most productive leads possible during an investigation.

In this case, for example, Samantha provided some important information in her mother's case as it related to the probability of Lucas being the offender. After reading through Lucas's confession, she noticed an important detail about the night of her mother's disappearance that she shared with us.

"He [Lucas] says that he picked her up hitchhiking," Samantha observed. "She didn't need to be hitchhiking. She had a car."

Samantha also discovered an inconsistency regarding Lucas's description of Jean's appearance that night.

"He said that she was wearing pigtails," she noted. "Mom was not wearing pigtails."

As Dean and I discussed the case, we identified some additional key facts of the case that were of particular importance to the investigation.

"They found her car," Dean said. "There were some key items, as I understand it, in that vehicle. Things she just never let go of, her cigarettes being one of them. So, that really raised the alarm."

"So, then there was some suspicion that, is it possible that Henry Lee Lucas would be involved in this?" I queried. "And, if he didn't commit this crime—or any of the others he confessed to for that matter—then how would he benefit from confessing at all?"

As I went on to tell the producers of *The Confession Killer*, oftentimes these types of criminal personalities will take responsibility for crimes they've never committed because it gives them recognition.

"For the first time in their life, they've been recognized," I said. "And, for them, it's better to be known for a crime than to be known for nothing at all."

As we close this chapter, it's important to realize this is not an investigative critique of any of the law enforcement agencies involved in the Henry Lee Lucas Task Force cases. Hindsight is 20/20. Given the circumstances, the knowledge and investigative technology at the time, who knows what any of us would have done?

I, myself, was a young police chief in Delta, Utah, during the 1980s, and I can tell you that the advancements in technology alone have made detective work much more efficient than it was when I started. Scientific evidence, such as DNA technology, has made cases much easier to solve. In addition, video evidence is much more widely available than it was during that time. With more cameras being installed in public areas and places of business, as well as most everyone having cell phones with video recording capability, evidence has the potential of being more widely available to law enforcement investigators than it ever has before.

But it also means that our reliance on cooperating with the public is much more critical to solving cases, as well.

The key thing that we wanted to point out with the Henry Lee Lucas cases was the principle of cooperation. This was highlighted by the forward-thinking of the Texas Rangers in putting together the Lucas Task Force. Bringing in different agencies to cooperatively share evidence and information was a less-than-common practice at the time. And the cooperative sharing of information and resources is a critical element that helps solve cases today.

A law enforcement agency's primary client is the victim, and their secondary client is the victim's family. When properly nurtured, they can serve as investigative motivators, support mechanisms, and critical information resources. As a result, developing a cooperative relationship based on trust is vital. A trusting relationship ultimately leads to the disclosure of vital public, private, and secret information about the primary client over time.

And, in the end, that is what helps bring these cases to a resolution for the victims' families, law enforcement, and the communities we serve.

CHAPTER SEVEN

COMMUNICATION AND OUR MOST IMPORTANT CUSTOMERS

"What in the world is all that screaming out there? It's eleven o'clock at night!" Harvey Dole complained to his wife, Glenna, who was finishing her nighttime routine in the couple's master bathroom.

"I'm not sure," she answered, looking out the upstairs bedroom window into the back yard of their next-door neighbor. "Oh my gosh, it's Dennis and Alyssa's kids. What are they doing out there so late?"

"And on a weeknight, no less," Harvey said, shaking his head.

"Well, I guess it's better than the screaming we have to hear from their parents," Glenna joked, eliciting a chuckle from her husband.

"True enough," he said. "By the sounds of it, at least those kids seem to be having a lot more fun than Dennis and Alyssa do during one of their grudge matches."

"Well, if they don't bring them inside in the next few minutes, I'm going to call them and tell them we're about to go to bed."

"Sounds good to me," he responded.

Just then, someone opened the neighbor's back door and called for the kids to come inside.

"Finally," Harvey said. "Now, maybe we can get some sleep. I swear, the Bayers are nice enough people, but it's a madhouse over there sometimes."

The couple, recent empty nesters, looked at each other one more time and smiled before turning out the lights to get some sleep.

The next morning, all seemed normal.

As Harvey was taking his trash can out to the street, he saw the Bayers' garage door open, and their minivan pull out of the driveway. Harvey presumed that Dennis was taking his kids to school. But he thought it was odd to see him behind the wheel of the vehicle and not Alyssa.

"Hmm, it's good to see Dennis finally picking up some slack," he thought to himself. "Maybe he's finally figuring it out. Hopefully, that will lead to less arguments and more inside time for their kids at night."

Harvey thought nothing more of it until about a week later when a man came knocking on his door to ask him some questions about the Bayers.

"Alyssa's family is worried because she hasn't answered their calls over the past couple of days," he said. "I was wondering if you or your wife had maybe seen or heard something?"

Harvey was surprised and taken aback. Not quite sure how to respond, he blurted out the first thing that came to his mind.

"Who are you again?" he asked quizzically. "Are you with the police?"

"No," the man answered. "I'm just a friend of Alyssa and her family. But I've worked with the police before so I kind of know the drill when it comes to missing person situations."

"Alyssa's missing?" Harvey asked, with an alarming tone of surprise in his voice. "How long has she been missing? I just saw her out with her kids the other day."

"Well, it seems that she is," the man said. "I'm not at liberty to say much more than that because we're not sure, but that's why I'm out here knocking on neighborhood doors and asking questions on behalf of her family. I told them that I would help and that, if we could find out if anyone has seen or heard anything, then I can help get that information to the police."

"Oh, I see," Harvey replied, still not sure what to make of the situation. "Well, my wife and I did hear their kids playing in the yard a couple nights ago. It was strange because it was eleven o'clock in the middle of the week. That's pretty late for young kids to be out playing."

"Yeah it is. I see you have a doorbell camera. If the police wanted to look at data from that, would you be willing to let them take a look at it—just to see if they pick up anything unusual?"

Harvey, now curious about the Bayer family, agreed.

"Sure, I guess so. I guess it couldn't do any harm. Just have the police call me if they need any information from me."

"I will. Thank you."

As the gentleman left, Harvey closed the door behind him and wondered why, if there was truly something to be alarmed about, the police weren't looking into any suspicious circumstances related to Alyssa's disappearance.

It seemed to him that, if her family were concerned, they would have contacted the police instead of having a friend canvas the neighborhood looking for clues.

Harvey thought about walking over to the Bayer household and checking on Dennis. Even though they had been neighbors for the better part of four years, they weren't particularly close. Alyssa was always friendly and much more outgoing than Dennis. But the truth was that the families didn't really have much in common. The Bayers were in the early stages of raising a family, while the Doles had just become empty nesters a couple years before the young family bought the house next door. Plus, living in a wide cul-de-sac in a smaller community, the homes were kind of spread out, and in this type of exclusive neighborhood, people tended to keep to themselves.

Still, Harvey hoped all was well and figured that Alyssa would probably be home soon—especially with young children to raise.

"They probably had one of their fights and she probably needed a break from Dennis," he told himself. "But maybe I'll see if there is anything I can do to help."

A few days later, Harvey saw a few cars parked in front of the Bayer home. It looked like the family was gathering together.

Could Alyssa still not have come home?

Since he hadn't heard anything more from the family's pseudo-detective friend or the real police, he assumed she had probably returned home and he just hadn't noticed. Harvey wasn't typically one to pay attention to what the neighbors were doing anyway.

He peeked out the window and saw some people who could have been a couple of Alyssa's family members—someone that looked like she could be her mother and possibly some siblings—he wasn't quite sure. What he was sure of was that they didn't look happy. In fact, they looked distraught.

He watched them as they stood at the front door of the Bayer home and talked to Dennis. They seemed to be discussing something, and it was a solid minute or two before Dennis let them inside.

"That's odd," he thought. "Why were they standing at the door for so long? Why didn't Dennis just let them inside? Doesn't he get along with Alyssa's family?"

Now he was really curious.

Harvey decided to pick up a book and read by the window, so he would see when Alyssa's family members exited the home. He put his shoes on and removed the kitchen trash bag from under the sink, bringing it into the living room near the window.

He wanted to be ready when the family made their way to their cars. This way, he would have an excuse to talk to them and maybe find out what was going on.

Harvey wanted to see if Alyssa was still missing, and he didn't want to miss his opportunity to find out. But he also didn't want to cross a line and insert himself where he didn't belong. If he had an excuse to be outside, he could just casually make conversation and see if they would tell him something.

When he saw the first couple of family members exit the home an hour or so later, he quickly picked up the trash bag and made his way outside toward his garbage can sitting curbside on the street. Then he nodded and gave a friendly wave to them as they made their way toward their vehicles. One of them glanced his way and waved back.

Harvey had his opening.

"Hi," he called over to them. "I'm Harvey Dole. I'm Alyssa and Dennis's next-door neighbor."

"Hi," replied one of the family members. "It's nice to meet you."

In the moment, Harvey was a bit annoyed at himself.

"What a dumb thing to say," he thought to himself. "Of course, you're the next-door neighbor. Who else is going to take a bag of garbage out to your curb?"

But, since the family member seemed nice enough, Harvey decided to make his way over to the group.

"I don't mean to pry, but how are things going over here?" Harvey asked, trying to show concern without overstepping.

The family members looked at each other for a moment, before one of them—a taller woman with short dark hair—answered, "It's not good. Alyssa has been missing for a few days now and we're not sure where she is."

"Oh, I'm sorry to hear that," Harvey responded, his curiosity immediately changing to concern. He had hoped that she had returned home by now. "Is there anything we can do to help?"

"We're not sure," answered the woman, who identified herself as Alyssa's mother. "We're still trying to figure all this out."

"Have you called the police?" Harvey asked, suddenly realizing he might have just crossed a line.

"Yes, but right now we're not getting a lot of response," she answered. "They told us that they would look into it and that's all we've heard so far."

"I'm sorry to hear that. Hopefully, you will hear from them soon and it will be good news. Is there anything we can do for Dennis or the kids?"

Once again, family members looked awkwardly at each other as if they weren't sure what to say or if they should even say anything at all. Then Alyssa's mother smiled politely and responded, "I'm sure Dennis would appreciate it if you checked in on him."

"Okay, then I will do that," Harvey said, still unsure whether he had made the situation better or worse. "Well, it was nice to meet you. If you can think of anything, please don't hesitate to knock on our door. My wife, Glenna, and I would be happy to help in any way. I hope that you find Alyssa soon."

"Thank you," she answered. "And, by the way, my name is Sandra, and this is my husband, Gerald. Once we hear from the police, I'm sure we will be in touch."

With that, the family drove away, and Harvey returned to his house to tell his wife about his encounter with Alyssa's family.

"How did it go over there?" Glenna asked.

"Not good," he answered. "They said that Alyssa has been missing for a few days."

"What?" Glenna responded in a surprised tone. "How come we haven't seen the police over there? I thought that the guy you talked to said he was going to call the police and that, if this was serious, they would get involved."

"I know. That's what I thought, too. So, when I hadn't heard or seen anything, I figured she had come back like most married couples after they have a bad fight."

"Did they say anything about what they thought might have happened?"

"No, they didn't really say much of anything," Harvey answered. "But I did get some odd vibes. After they told me that Alyssa's been missing for the past few days, I asked them if there was any way I could help Dennis and the kids. They just kind of looked at each other and Alyssa's mom said it would be good if I checked in on him. But I got the feeling there are some issues between them."

"Well, maybe you should go see Dennis and see how he's doing," Glenna said. "The poor guy. If Alyssa has gone missing, he's probably beside himself. I know I would be."

"Yeah, you're probably right. I'll go see him tomorrow after work."

The next day, Harvey happened to be pulling into his driveway just as Dennis had stepped outside to get the mail.

"Hey, Dennis," Harvey called as he walked over to him. "I heard about Alyssa. I'm so sorry. How are you and the kids holding up?"

"We're fine," Dennis said with no real tone to his voice and seeming to be somewhat surprised at the degree of concern his neighbor was showing.

"I'm glad to hear that," Harvey replied. "Is there anything we can do for you?"

"No, not really."

"Man, you're doing better than I would be. Have you told the police what's going on? Maybe they can help you find her."

"They've been by, but there's really not much to tell. She likes to get out by herself sometimes. I'm sure she's fine."

Surprised by Dennis's aloof demeanor, Harvey wasn't quite sure how to respond.

"Are you sure?" He once again found himself blurting out—this time unapologetically. "I mean, a week is a long time. If it were me, I'd be pretty worried and I'd want all the help I could get."

"Well, I'm not you. And Alyssa is not Glenna," Dennis responded curtly. "She likes to be on her own and she is fine."

Harvey couldn't believe what he was hearing, but he thought about the Bayer children and decided that it wouldn't hurt to offer some sort of help one more time.

"Well, can we maybe bring over a meal or something for you and the kids? Glenna makes an amazing lasagna."

"No, we're good. But thanks."

"Okay, well, if you change your mind, just let us know. We'll be happy to help."

"Sounds good. I'm going to go inside now. Have a good night."

Harvey watched in disbelief as his neighbor abruptly turned around and went inside.

On his way home, he was perplexed at what appeared to be Dennis's utter lack of concern for his wife's well-being. Even worse, he didn't know what to do about it or if he could do anything about it.

All he knew was that he was shocked, saddened, and frustrated. Harvey had always been the guy whose life motto was "live and let live—and mind your own business."

But this was different. There were children and possibly an innocent life at stake. And the man who should have cared the most didn't seem to care at all. For some reason, that made Harvey angry. Something that was none of his business got his blood boiling and he felt the need to do something about it.

"What a sad mess," he thought.

Not more than an hour later the doorbell rang.

When he answered the door, Alyssa's parents were standing at his doorstep.

"Did you mean what you said?" Sandra asked. "Are you really interested in helping us?"

Harvey didn't hesitate.

"Absolutely," he said in a determined voice. "What do you need me to do?"

Sandra explained that the family had contacted the local media and that they were hoping to rally as many people in the community as possible to search for Alyssa. They would be meeting at a park close to the neighborhood and would give more details about the search then.

"We're so glad you can help," she told Harvey.

"I wouldn't miss it," he answered. "I do have one question, though, if you don't mind."

"Yes, of course."

"Is Dennis planning on being there?"

The couple looked at each other, then Sandra turned to Harvey.

"No, he doesn't have any interest in participating in the search. Does that change your mind on helping us?"

"Well, I had a chance to talk to Dennis about an hour ago," Harvey said. "After my conversation with him, let's just say it makes me want to help you folks even more."

"Me too!" Glenna interjected from inside the house. "Count us in."

"Okay then," Sandra replied. "I guess we'll see you both at the park soon."

When Harvey and Glenna arrived, there were well over a hundred people at the park. Some were holding signs, while others just mingled and talked to each other. Never one for large gatherings, Harvey felt very much out of his element. But there was no way he was going to let that stop him. Not after his experience with Dennis and not while there were two kids who hadn't seen their mother in over two weeks.

Thinking about the Bayer children was the hardest part for Harvey. He realized that, with the exception of seeing them drive off to school, he hadn't seen them outside at all.

He wished he had never complained about the noise they made.

"What I wouldn't give to hear those kids laughing and playing now," he told Glenna. "I wouldn't care what time of day it was."

Glenna squeezed his hand and gave him a reassuring nod. They were in the right place doing the right thing for Alyssa and her children.

Just then, Sandra and Gerald approached the microphone that was set on a makeshift podium that one of the television news crews had brought. The news station producer counted down with his fingers, then gave them a nod, a cue that they could start speaking.

Sandra was the first to speak.

"We want to start by thanking all of you for being here this evening," she told the crowd. "It means so much to our family that so many of you would take the time to be here."

After a few more words of gratitude and encouragement, Sandra handed the microphone to Gerald, who explained that Alyssa had been missing for two weeks and no one had heard anything from her. He told the gathering that there were people handing out stacks of flyers with Alyssa's photo and the parents' contact information.

"If you will please post these around town in public areas with the most visibility," he requested. "That way, if anyone has seen Alyssa, they will know how to get in touch with us."

Just then, someone from the crowd shouted, "Where are the police? Have you called them?"

Sandra, unable to contain her emotions, told the gathering, "We have called the police. They told us they opened an investigation. But we feel like more has to be done. Right now, we feel that it's up to us to help find Alyssa."

Harvey couldn't believe what he was hearing. Why wouldn't the police get involved?

"At the very least, they can look into what's going on," he said to Glenna. "They've got to at least acknowledge the family, right?"

Glenna could only shrug her shoulders.

As for Harvey, within two weeks, he had undergone a complete transformation. He had gone from being an unconcerned neighbor, just wanting to maintain his space, to a curious neighbor, and then a concerned citizen who wanted to help. Upon hearing this news, he was now an outraged neighbor who had been transformed into a man on a mission.

Just then, he bumped into the man who had rung his doorbell nearly two weeks ago asking questions and requesting information.

"It's you," Harvey said.

"Yeah, it's good to see you out here," the man said, this time introducing himself by name. "My name is Louis. It's good to formally meet you."

"You too," Harvey said. "In case you didn't catch it when you were at my house, the name's Harvey."

"Harvey, it's good to see you here," Louis replied. "I've got to be honest; you didn't strike me as the get-involved type."

"I wasn't until you showed up," Harvey said. "Now I see why you were knocking on our doors. I feel so bad for this family. I just hope the police are doing everything they can to find out what happened to Alyssa."

"Well, it's hard to know how much they're doing," Louis answered. "They have been by the Bayer house, so they are probably doing more than we are aware of. But it would be nice if they would talk to Alyssa's family and let them know that."

The truth is that, behind the scenes, police detectives were in fact working on Alyssa's case. They just weren't communicating with anybody about it—including Alyssa's family.

Over the next few weeks, one rally turned into more and those rallies turned into multiple protests in front of the police department. As the public appearances became more frequent, the complaints about the job detectives were doing grew louder. The claims about the department not doing enough to find Alyssa or potentially bringing her killer to justice began to be frequent narratives on the nightly news and the constant media requests were beginning to interfere with the detectives' ability to investigate Alyssa's disappearance.

It had been more than a month since anyone had last seen Alyssa, and a rift had developed between Dennis and Alyssa's parents, family members, and close friends, many of whom were now suspecting that he had something to do with Alyssa's disappearance. To make matters worse, Dennis had hired an attorney and had stopped openly cooperating with police. Worse yet, he began to limit contact between Alyssa's family and his children.

Tensions were getting high, and frustration was mounting to a boiling point between Alyssa's family, her friends, Dennis, his neighbors, and the police department. And it was becoming very public to the point of daily protests in front of the department.

That's when a friend of Sandra's told her about our foundation. He told her that he had been listening to a true crime podcast episode that talked about the Cold Case Foundation and thought it might be a good idea to reach out to us.

Not long after their conversation, Sandra contacted us and asked if we could assist with Alyssa's case.

Of course, we were happy to lend our expertise and experience in whatever way we could, but we would need to reach out to the investigating agency first. "It's important that we establish a cooperative effort," we told her. "We would need to be there to assist the department in a supporting role. That's the most effective way to approach the investigation and the best chance to find out what happened to Alyssa."

After some more discussion, the family agreed that this would be the best course of action and agreed to let us reach out to the department on their behalf. At first, department administration was hesitant. But, as we continued to communicate with them and reassure them that we were only there to function in a support role behind the scenes, they eventually warmed to the idea and decided to take us up on our offer to help. They told us that while they could use our services with the investigation, their most urgent need was to calm the contentious situation that was developing between Alyssa's family, the public, and the police department.

"It's been brewing for a while, but it's starting to play itself out in the media to the point that our detectives aren't able to interview some of the people they need to without it becoming a spectacle, and as you know, that won't be good for anybody," the lieutenant overseeing the investigation told us.

One of the members of the department's investigative team was familiar with an individual on our team, Chris McDonough, who had been a homicide detective for more than twenty years. The two shared a mutual respect, and he thought Chris would be a perfect fit for the task at hand.

The respect for Chris was well earned. Chris had a distinguished career as a homicide detective in Southern California, having worked over a hundred homicide cases and solving the vast majority of them. Many of those cases were high-profile murders that made national news, such as the harrowing murder case involving Matthew Cecchi, the nine-year-old boy who was murdered in a public restroom while at a family reunion. Chris arrested Brandon Wilson for the boy's murder and elicited a confession from him, convincing him to reenact the crime while knowingly being video recorded in the police department interrogation room.

That confession led to a conviction, and Wilson was sentenced to the death penalty, which was never carried out by the state because he took his own life thirteen years later. It was an incredible piece of detective work, and Chris was able to get the confession in such a dramatic way because he understood the mind of the perpetrator and played upon Wilson's self-delusions of grandeur. This is what makes Chris so great at what he does. He has a knack for reading people and situations, yet also has an empathy for those he serves and a vision for what he wants to accomplish and why.

The Matthew Cecchi case was one of several that involved children, and it was no coincidence that Chris became well known in law enforcement circles for his work in violent criminal cases against children. Several years before he became a detective, while a young father and police officer, Chris had an experience in which a stranger had pulled over in front of his house and invited his son to get in the car with him. Fortunately, Chris, who is a large man at six feet five, happened to be watching through the window and immediately intervened to stop his son from getting into the car. When the driver saw Chris coming, he quickly abandoned his designs and drove away. "I can never say for sure what would have happened if I hadn't been there that day," Chris said when sharing that experience with us. "But I can say that it probably wasn't going to be good."

As a result of that experience, Chris also had an "aha" moment that would shape the rest of his life and career. "I just got this strong feeling that I had been given a set of talents and drawn to use those talents in law enforcement for a reason," he said. "And, in that moment, I knew that reason was to be an advocate for children. Whether it was protecting them, helping them get out of bad situations, or working to get justice for those who had been victimized, I felt that that needed to be my life's work."

Chris certainly made it his life's work both throughout his career and even in retirement. Not only does he currently donate his time and expertise to our foundation—as he did in this case—but he also continues to help solve cases and teach safety principles to the general public through his podcast, "The Interview Room." This is why he was recommended to be a liaison between Alyssa's family and the police department. Because of his sensitivity to helping families and children, he was the perfect fit for this situation.

"I can't think of anybody better, but we will have to run it by the chief first," the police department's representative said.

He did and, after some discussion, it was agreed that Chris would meet with the family and see if they could find some common ground. But before Chris set up the meeting, the chief of police wanted to talk to him and make sure they were on the same page.

"What approach are you thinking about taking?" the chief asked Chris.

"Well, the first thing is to understand that the natural instinct of the family is to engage in some kind of service," he answered. "Because there's a sense of hopelessness, they don't want to just sit around, wait and do nothing."

"So, what are you suggesting?"

"Let's give them some appropriate direction," Chris said. "All this energy is going in one direction right now. They're out looking for Alyssa right now. They've been out looking for her for weeks with very little guidance from the department's end. So, to them, it feels like we don't care."

"But we do care. Anytime we talk to the media, we reinforce that message."

"I know you do, but they need more than that. They need to see it. They need us to show them that we are on their side. Sometimes saying it just isn't enough."

"So, what do you suggest we do?"

"First, assign someone from the department who is familiar enough with the case that they can give regular updates to the family, but not so familiar with the intimate details of the investigation that they will slip and give information that would compromise it. This will give the detectives assigned to the case the freedom to investigate it knowing that the family is being taken care of.

"Second, have that person help guide the family in a way that brings them toward working with the police—not against the department. It's my experience that, if we show them that we are advocates for them, then they will work with us. But we have to start by setting up a constant line of communication with them. Will you trust me to do that?"

"I've heard about your record, and I've been told that this is your area of expertise," the chief told Chris. "It's been an uphill battle so far, so if you can build a bridge between the family and the department, I think that will resolve a lot of issues."

With that directive, Chris set up a meeting with Sandra, Gerald, and other family and friends that the couple requested be there at their home, including Harvey Dole, the outraged neighbor who went on to become unabashedly publicly critical of the department.

The minute Chris entered Sandra and Gerald's home, Harvey, who had developed a close friendship with Sandra and Gerald over the weeks after Alyssa's disappearance, was demanding answers.

But Chris came with one agenda: Listen to the family's grievances and report back to the department.

As Chris met with the family, there was palpable tension in the room. He knew that the only way to diffuse that tension was to ask questions and listen. So, he did.

"We just don't understand why nobody will talk to us or tell us anything," Sandra told him. "They have just shut us out from the beginning. I'm Alyssa's mother. We're her family, her friends. I know you can't tell us everything, but why won't you at least tell us something? Let us know that you're doing something to find our daughter."

"That's a fair point," Chris told them. "Knowing that the detectives can't divulge certain details about the investigation, what would be an acceptable system of communication between you and the department? What would that look like to you?"

"Just update us regularly," Gerald told Chris. "And let us know how we can help. We're not trying to get in the way, but if we don't know how we can help, what else are we supposed to do?"

"We just want to know what happened to our daughter," said Sandra, her eyes now filled with tears. "We know that something has probably happened to her. She wouldn't just up and leave her kids and family and never talk to anybody again. So, just tell us what you're doing to find her and find out who is responsible for her death. We just want to know that she matters to the people who can do something about this. Because she matters to us."

After spending a few hours with Alyssa's family, Chris said he would talk to the department administration and see if he could set up a meeting with them and the family. Either way, he would get back to them within the next couple of days.

The next morning, Chris spoke with the chief of police and briefed them on his meeting with the family.

"Like we discussed," he said. "they just want to be heard. They want some direction. And they want to know that this case is important to the department."

As Chris closed the debriefing, he recommended that all the principal parties meet together at the department.

"You, the detectives, and any other personnel essential to the investigation should be there," he said. "And, chief, it will go a long way if you acknowledge that the communication should have been better. I believe that, if they hear that from you, they will become an advocate instead of an adversary."

"I'll take that under advisement. Set the meeting up and we will hear what they have to say."

Two days later, a meeting between Alyssa's family and the department was convened in a conference room at department headquarters. Sandra and Gerald brought a list of grievances and of things they would like to see happen going forward.

To the agency's credit, they listened and were upfront and sensitive in their responses. When the meeting ended, the chief of police shook each family member's hand and apologized to the family.

"We should have communicated better. I'm sorry. You deserved better. You have our commitment that we will be better in this area going forward."

At that moment, the family was on the team with the investigation, which allowed Chris to walk the family through some important next steps and set up a plan to work with the department as the case developed.

"The important thing to remember," he told them, "is this is going to be a long-term process with multiple phases to it. I know we don't want to think that way, but right now, I think you all understand why it's being treated as a homicide investigation."

Chris went on to articulate to the family why there may not have been the type of contact they had expected.

Sometimes, victims' families have the expectation that investigating officials should treat the family as an ally. While, on the surface, that might sound like a well-intended plan, sometimes the best intentions lead to unintended consequences.

Detectives have to remain objective in the facts and evidence of the case. If they stray outside that mindset, it can create a conflict of interest. If the lead investigator of the case gets too close to the family, it can skew his objectivity, which is essential to the investigation because, unfortunately, in a lot of cases, it's a family member who has committed the crime.

As Alyssa's family came to understand that principle, Chris outlined each of the four phases of a homicide investigation, so they would have a roadmap of what to expect going forward.

- investigation
- suspect's arrest
- court trial
- impact statement

"What you need to keep in mind is that, if an arrest is made and the case goes to trial, then there are going to be twelve jurors who have probably been watching your interactions with the police and prosecutors on the nightly news," he explained. "If you aren't walking arm-in-arm with the authorities, then some of those jurors aren't going to believe a word they say in court and that could damage the outcome we all want, which is a conviction."

That message was received by Alyssa's family and loved ones and, because the department assigned a liaison to keep in constant contact with the family, the relationship between the family, the police, and the community as a whole changed from an adversarial one into a productive partnership. Even the staunchest opponents of the department, like Harvey Dole, changed their narrative in regard to the work the detectives were doing on behalf of Alyssa's family.

Detectives eventually found enough incriminating evidence to make an arrest for the murder of Alyssa Bayer. The district attorney charged Alyssa's husband, Dennis, with first degree homicide in the case, but because court proceedings had not yet started at the time of this book's writing, we aren't at liberty to divulge details of what that evidence was or how it was obtained. What we can say, however, is that the strength of the relationship between Alyssa's family and the police department played a key role in moving the investigation in a positive direction that led to the arrest. Alyssa's case illustrates how communication is key to creating a productive relationship between law enforcement and families who are going through so much and how communication—or the lack thereof—can help or hinder an investigation.

We have to communicate regularly with the victims' families. And we have to do so for a couple of important reasons. First, it is the right thing to do. We should always keep them in the loop and keep them informed as to how the case is progressing. That doesn't mean we share critical information that is vital to the integrity of the investigation, but we can share updates on the investigation's progress.

Most important, we need to let them know that their loved one hasn't been forgotten and that we are doing everything possible to solve their case and find out what happened. Just as critical, staying in contact with the family allows them to be heard. We should always listen to what the family has to say and keep an open mind.

I like to say that, if police work was a business, then the primary customer is the victim and the secondary customer is the victim's family and the communities we serve. That principle holds even more true in how we interact with victims' families and loved ones because, what successful business doesn't want to receive feedback from its customers so that they can keep improving?

We see that everywhere. Whether it's the grocery store, a restaurant, or even a doctor's office, businesses are asking us to go online and give them a review. Why should police agencies be any different? If we don't listen, we won't receive the information we need to get better, and it is imperative that we continue improving on a consistent basis. That's the only way for us to better serve our communities.

Second, as a detective, you never know when a new development is going to occur or when something is going to trigger a loved one's memory. That's why it's important to stay in contact with family members so that we can be there to help guide that process in ways that will be productive to the investigation.

In my experience, the last thing family members want to do is sit around and wait for updates. They want to actively be doing something. That's why it's important to find constructive ways that the families can contribute to an investigation. Having them make a running list of known friends and associates, for example, is a very important way they can help. And, not just in the immediate aftermath of the loss of a loved one, but for the long term, as well. In most cases, a victim's family members don't know every single person the victim spent time with. Often, months—or even years—pass before an acquaintance or two is mentioned that they weren't aware of. And that's when new information can come to light that can sometimes point the investigation in the right direction. So, communication with the family is crucial in that regard.

After I finished my career with the FBI, I brought that philosophy with me to the Provo, Utah Police Department as chief of police and instituted a community policing program in which patrol officers were given an area of the city that they were responsible to become involved with. Their role was to get to know the residents of their neighborhoods of responsibility and make them aware that they were their liaison between the neighborhood and the police department. If the citizens of that area needed anything—or saw anything—they knew that they could contact that specific officer. Unfortunately, a lot of departments around the country have discontinued this practice. I think that's unfortunate.

With police departments around the country facing depleting resources, manpower has generally been reduced. Sometimes that means there are fewer detectives at a department's disposal. So, how do the detectives who are working in that department work their current case load while keeping up with cases that have grown older? And how do they do so in a way in which the families of those victims are being communicated with?

It's not easy, but there is a way.

We used to utilize our community policing patrol officers. Patrol is typically where most law enforcement officers get their start. Most of them aspire to someday become detectives. So, putting them in charge of updating victims' families on the progress of a case is a great way for the department to keep in communication with families and loved ones.

For one, if an officer is assigned to a specific area of the city where the crime has been committed, there is a chance that the family knows them by virtue of them being their community policing liaison, so there might already be some familiarity there. And, if they don't know the officer directly, there is a good chance that someone in the neighborhood does, so there is still a friendly face during a time of need.

That is crucial to the officer being able to guide the family through activities that can be helpful in the investigation. For example, officers can ask questions to see if anything has changed or if the family remembers anything new. Maybe someone has heard from someone who has heard something. There are just so many directions a case can go.

These communication skills are essential and, by filling this role, that patrol officer gets some much-needed experience in the area of detective work. Some of our department's best detectives grew from within because they got exposure to the work before officially being promoted to the detective role.

Finally, because communication plays a key role in the human experience, who is more important than a first responder to be able to communicate effectively and sensitively to those who have just suffered a traumatic loss? Even though we have an investigation to do, it is important that, as representatives of our local and federal law enforcement communities, we are mindful of the needs of victims' families.

The department that handled Alyssa Bayer's case is an excellent example of the positive effect that communicating with people outside your agency can have on both the department's investigation and their relationship with the families. Historically law enforcement has been reticent to seek outside resources and expertise during the investigative phase based on prior negative experiences. As the department administration engaged our resources and collaborated with us, we found that the benefits far outweighed any potential risk.

At the press conference announcing the arrest of Dennis Bayer and the charges against him, the police chief was kind enough to thank our organization by name, which is something we don't actively seek out, but we appreciate it when it is given.

"I'd like to give a special thank you to the Cold Case Foundation, who also helped through this process," the chief said. "Their support of all our partners, and their commitment, has been invaluable to this case."

The police chief's statement is a great reminder that so much heartache and distrust between families, police agencies, and the people of our cities and towns can be avoided if we make the effort to effectively and sensitively communicate with our most important customers—the victims of these horrendous crimes, their families, and the communities we serve.

CHAPTER EIGHT

COLLABORATION

"Tell me about your son."

"Well, I'm not sure where to begin," Barbara Petero timidly told the young gentleman seated across from her.

"Just start wherever your thoughts take you," the young journalist responded, notebook and pen in hand. He could see that his subject was tense, and he wanted to put her at ease.

It was the first time Barbara had ever spoken to a newspaper reporter—or a media member of any kind for that matter. She was nervous, and her thoughts seemed scattered. She knew what she wanted to but was worried the words wouldn't come out the way she wanted.

Would she do her son justice?

"This might be my one chance to tell the world about this amazing young man I had the privilege of raising," she thought to herself.

She wanted to speak about her son, give him a voice, but she never felt confident about how she articulated things. Everyone else seemed so well spoken and she was—well, she was her. Everything in her mind was so jumbled.

But she was also Brent's mother, darn it! And if anyone was going to speak for him it should be someone who speaks from the heart, someone who knew him better than anyone. Who better than his mother?

So Barabara, the oldest daughter of Czechoslovakian immigrants, composed herself, took a deep breath, and did what she did best. She spoke from the heart.

"From the time he was born, he was just such a sweet boy," she began, looking around the room at some old photos displayed on the shelves of her decades-old Midwestern home. "He always wanted to make people smile and laugh; never wanted to see people cry. Oh, he hated to see anyone sad."

The mere thought of what she had just said brought images of her now-deceased child to her mind. Pictures of him flashed back to his days as a small child.

"It's okay, mommy," she remembered him telling her when her mother had passed away. The image of her six-year-old son handing her a tissue to "wipe away the tears and make it all better" immediately came to mind. All he wanted to do in that moment was take the sadness away. All his life, that's all he ever wanted to do.

Now he was gone, and the very thought of her loss made it impossible to continue speaking as she fought back the tears welling up in her eyes. Barbara paused for a moment to regain her composure, then continued, "Especially me. He was always my champion. Even up until the day he died."

As she told the story of her son, Brent Petero, the words that she was so worried would never come now flowed freely, and the images of the years raising her son ran through her mind as if she were watching it play all over again on a movie screen.

She talked about how he would light up at the smallest gift for his birthday and on Christmas, how he gave the biggest hugs for the slightest act of kindness. "He was really something," she said. "When he was a little boy, we'd go to a restaurant and, because he was always so polite and told the waitresses thank you for every little thing they did, nine times out of ten they would bring him a free dessert on the house. Can you believe that? He was just so good that way. And that was always a part of him."

"I take it you raised him as a single mom?" the reporter asked, pointing to an array of pictures she had on the wall, most of them of just mom and son.

"Oh yeah, his father and I divorced when he was seven years old. He really took it hard. Can you imagine? Seven years old and, all of a sudden, you have to be the man of the house? Of course, he didn't really, but I know he felt like he did."

Barely out of high school, Barbara had married Brent's father, Arthur Petero, and within a year, she was pregnant with Brent.

The pregnancy was difficult. Barbara spent most of it on bed rest. When it came time to deliver her son, there were severe complications that left Barbara unable to have more children.

"Maybe that's why I treasured him so much," she said. "He made me realize just how fragile and precious life can be."

Barbara bowed her head slightly and stared at the floor, forgetting for a moment that she was actually doing a media interview.

"I'm sorry," she said, quickly catching herself in what she perceived as a moment of weakness. "I didn't mean to drift off like that. It's just that the last twenty years have been so hard, you know?"

"It's okay," said the journalist, a young man in his mid-twenties, about the same age as her son when he passed away. "Take your time. Do you need a minute?"

"No, no, I'm fine," she said. "I just got lost in thought for moment there. Go ahead and ask your questions."

"Okay, maybe you can tell me what he was like as a teenager?"

"Oh my goodness, teenage boys!" she exclaimed. "Now, that's an adventure. Of course, you know exactly what I'm talking about. You were one once, right?"

The young journalist smiled in agreement, nodding his head in a reassuring way.

"Oh yes," he said. "I'm sure my parents tell a lot of stories about my high school years."

"I'm sure they do. And I'm sure they're proud of you. You seem like a very nice young man."

"Thank you. I try."

"Well, I actually don't have many stories about Brent getting into trouble. Not that he was perfect, but he was a good kid. He was always very helpful, and he could take on some pretty heavy responsibilities when I needed him to."

She told of Brent's seventh-grade year when she had broken her right leg in three places, the result of a mistimed step on the front stairs. Just before the school year began, Brent suddenly found himself having to do the shopping, cleaning, cooking, laundry, and all that goes with taking care of a household.

"How did he get the shopping done when he wasn't old enough to drive?" the reporter asked.

"Oh, he would ride his bike," Barbara answered. "He had to go shopping several times a week because he could only carry so much on his bike. And he had to shop for everything. You should have seen the look on that kid's face one day when I gave him the grocery list and he saw that tampons were on the list. I thought he was going to fall over right then and there! Can you imagine? A thirteen-year-old kid having to buy tampons for his mom? Not many boys would be willing to do that for their mothers, I tell you. But he did. And he never complained. I could tell he wasn't happy about it, but he never complained."

"It sounds like he was a better kid than I was at thirteen, because I don't think I would have been up for that," Barbara's guest said.

"Oh, you'd be surprised what you can do when you need to," she replied. "Brent would always step up in a pinch. He was definitely the kind of person you wanted to have around when the chips were down. And, when he got older, Brent was that way at work too. Everybody knew they could count on him. He was that kind of person."

After high school, Brent worked at an appliance parts warehouse, Barbara related. First, as a clerk, then later being promoted to assistant manager.

"He was still working at that place the night he died," Barbara said somberly. "He worked late that night because they had to do inventory. He probably worked fifteen hours that day helping them get everything ready for their inventory audit. He could have just made his employees do it, but that wasn't him. He would never have them work later than they had to if he could chip in and help them get it done faster. I'm sure he was exhausted. But, you know what? He still called me after he got off work. What a good son, huh?"

"He definitely sounds like a great guy," said the young newspaper man before shifting somewhat in his chair.

Barbara immediately noticed the awkward change in the young man's demeanor. She knew the hard questions were coming.

"You want to ask about that night?" she asked, referring to the night Brent died under suspicious circumstances.

"If you don't mind," he said, clearly uncomfortable in bringing up the topic, "I do have a few questions."

"It's okay. Go ahead. That's why I asked your boss to send you here. I need to talk about it."

"Okay, um, I have the details from the police and fire investigators, so I know the official report," he said. "But I wanted to ask you about your recollection of events the night he passed away. What can you share with me about that night?"

"Well," Barbara began, "first of all, technically, it was the early morning hours that it all happened."

She told the journalist how Brent had called her after midnight, but that she had missed the call. But she did get to talk to him the day before. They talked about work, life, and his new house. It was a small home in an older part of town, a fixer-upper.

"It wasn't much," she said. "But to be in your twenties this day and age and to be able to get into a house of any kind is quite an accomplishment. And he was really something of a handyman, so fixing things up was right up his alley."

Barbara didn't remember much about the details of their conversation. Mostly, she remembered that he sounded tired on the phone and that she was worried that he wasn't getting enough rest. Then her attention turned toward the call she got the morning of his death.

"It was devastating," she recalled. "I remember getting a call that his house had caught on fire overnight. My heart was in my throat. I couldn't even get the question out. But I already knew. He was gone."

Firefighters were tasked with telling Barbara that her only child had passed away in a house fire. They had found Brent leaning against a wall near his bed and hunched over. The fire had started while he was asleep. It appeared that, when he awoke and became aware of the fire, he got out of bed in an effort to flee the house. But he had already breathed in too much smoke and didn't make it any further than just a few feet from his bed.

Several days later, the fire marshal's investigation determined that the cause was arson. They had found evidence of what appeared to be a fire accelerant in the front room of the house and standard operating procedure dictated that any death resulting from arson be classified as a homicide investigation. In Brent's case, that's when the police took over and started looking into the circumstances of his death. They needed to find out who would have had motive to murder the young man and who would have had access to his house.

They started by working with Barbara to get a list of his closest circle of friends and associates. From there, they would conduct interviews and widen the search as circumstances dictated. But, despite their best efforts, detectives were unable to identify any legitimate suspects.

As with most cold cases, weeks turned into months and months turned into years. Nearly two decades had passed, and Barbara still wasn't any closer to finding out who had taken her son away from her. She stayed in touch with the police, who over the years, had tried a number of strategies to keep the case alive—social media posts, news stories, rewards for information, and even reinterviewing previous people of interest to see if something new would surface. But nothing did. Now, Barbara was in her home—nearly ten years later—talking to a newspaper reporter in the hopes that somebody would come forward with information that would lead to a break in her son's case.

"This must have been a very difficult time for you," the journalist said to her. "I'm sorry you've had to go through all that."

"You can't even imagine," Barbara replied. "It's the worst thing ever to lose a child. This should never happen to any parent. But to lose him like this? I just miss him so much."

"So, what is your message for people today? What are you hoping will come from this article?" the young man asked.

"I just want someone to do something," she offered, clearly frustrated. "I feel like everyone's forgotten. The police have been kind to me, and they've stayed in touch all this time, but it just seems like they could do more. There has to be something more somebody can do to find out what happened to my son."

Feeling sympathy for Barbara, the young journalist ran an article in the local newspaper telling the story of that twenty-year-old cold case. At the bottom of the article, he published the police department's tip line phone number and email address, urging anyone who knew anything to share any information they had with local authorities. He was hopeful that the article would trigger some kind of lead in the case.

Having supported Barbara's decision to go to the media with her story, police detectives and firefighters were hoping for the same thing. Unfortunately, despite an offer of a $25,000 reward for anyone who could provide a tip that would lead to the resolution of the case, no one came forward with anything.

Eventually a new detective, Lance Nettles, was assigned to the case. In thinking back to this case, it has always been fascinating to me that Lance was the one who was assigned to this case for a couple of reasons.

First, this is the only cold case that Lance ever worked, which was astounding to me because he did such a good job of letting the evidence lead the investigation. That is sometimes the hardest part for any detective regardless of their experience. It's human nature to develop theories and then try to find a way to make the evidence fit that theory. But, even though this was the only cold case he had ever investigated, he never fell into that trap.

Second, Lance did an outstanding job of collaborating with any credible source he could find—including our organization—to find the true cause of Brent Petero's death.

"I started as what we called a technical hybrid detective," Lance told us during a recent discussion about this case. "Then I moved to a general assignment detective with the department. For some reason, this case caught my attention and I asked to be assigned to it. At the time, this was a legacy case for our chief that he really wanted to see solved before he retired. And I wanted to help make that happen."

Lance was still a relatively young detective when he approached us with this case. It wasn't long after he took Brent's case that Lance was watching the Netflix series *The Confession Killer*, when he saw the Cold Case Foundation featured on the series' final episode. Thinking that we might be able to help, he sought approval from department administrators, who gave him the go-ahead to reach out to us. Within a few weeks we assembled a team to review the case with Lance.

Fortunately, we have two of the best arson specialists in the country donating their time and expertise to our organization. Between them, Bryan Crump and Gary Hodson have decades of experience specific to the area of arson investigation.

Bryan, who has been known over the years for his Sam Elliot–like mustache, has had a distinguished twenty-five-year career that not only included arson investigation, but also saw him serve as a board member of the International Association of Arson Investigators.

Following a multimillion-dollar fire at a lumber yard, Bryan also had the unique opportunity to work as a task force officer with the FBI's Joint Terrorism Task Force, Salt Lake City Division. He was assigned to the domestic terrorism section, where he provided investigative expertise related to environmental and animal groups. His wide range of experience has been extremely beneficial to the foundation.

Gary's experience in fires has been particularly valuable to us. He investigated over one thousand fires during his thirty-four-year career in arson investigations and law enforcement. Gary has a wide range of experience in that, in addition to arson cases, he has investigated numerous major criminal cases, including bank robberies, homicides, and suspicious death investigations. He also authored a book on arson investigation titled, *Fire Investigator: Principles and Practice.*

With all that Gary and Bryan have accomplished in their careers, their combined experience proved to be extremely instrumental in resolving this case. As we gathered to review the case with Detective Nettles, we started by analyzing the case materials, which included the following:

- police and fire marshal investigative reports
- crime scene photographs
- crime scene diagram of the house
- autopsy report and photographs
- notes from the initial detective
- phone records
- recorded phone calls of tips they had received

After reviewing the evidence, we went through the victimology and discovered some important information about Brent Petero, who was twenty-six years old at the time of his death. All indications were that he was basically the type of person his mother characterized him as in the newspaper article. He was responsible, hardworking, and had ambitions in life.

Brent had been married and had a daughter, but he and his ex-wife had divorced a couple years prior to his death. They had joint custody of the child, and Brent was hoping to fix up his current house so that he could eventually flip it and get into a home closer to his daughter. That way, he could spend more time with her.

In looking at his life, it was clear that the victim had plenty to live for and had made plans for the future, so we determined that, from a behavioral sciences perspective, the probability that he committed suicide was very low. A note in one of the previous detective's reports indicated that family members and friends did tell detectives that there was some friction

with the ex-wife's boyfriend, but there had not been any physical altercations between the two. All of this information pointed to us classifying him
as low-risk for being a person that would be targeted for a homicide.

In terms of his activities during the night of his death, he did have a few
drinks with some friends from work after they had finished their shift. They
went to a nearby bar for an hour or so and then his friends dropped him off
at his house. That was a significant piece of information because toxicology
reports showed his blood-alcohol level at .115 percent. Couple that with a
long night at work and his reaction time during the fire would have been
slowed significantly.

"These factors would have contributed to his slow response to the fire,"
we wrote in our report, "and therefore contributed to his death due to smoke
inhalation. Finally, the amount of smoke after a long-burning fire would
have added to his confusion, impaired visibility, and breathing difficulty as
noted in the coroner's report."

We also saw another significant piece of evidence that indicated that
Brent had been in his bed for a long duration while the fire was burning.

"Look at the post-fire photo of the bedroom where the decedent was
found," one of our team pointed out. "There is a large area in white on the
middle of the bed that is devoid of any soot. The rest of the bed is covered
with it, forming an outline that is consistent with the decedent sleeping in
the bed during the fire."

As a team, it wasn't hard to visualize him being sound asleep and taking
a long time to be awakened by the smoke and flames around him. By then,
he would have breathed in a lot of smoke and would have had a difficult
time finding his way out of the house in such a state of confusion. It's probable that, by the time he realized what was going on, his body shut down
before he could even leave the bedroom.

"Looking at the coroner's report, his carbon monoxide level was at 80.5
percent," another member of our team observed. "That would have contributed to his incapacitated condition and likely would have resulted in his
inability to escape. It's remarkable that he had enough wherewithal to even
get out of his bed."

After our thorough examination of the victimology, we turned our attention to the crime scene. Specifically, we addressed the level of probability that
someone committed arson with the intention of murdering Brent Petero.

And, in studying the original fire marshal's report and crime scene photos, our arson specialists quickly identified some important evidence related to the fire itself.

They noticed that laboratory tests on the charred debris collected by investigators were "inconclusive" for the presence of an accelerant. Typically, arsonists use accelerants as a way to get a fire burning quickly—especially if they are starting the fire with the intent to commit murder and then burn the evidence later in an effort to cover their tracks.

"In the team's experience, burglaries and home invasions are not typically carried out in conjunction and without evidence of trauma to the victim, which would have incapacitated him," we wrote in our report. "It would be highly unlikely that the offender would sneak in while the decedent was sleeping and then decide to set a fire on the way out."

Our arson specialists also pointed out that the legal standard for ruling a fire an arson had changed between the time of this fire and the time we gathered to review this case. We had to take that into consideration.

So, what did the fire marshal investigator see at the time of the fire that would have caused him to classify the fire as the work of an arsonist? Also, what would have qualified under the old standard of arson, but maybe would not have after the change in the legal standard? With those questions in mind, our arson experts examined the information in the report and compared them to the photos from the scene.

"As you can see here," said a member of our arson team, pointing at one of the photos, "the living room sustained the most significant damage and contained furnishings that created a significant fuel load."

He also pointed out that the carpet and the padding would have significantly added to that fuel load. Carpet and padding alone would cause the fire to burn quickly, but the glue used to secure the carpet padding would have also been a heightened accelerant.

"And when we look at the fire patterns," another member of the team added, "there is a strong indication that the living room went to flashover, meaning that the fire spread very rapidly across the room due to the intense heat."

That was significant, they explained, because in the original fire marshal's report, investigators had identified "pour patterns," which are patterns in an area where it appears that someone deliberately "poured" an accelerant in a specific spot so that the fire would move more quickly through the intended target—in this case, the house and, more specifically, the room where Brent was sleeping.

But we didn't believe that was the case. Because lab tests were inconclusive in determining the presence of an accelerant, our experts didn't see enough evidence under the modern legal standard that someone had poured anything on the floor in an attempt to commit arson. Under the old legal standard that existed during the time of Brent Petero's death, fire accelerant patterns were all that were legally required to rule arson.

"So, why do you think they originally ruled arson?" I asked.

"If you look at the area of the living room where they identified the pour patterns," one of our arson experts answered, "you will see that the pour patterns described in the report were in the path toward the front door, the highest traffic area of the room." He went on to explain that such patterns can be mistaken for the pool or halo patterns formed by burning ignitable liquids. The localized flames from such floor coverings are sustained long enough to melt and oxidize aluminum floor molding.

"This could be what they saw," he said. "And what led them to rule the fire an arson."

The probable lack of a planted accelerant led our experts to determine that the fire had started slowly—perhaps in the interior wall of the living room—and then gradually spread to the living room floor before picking up speed and spreading through the house where it eventually made its way into Brent's bedroom.

"There just isn't enough sufficient evidence to rule this an arson," another of our arson experts concluded. "In fact, this shouldn't have been ruled arson. Based on all the evidence we have here, even though the exact cause of the fire was never determined, the most probable conclusion is that this was an accidental fire."

That was the consensus among all the investigators that had gathered to review the case. But we did recommend that a comparison sample be obtained from the charred debris of the living room area near the front door for laboratory analysis just to confirm that there was no accelerant beyond the furnishings and carpet that already existed there. The lack of a poured accelerant was a key finding as we went through the evidence, and it likely explained why no one had come forward to provide tips in the case despite the generous offer of a $25,000 reward. Perhaps there was nothing to come forward with.

But we had to be sure, so we moved from the evidence of the arson itself to the autopsy report. We were looking for anything suspicious that an examination of the victim's body could tell us. We wanted to see if there were other potential factors that might have led to Brent's death. As we studied the autopsy results, there were no signs of trauma to the body beyond the burns. There was no evidence of blunt-force injuries, sharp-force injuries (such as stab wounds), or gunshot wounds. Additionally, there was no evidence to show forced entry into the home.

A neighbor reported that the door had been somewhat ajar, but there was no sign of forced entry, and there was nothing in the reports or photographs that we reviewed to suggest that the door had been forced open.

In short, we didn't have any evidence that

- the victim's life had been threatened previous to his death
- his home had been broken into on the night of his death
- he sustained any life-threatening bodily injuries beyond the burns he sustained in the fire
- the fire was set by an arsonist

"It's our experience that, in arson cases, the offender typically attempts to incapacitate the victim first," I pointed out. "Here, we don't see any sign of that. No blunt force trauma or wounds of any kind on the victim and no forced entry. On top of that, he lived a low-risk lifestyle with no known threats to his life. So, if we can't definitively prove arson, then it can't be ruled a homicide."

With that information in hand, Lance thanked us for our time. We told him that we would draft a report of the team's findings, including our recommendations, and send it to him so he could present it to the department's administrators.

A few days after we sent the team's report to them, we got a call from Lance about the case. He had presented the report to the police chief, and he told us that police administration concurred with our team's findings.

Not long afterward, police officials met with fire marshals on the local, state, and federal levels to review the case. In the end, they agreed to amend the conclusions of the original investigation. Brent Petero's death was ruled accidental due to the house fire.

When detectives contacted Brent's mother, she was devastated. And angry. She had spent nearly twenty years believing her son had been murdered.

"How in the world do you spend all these years telling me you're looking for my son's killer and, all of a sudden, now you're telling me, 'Oh, it was an accident?'" she responded when the detectives came to deliver the news. "It just doesn't make any sense. Why did we even go through all this?"

They explained that investigative technology had advanced quite a bit over the past twenty years and that they had applied that technology and modern expertise to the case.

"We wish we would have had these resources back when this happened," Lance told her. "Then you wouldn't have had to go through this for all this time. But they only recently became available to us, and that's why we have this outcome now."

But Barbara didn't want to hear the explanation. Understandably, she was upset. This is a woman who had lost a child and she believed that someone had something to do with his death. Twenty years is a long time to believe that your loved one was murdered.

In my experience, when family members believe that their loved ones have been a victim of homicide, sometimes it can define their identity. It's one of the unexpected psychological effects of believing you have lost a child at the hands of another who had homicidal intentions. Then, to find out that it was accidental, it can be difficult for a parent to cope with.

That's not the fault of the detectives. Their job is to follow the evidence to wherever it leads them, no matter how long it takes. But it can be hard for families to cope with, especially when a case takes a long time to solve.

It should be noted that, in this case specifically, police investigators did everything a victim's family could ask. They collaborated with the family in varying degrees throughout the entire twenty years of the investigation. Detectives touched base with Barbara regularly, checked in and kept Brent's loved ones apprised of any updates. As a homicide detective, you have to keep the investigation open and continue to work the case until you either solve it or, as in this situation, some evidence comes to light that shows that no murder was committed.

We hope that, over time, Barbara will be able to find some peace in knowing that the investigative agency stuck with her son's case for so many years and never gave up on it. Hopefully, when she is ready to receive that message, maybe it will come through the kind words of a friend during the course of a heartfelt conversation. Maybe the friend would say something like this: "You know, Barbara," her friend might say, "I know that what you've been through is hard, and I wouldn't wish it on anybody. But even though it took so long to find out, isn't it better to know the truth about what happened to Brent than to just have the police rush to close the case? I know it was a long time, but they never stopped looking into Brent's death. And don't you think that's what Brent would have wanted?"

Though that sentiment might be hard to hear, hopefully Barbara would come to see the wisdom in her friend's words. It might even lead to her calling the detective to get some closure and healing, her pain and anger turning to acceptance and gratitude.

I could visualize the conversation going something like this: "I've been thinking about this for some time, and I just wanted to call and thank you for the lengths you and your colleagues have gone to close my son's case the right way," she might tell him. "It had just been so long thinking that someone had done this to my boy. When you told me it was accidental, it was just so hard to hear. I'm sorry I took my frustration out on you, and I just want to thank you for all you and everyone at the department did for my son and our family."

On the detective's end, I could see there being an immense amount of gratitude—both for her calling, but most importantly, gratitude that she had found peace.

"Thank you for calling. We all truly wish we could have solved the case a lot sooner than we did—especially for you and for your family. Just know that, if you ever have any questions or want to talk about Brent's case, we would be happy to go through the details with you."

"I'm not sure I'm ready for that just yet," Barbara might reply. "But I will definitely let you know when that time comes. Thank you."

It's not hard for us who worked with these detectives to see a scenario where a call like that is placed and that kind of conversation is had, which is what we ultimately hope on behalf of any victim's family—a resolution where the family finds some degree of healing and peace.

The department that handled Brent Petero's case is an excellent example of the positive effect collaborating with people within and outside your agency can have on both the department's investigation and their relationship with the families. When the investigating agency made the decision to reach out to our foundation for assistance, they were earnestly searching for a way to solve this case. It worked, and ultimately, everyone involved with the case benefitted from it.

After closing the case, the ranking Detective Commander of the police department we worked with wrote to us and had some kind words of gratitude for our assistance. "The expertise your group provided us with was priceless," he wrote. "We have had several investigators assigned to this case over the years. But, as you know, it is sometimes good to have someone not familiar with the investigation to review the details and maybe see things from a different perspective. Being able to receive help from the experts you have on staff was huge for our agency. We will gladly recommend the Cold Case Foundation to any other agencies in need of your services."

His words are a great reminder that it is possible to collaborate with qualified multidisciplinary experts to enhance the investigative outcomes. By so doing, the door can open up to an array of potential ideas and resources. Experience tells us that the more eyes and ears that we have on a case, the more expertise you can bring to it, the more likely we are to solve these cases and bring an increased level of resolution to that difficult chapter in those families' lives. And that's what we all really want.

CHAPTER NINE

THE EVOLUTION OF COLD CASE INVESTIGATION

On a long stretch of desert highway, the tractor-trailer traveled deep into the night through the heart of West Texas. One could only guess the rig—whose cargo was a mystery to passersby—was transporting perishables, furniture, or electronics.

This trip had been particularly taxing on the driver, a middle-aged man with an outwardly friendly demeanor. He had been hauling goods across the country for nearly twenty years and was well aware of the dangers associated with his occupation.

Despite the pressures of getting a load delivered on time, he knew that sleep deprivation was a trucker's worst enemy. He also knew that strange people traveled the highways, and he had definitely seen his share of them. But as the night wore on, Ben thought it best to stop and get some much-needed rest. He pulled over to the side of the highway and stretched out to get some sleep. Just a few hours later, he heard a noise that startled him awake.

"Hello? Is anyone in there?" shouted two voices, a young man and a teenage girl. Cautious, yet curious, the truck driver poked his head out the window.

"What can I help you with?" he asked them, putting on a hospitable front. "We were wondering if you could give us a ride. You're headed south, right?"

"Sure, but you two look a little young to be out hitchhiking. That's dangerous for anybody, much less someone as young as you two. I've got a radio in here. Do you want to call your folks?"

The couple looked at each other for a moment then turned to the seemingly kind trucker.

"It's our parents that we're trying to get away from."

The two hitchhikers seemed harmless enough. The girl had a soft, friendly way about her, and the young man had a calm and quiet demeanor.

Ben didn't think that they would be a problem, so he decided to give them a ride.

"Well, I don't want to pry into your business. You two look like good kids. Why don't you get in, and I will take you as far as I can."

As they pulled onto the highway, the truck driver began to make polite conversation with the young couple.

"My name is Ben. What are your names?" "I'm Regina, and this is Ricky," the girl answered.

"Well, it's good to meet you two," he answered, maintaining a friendly tone.

As they traveled over the next couple of hours, the pair began to feel comfortable with the driver. He was very pleasant and wasn't at all judgmental. Things seemed to be going well, but Ben noticed that the young man was becoming fidgety and restless.

The trucker stole a glance at him to make sure he wasn't carrying a weapon. Not seeing anything suspicious, Ben determined that the boy was probably just trying to get comfortable. Still, Ben knew it could be dangerous to pick up hitchhikers, and he wanted to make sure the couple wasn't concealing anything.

As they drove on, the couple began to doze off, giving the driver the opportunity to size up the situation. Finally, when he was sure the couple didn't pose a threat, Ben made his way to a secluded location and abruptly pulled his rig over to the side of the road.

"What's going on?" they asked in unison.

"I'll tell you what's going on," he growled. "This is going on." In an instant, the driver pulled a gun out of his jacket and the face of a kind and helpful gentleman abruptly transformed.

While holding the gun on the young man, Ben handcuffed fourteen-year-old Regina Walters to the inside of the sleeper cab. He then ordered Ricky to get out of the truck.

"Do it slowly," he warned, following the young man out the passenger's side of the cab while keeping the gun fixed directly on him.

The hitchhikers, once on an exciting romantic adventure, suddenly found themselves prisoners. Their romance had turned to terror. In a matter of minutes, from inside the cab, Regina heard gunshots in the distance, maybe a hundred yards or so off the sparse highway. Her heart sank, and she felt an immense lump in her throat. She had a bad feeling Ricky wouldn't be coming back.

As she heard footsteps draw closer to the truck, she had no idea what lay in store for her, but she could sense that it wouldn't be good. Tears began streaming down her face as she began to tremble, and her breathing took on a rapid pace.

The driver opened the door, stepped up into the cab and quietly moved in close, his eyes eerily fixed on her. Slowly, he held the handgun up to her face and gently stroked it up and down her cheek. The man, who seemed so friendly and helpful just hours earlier, leaned back and ogled the young teenage girl.

"I think you and I are going to have some fun, little lady," he said, before closing the door and assuming his position in the driver's seat.

Paralyzed with fear, all Regina wanted to do was flee. But she couldn't. She couldn't do anything. There wasn't a muscle in her body that dared move as she realized that her nightmare was just beginning.

Had the young couple known what they were dealing with that night in February 1990, they never would have approached the truck of this man, who would turn out to be one of the most infamous highway killers in US history. This is the case I referred to in the introduction to this book and it's the one I have used as an illustration for investigative technique trainings I conduct throughout the country and internationally.

While we don't specifically know the exact detailed wording from the conversations that led to Regina and Ricky getting into Rhoades's truck— or from the events afterward—the depiction that you just read comes from our visualization of these events based on the facts of the case and of our criminal profile of Rhoades as a sexual sadistic killer. We know that long-haul truck driver Robert Ben Rhoades picked up the couple, eighteen-year-old Ricky Lee Jones and fourteen-year-old Regina Walters of Palestine, Texas.

We believe that, after killing Ricky and leaving his body lying in a secluded West Texas desert, Rhoades turned his sinister attention to Regina, whom he imprisoned in a makeshift bondage chamber in the sleeper birth of the truck. It is believed that for over a week, he mercilessly raped and tortured the young girl before finally taking her to an abandoned old barn just off Interstate 70 in a remote location in Illinois.

While holding her captive, Rhoades dressed her in selected clothing, cut her hair, and shaved her pubic area—his way of physically and psychologically controlling her. At the barn he dressed her in a conservative black dress with high heels reminiscent of something someone would wear to a funeral as part of the mourning process, then he forced her to pose for photos in front of the barn in that clothing. In the end, he strangled her, using a stick that he had inserted through a double loop of baling wire. He twisted the board clockwise tightly around her neck until he was sure she was dead. Then he took the clothing from her body and left her in the barn. Her corpse was eventually found, badly decomposed, more than six months later.

In a chilling twist, Rhoades made two anonymous phone calls to Regina Walters's father just days after her murder, one to his place of employment and the other to his unlisted home number.

"I made some changes," the cold-blooded killer told the girl's father. "I cut her hair."

Taunting the grieving father, Rhoades told him that his daughter was in a barn loft, but he did not give him any indication where the barn was located.

"Is my daughter still alive?" her father desperately asked.

After a short pause, Rhoades hung up the phone without uttering a word.

That was the last the Walters family would hear about their daughter until she was discovered on September 29, 1990. None of this information would have come to light, however, had it not been for one fateful night on an Arizona highway.

Arizona Highway Patrol trooper Mike Miller was patrolling Interstate 10, just outside Casa Grande, on April 1, 1990—just six weeks after Rhoades had picked up the young couple. Everything seemed normal until he noticed a parked tractor-trailer's hazard lights flashing in a rest area off the interstate. Because it was during the wee hours of the morning, Miller decided he would do a wellness check on the driver.

"Hello!" the trooper called out. "Is anyone here?"

When no one answered, Miller decided to see whether he could find the driver. As he walked around the rig, he couldn't find anyone around the vehicle or in the driver's area of the cab. But when he noticed that the cab door was unlocked and heard some commotion within the sleeper portion of the cab, Miller became suspicious and decided to investigate.

The trooper carefully climbed up onto the runner, pointed his flashlight toward the back, then nearly fell backward when he caught sight of a naked woman shackled and chained to the wall of the cab.

She screamed uncontrollably when she saw the trooper.

Then he saw Rhoades scurry from around the front of the truck, hands raised.

Miller quickly drew his firearm. "Keep your hands up!" Miller ordered.

"Okay, okay, everything's cool, officer," Rhoades insisted.

"Keep your hands where I can see them and move slowly," the trooper reiterated.

"I am, I am," Rhoades said. "Look, just so you know, I have a gun with me. I just didn't want you to freak out, okay?"

"Okay, let me see your hands," Miller said as he cuffed Rhoades and secured the weapon.

Through all the commotion, the trooper couldn't believe what he was seeing.

The woman, still in hysterics, was chained against the wall, her hands and ankles handcuffed, and a horse bridle strapped around her neck, with a long chain padlocked to the horse bit.

The trooper noted the red welts on her body and blood trickling from the severe cuts on her mouth. She had clearly been whipped several times and orally tortured with the horse bridle.

"Hey, man, I promise, this isn't what it looks like," said Rhoades, trying to reassure Miller as the trooper led him to the patrol car. "She wanted me to do this to her. I swear. She told me she likes it this way. I was just playing along, then she started freaking out on me. That's when you got here."

"Okay, sir, I need to sort this all out," Miller told Rhoades, placing him in the backseat of the patrol car. "I'm going to check on the lady. I'll be right back."

He had cuffed the suspect—behind his back—and closed the door to the patrol car. When he returned to the rig to check on the victim, she was still uncontrollably frantic.

"He's coming back!" she screamed. "Get me out of here! He's coming back!"

"Ma'am, I've got him locked up in my patrol car," Miller replied, trying to reassure her. "He's not going anywhere. Now, I'm going to get you out of here, but I want to cover you up with this blanket first, okay?"

"No! No!" she shrieked. "He's coming! He's coming! He's going to kill me!"

It was clear that the trooper wasn't going to be able to calm her down anytime soon—and understandably so.

Whatever had happened certainly wasn't consensual, Miller surmised.

After he covered the woman with the blanket, he went back to check on Rhoades, who had slipped his hands, still handcuffed, from behind his body to the front and had just undone his seat belt when Miller returned.

"Hey, what are you doing?" he asked Rhoades.

"I was just a little uncomfortable, that's all."

Miller shuddered as he thought about the horrific scenarios that could have occurred had his suspect escaped.

"I'm going to need the keys to the handcuffs you used on the lady," he told Rhoades. "Where do you keep them?"

"They're in my pocket, on this side," Rhoades responded, motioning with his chin to the left.

The highway patrolman dug the keys out of the suspect's pocket and secured him in the vehicle. Just then, another police car pulled up.

Officer Robert Gygax of the Casa Grande Police Department had gotten Miller's call for backup and had arrived within minutes.

"What do we have here?" he asked.

"You're not going to believe this," Miller said. "It looks like we've got a rape and torture victim. She's frightened out of her mind. Here, I've got the keys to the handcuffs. We're going to need them to get her out."

"The victim is handcuffed?" Gygax asked, somewhat perplexed.

"Yeah," Miller replied, glancing over at the suspect. "Thanks to him."

Gygax looked over at Rhoades, wondering just what they had on their hands.

The officers called an ambulance, and the woman got some much-needed medical attention. Once at the hospital, she began to calm down, finally realizing she was safe, and that Rhoades was securely in custody.

The twenty-seven-year-old victim, Jenny Harris, had regained enough composure to talk to the authorities about her ordeal.

She described how she had met her attacker at a truck stop just north of Phoenix. She told them that she often hitched rides to visit friends but that she was usually careful not to accept rides from "creepy" guys.

"He was very nice to me, very polite," Jenny told Rick Barnhart, the detective who questioned her. "He was more polite than most of the guys I usually meet there. But then all of the sudden, he changed."

"What happened?"

"I don't really know," she replied. "We were driving along toward Tucson, and we were talking. But I got tired and fell asleep. The next thing I knew, he pulled over, grabbed me, and shoved me into the back. Then he shackled me up like a wild animal. Then he took out this briefcase and started pulling things out of it."

"What kinds of things did he take out of the briefcase?" the detective asked.

"Handcuffs, a horse bridle, a whip, and these large pins."

"What did he do next?"

"He took off my clothes, chained me up, then he pulled out the whip—"

At that, the young lady choked up and began to cry.

"It's okay, take your time," the detective reassured her. "Do you need to take a break?"

"No, no, I'm fine," Jenny sniffled. "I want to finish this."

After a moment, she continued.

"He took out the whip, and he started hitting me with it."

Jenny began to cry some more but reassured the detective that she wanted to continue. "I just want to get this over with."

She paused for another moment, took a deep breath and, with a determined look on her face, finished her thought.

"Then, he put the bridle in my mouth and started to whip me some more."

As the interview continued, she related how she had been tortured on and off since he had picked her up earlier that day.

For the purpose of collecting evidence, police photographed the long red welts that covered her chest and back from the vicious whipping, as well as the grotesque piercings of her nipples and labia.

Finally, Jenny said, "He told me he has done this for fifteen years. He said he was a real pro."

"Did he tell you his name?"

"Whips and Chains. That's what he called himself. I think that was his CB radio name, too."

"Okay, I think that's all we need for now," the detective said. "Is there anything else, anything that stands out, that you can tell me?"

"Not really. Just that it seemed like he really got off on the torture and bondage stuff. That turned him on more than anything."

"Jenny, I know this was difficult for you, but we really appreciate your cooperation," Barnhart told her. "You did great, and you were very brave."

It was about 3 a.m. when Rhoades was ushered into the interrogation room and, immediately, the suspect began trying to minimize what he believed was circumstantial evidence against him.

Upon entering the room, Rhoades casually slumped onto a nearby chair and let out a huge yawn, as if to say, "You guys don't have anything on me. This is no big deal because the whole thing was all her idea."

"Mr. Rhoades, why don't you start by telling me how you met up with Ms. Harris," Barnhart said.

"I was just getting a bite to eat at the truck stop, and she came up to me and asked if I could give her a ride."

"Just like that, she asked you for a ride?" the detective asked.

"Well, no. She spent some time talking to me first, then she asked for the ride."

Barnhart didn't immediately respond, giving pause to allow Rhoades to keep talking.

Then Rhoades leaned over, trying to be chummy with the detective.

"Look, I know you've got a job to do," Rhoades said. "But that lady is not playing with a full deck, you know what I mean? She's a lot lizard."

"What's a lot lizard?" the detective asked.

"You know, a woman who hangs out at truck stops trying to pick up on truckers. She gets around if you know what I mean. That's what that woman is. I normally don't like to get involved with that kind because I've got too much work to do, and I don't want to get any diseases, you know what I'm saying? But I thought I'd give that woman a ride just to help her out. But she came on really strong, and, you know, I'm a man, so I thought I'd go along with her just this once, have a little fun on the side."

Undeterred by the bizarre nature of Rhoades's answers, the detective continued to question the suspect about Jenny's injuries.

Rhoades never directly answered that line of questioning, and the interrogation came to a halt when Rhoades said, "I took you up to the point where I stopped the truck. Now, I'm not gonna cross that line. I stopped the truck."

The detective finally booked the suspect into jail for aggravated assault, sexual assault, and unlawful imprisonment, but Barnhart suspected that Rhoades had done far more, and he needed time to confirm his suspicions.

Shortly after the interrogation, Barnhart sent a nationwide teletype, then he faxed a letter to a superior court judge in Florence, Arizona, to detain Rhoades at least until some information came in.

Then he called Rhoades's hometown police department in Houston, Texas, hoping for some kind of information. It wasn't long before detectives from the Houston Police Department called to relate the details of a similar case that also involved the suspect.

Rhoades had been suspected of kidnapping an eighteen-year-old woman in California and holding her captive for two weeks.

As he did with Jenny Harris and Regina Walters, he cut the eighteen-year-old victim's hair short and shaved her pubic hair. Rhoades also systematically tortured her and had threatened to kill her.

She eventually escaped when Rhoades forgot to close the handcuff that kept her chained inside the truck. Unfortunately, the woman had been so brutalized that when officers brought her face to face with the detained Rhoades, she told police that he was not her attacker. Without her testimony, police were legally unable to hold the suspect and were forced to release him. A few days later, the victim came forward and admitted that the man they had detained was indeed her attacker, but when she had to identify Rhoades, she had been too intimidated to implicate him. After two weeks of torture, in her mind, there weren't enough officers in the world to protect her.

Because of the inconsistencies in her testimony, however, authorities were unable to bring a case against Rhoades.

The Arizona case, however, would prove to be a huge breakthrough for investigators—not only in Houston, but eventually in other parts of the country as well. On April 6, 1990, police obtained a warrant to search Rhoades's apartment in Houston and the horror of what they found would stun even the most veteran law enforcement officer. During their search, they found numerous items of women's clothing, obscene magazines and books, instruments used for bondage, and white towels, some with blood on them. The search also produced photographs of nude women, one of whom was Regina K. Walters. Some of the clothing investigators found resembled that worn by Regina in other photographs in Rhoades's apartment, including one of Regina standing in front of the barn where her body was discovered.

Authorities also obtained phone records that linked the infamous calls made to Regina's father, tracing them to Oklahoma City, Oklahoma, and Ennis, Texas. Detectives were able to obtain Rhoades's work logs from the trucking company he worked for and pinpoint where he had been on the days the calls were made. The first call to Regina's father was from a pay phone at a truck stop in Oklahoma City on March 16, 1990.

On that day, Rhoades had fueled up at the same truck stop. The next day, the logs indicated that he had been in Ennis, Texas. Ben Rhoades was indeed in both locations on the days in question, effectively proving that he had made those calls. He had gotten the unlisted numbers from a notebook Regina had written them in. Police found the notebook among the other items in the suspect's apartment.

In the notebook, Rhoades had crudely drawn a picture of a gun with drops of blood next to the message, "Ricky is a dead man." There were also other cryptic notations that seemed to indicate directions and other unknown meanings, such as "water tank, Fun and Hide," which could have meant he toyed with the young man before killing him. Rhoades's wife was shown the handwriting and identified it as his. Months later, these key pieces of evidence would be used to link Rhoades to Regina Walters, and, in 1992, Rhoades was sentenced to life in prison in Illinois.

As I described in my introduction to this book, more than five years later, in late 1997, I presented this case to several dozen sheriffs and police chiefs at the Utah Chiefs of Police and Sheriff's Conference in St. George, Utah.

That was the same conference that my old friend and colleague, Millard County (Utah), Sheriff Ed Phillips, and I reunited.

During my presentation, I went through all the evidence and behaviors of Ben Rhoades to illustrate the behavioral profile of the sexual sadist serial killer.

"To be clear, this type of offender is one who is outwardly friendly," I told the audience. "He is not going to outwardly appear or behave in a deviant manner, like the quiet, creepy guy who keeps to himself that we frequently see in the movies. Ben Rhoades's victims said that when they first met him, he was a very nice, polite man. That's how he cons his prey. But once he secures and isolates his victims," I continued, "the sexual sadist in him will use torture devices and scare tactics. He uses a voice that is non-emotional to unsettle his victims. If you can find them, this type of offender often tends to keep trophies and souvenirs from their crimes. They also utilize photographs or recordings of their victims so they can fantasize and relive their crimes. The sexual sadist is often difficult to distinguish from the rest of society because, like a wolf in sheep's clothing, he can adapt to his environment and fit in so well."

I then walked over to the video screen and made one last, unsettling point.

Directing the audience's attention to one photo in which Rhoades's teenage victim wears an expression of deep despair, I said, "A telling characteristic of sexual sadists is that they often tell their victims what they're going to do to them ahead of time. That very likely was the case here as he snapped this photograph of his victim."

As I began to finish the presentation on Rhoades, I went through the victimology of a person most likely to be taken by this type of killer.

"When you look at the victims Rhoades selected," I began, "you will find that there are some commonalities among them. Both of the victims who survived his attacks were especially vulnerable: Either they'd had emotionally upsetting incidents around the time they were abducted or were very young and naive, and easily manipulated. In the case of Regina Walters and Ricky Lee Jones, there is no question that Rhoades preyed on their naivete and their dependency for transportation."

I concluded that portion of the presentation by showing some photographs collected at Rhoades's apartment and a map created from his trucking log that displayed his travel routes by state and year. Using his trucking logs, investigators had tracked approximate dates for the portions of the country that he traveled through, including during the early months of 1990, when it is believed that he went on an abduction and killing rampage. The authorities who worked most closely on the Rhoades case believe he was attacking as many as three girls a month by early 1990.

"Those who investigated this case believe, as do I," I told the audience, "that Ben Rhoades left several victims in his wake. There are still nearly fifty missing people or unidentified bodies for which investigators cannot rule out Rhoades as a potential suspect." As I described in the introduction to this book, during my presentation of the crime scene photos, I highlighted the maps reflecting Rhoades's long-haul truck route in 1984, 1987, 1988, 1989, and 1990.

Just as I was emphasizing that Utah was included among the many states that he traversed in 1990, I noticed a hand raise up in the back of the room.

It was my old friend, Sheriff Ed Phillips, who I had worked with twelve years before when I was police chief in Delta, Utah. He related that he had a cold case of an unidentified female who had been murdered and whose remains were discovered in a rural area of Millard County in 1990.

After the class, we continued our discussion. "You know, I was looking at those photos and that map, and I wanted to talk to you a little bit more about that case we haven't been able to close since 1990," Ed said. "Do you have a minute?"

"Of course," I replied. "What's going on?"

"Well, I'm not entirely sure. As I said, the scenery in those pictures of Regina Walters is similar to some of the landscape in Millard County," he told me. "And in October 1990, a couple of hunters found a badly decomposed body in some bushes right off I-15 by Fillmore."

"Do you think this victim might have been one of Rhoades's?" I asked him.

"I'm not sure, but I think it would be worth looking into."

I agreed. After discussing additional details of Ed's Jane Doe case, I referred him to some contacts who I thought could help point his investigation in the right direction, and he said he would let me know how things turned out.

Ed followed up with the FBI and other law enforcement agencies associated with Regina's case, and about a year later I got a call from John Kimball, a detective from the Millard County Sheriff's Office. He asked if the case could be included in a review as part of a multistate joint task force conference that was going to be conducted into unsolved homicides in the Great Basin area. The conference included more than fifty law enforcement professionals from five states.

Our aim was to put our heads together to see if we could, as a collective group, solve some of these cold cases. We presented John's case before the group, and he was able to get some good information about Ben Rhoades.

As I mentioned in the introduction to this book, I had a rather contentious call with Rhoades when I promised him that I would do everything I could to make his life as miserable as possible. This was one of those moments when that promise came to fruition. John followed up on that information and, in 2003, finally caught a break in the case. Amazingly, one of the bloody towels found in Rhoades's Houston apartment contained the Millard County, Utah victim's DNA on it. After some jurisdictional legal issues were resolved, the matter finally went to court in Texas.

Rhoades was charged in 2006 with the murders of the twenty-four-year-old woman, Patricia Walsh, and her husband, twenty-eight-year-old Douglas Zyskowski, two newly wed Christian missionaries who were hitchhiking in Texas when Rhoades picked them up. Authorities believed that he shot and killed Zyskowski then dumped his body near I-10 outside of Ozona, Texas. They also thought that Rhoades then kept Walsh for about a week before shooting her multiple times in the head and dumping her naked body in Millard County, Utah.

This was a difficult case to solve because, although Zyskowski's body had been discovered months earlier, he wasn't identified until 1992. And because his wife's body had never been identified, the two slayings were not linked until 2003, when authorities were finally able to identify her through dental records.

In 2006, after exhaustive legal analysis, authorities from the states of Utah and Texas agreed that it would be best to try Rhoades for both homicides in Texas, where there would be a greater chance for the death penalty. In 2012, prosecutors in Texas agreed to waive the death penalty in exchange for Rhoades's guilty plea to two charges of capital murder. He was sentenced to life in prison without the possibility of parole.

As I mentioned during my presentation, there are still dozens of murders and unidentified bodies across the country for which Rhoades hasn't been ruled out as a suspect. This is one of the reasons I routinely highlight this case when I conduct trainings on cold case investigative technique. You never know if someone will see something that leads down an avenue toward solving cases Rhoades might have been involved with—or even cases unrelated to Rhoades where the evidence points investigators in a direction they haven't been led to pursue yet.

Think about it. Just by presenting this one case to a relatively small group of law enforcement officials in southern Utah, we had a breakthrough in 1997 that sprung from the Regina Walters case in Illinois that I was introduced to by Roy Hazelwood in 1990 when I was teaching at the FBI Academy in Quantico, Virginia. Even though the Regina Walters and Patricia Walsh cases were thousands of miles apart, we were able to tie them together simply because we came together.

And that was back in the 1990s during a time when most people were not using cell phones and camera phones. It was during a time in history when we had just barely started using advanced DNA technology to solve crimes and the internet was just getting started. The technology we have to collaborate on these cases is far more advanced today than it was back then. And, because of it, we have a better chance now to solve cold cases than we ever have before.

That's why this is the ideal case to present in a law enforcement training. It hits on all aspects of the kind of coordination, cooperation, communication, and collaboration necessary to solve homicide, missing persons, and unidentified bodies cases. And, while we have had some incredible results presenting this case, personally, I would love to find evidence that ties Rhoades to more unsolved cases. If that happens, I can think of no greater satisfaction than to see him held accountable for the pain and suffering he has caused the families and loved ones of the people he tormented and whose lives were so brutally cut short.

All that said, what is the evolution of the Cold Case Foundation? With all the technological advancements that are happening in the world, what would we like to see happen going forward in the area of cold case investigation? The answer: We need more resources to enable our local law enforcement agencies to better take advantage of existing technology and training.

As we pointed out in the first chapter, since the inception of the Cold Case Foundation, we have grown from 6 volunteers to more than 150—and counting. And these are people with impeccable resumes. Decorated FBI, CIA, and military homicide investigators, DNA analysts, criminal forensic scientists, attorneys, forensic psychologists and psychiatrists, and the list goes on. In short, we have the manpower. We just need the funding and resources to put them to work. And we are getting close.

When we started the foundation, we wanted to ensure that the demand for our services did not outgrow the network of volunteers we had to support that demand. Or, as we like to say, "We didn't want to get too far out over our skis."

So, we spent the first several years building our network of highly qualified experts. The next phase of our vision is to eventually have regional representatives—ideally one for each state—who will serve as first point of contact liaisons between the foundation, local law enforcement agencies, victims, and victims' families. This will better help us to connect those incredible resources to the victims, victims' families, and the local law enforcement agencies that serve them. That is why funding is so important to this effort.

As we have illustrated throughout the course of this book, the technology required to solve so many of these cases now exists. Whether the case is fifty days old, fifty years old, or even thousands of years old, we have demonstrated that if we can apply modern forensic science and techniques to the hundreds of thousands of cases of unsolved homicides, unidentified bodies, and missing persons that exist in this country, then we can assist in solving a significant number of them. And that means the families, who have been waiting decades in some cases, can finally get the answers they deserve.

Unfortunately, even though the technology and advanced training in investigative technique exists, numerous law enforcement agencies throughout the country haven't been given enough funding to adequately take advantage of it. A prime example of this is the use of technology to share information about violent crimes across jurisdictions and state lines. It's called ViCAP, but it is not being used to its full potential.

We know that the common characteristic that we have with the offenders responsible for most of these crimes is that they are roamers. They are free to roam from state to state, jurisdiction to jurisdiction, city to city, county to county—from one end of the country to the other. Consequently, if we are going to bring these offenders to justice, we need to have a system where agencies have the ability to come to one focal point, share that information, and identify the possibility of common offenders so they can work

together to resolve these cases. During my decades-long career in law enforcement training—whether it was in the FBI, as a police chief, and even
after I retired—I recognized that the main difficulty in providing information and training in advanced methods and technologies was primarily in
the funding and personnel.

Quite often, local police agencies don't have the resources to conduct
these types of trainings or to even send their personnel to attend. That means
that it's common that the law enforcement officers individually have to pay
for it themselves. This goes back more than thirty years when I was in the
FBI to my time with John Douglas. We used to talk about the same thing.

"Wouldn't it be great if we could do this type of training and provide
this service to law enforcement all around the country?" we would say.

So, I've wanted to do this for a long time, but could never figure out
how to do it in a way that would be accessible to any law enforcement
officer who would want to participate. Knowing it couldn't be a for-profit
company—that's always been the problem—we finally came up with this
consideration: If we created a nonprofit organization where the public has
an opportunity to see the types of services that could be made available
to assist victims' families and/or surviving victims, then everyone could
contribute and, most important, everyone would benefit. And if the general public could contribute to the training and resources provided to law
enforcement agencies in helping them work these types of cases, identify
offenders, and bring them to justice, then we just might be able to generate the funding needed to make this happen. And not only the training,
but as you've read in the previous chapters of this book, we also have the
manpower to provide assistance with case reviews that have contributed to
solving some very difficult cases.

That certainly doesn't mean we take over an investigation. But we lend
a hand to departments that may be understaffed. Imagine a police department that only has enough funding to assign one or two detectives to a
homicide case on top of the ones they are already investigating. It can get
burdensome very quickly. Now, imagine what can happen when they have
five or six experienced former homicide detectives, FBI profilers, and forensic experts assisting them with cold cases, with victims' families (as we
have seen in the previous chapters). Do you see the difference that can
make for the detectives and in the lives of the victims and their families?

And this especially applies to underrepresented communities, where funding for police agencies has been historically hard to come by. In 2018, we were approached by representatives from the Bureau of Indian Affairs about providing training and case consultation for tribal police agencies throughout the country. Due to the newly established Operation Lady Justice program, they sought training that would help with the many unsolved cases they have on their books. Of course, we agreed, and we have been able to conduct several trainings in various areas of the country already, with plans for several more in the near future that will include cold case consultations.

It's exciting for us to be able to assist the wonderful people of the BIA, National Tribal Police, and the people they serve. We truly hope to make a difference in their police departments and, ultimately, in the lives of those families who have been waiting and hoping to see justice done for their loved ones. In short, there is nothing more we would like to see happen than for every community throughout the country—and the world, really—to know that their corner of the world matters enough that every victim's case is being looked into no matter how long ago the crime against that person was committed.

That is our mission, and we are committed to working tirelessly to that end until as many communities as possible are able to see this mission accomplished.

CHAPTER TEN

WHAT CAN YOU DO?

Most of us have been in situations where we see a heartbroken family on the local news whose daughter or son goes missing or has tragically died. You may not personally know them, but they are members of your communities, and because of that, your heart goes out to them and you immediately wish there was some way you could help.

So, what can you do?

When you see a situation like this on the local news, you may be thinking to yourself, "I don't have law enforcement experience, and I don't want to get in the way of the investigation. So, how can I help in a way that is productive but that doesn't interfere with the work my local law enforcement agency is doing to help that family?"

It's a great question, and it's one of the main reasons we founded the Cold Case Foundation.

One of our primary missions is to provide an avenue for you to take action and make that direct contribution. You can do so certainly by providing information that you may be aware of about crimes. You can also contribute and be an active participant in resolving unsolved crimes through your generous donations.

One way is by joining https://coldcase.live/. When you become a member of Cold Case Live, your membership helps support the work of the Cold Case Foundation. For less than the cost of a cup of coffee a month, you can support our efforts to support victims, their families, and law enforcement. Additionally, members get access to all of our podcasts, articles, web series, blogs, and classes. All of our content features the investigators and experts at the Cold Case Foundation, some of whom you have read about in this book. Whether it be $1 a month, $5 a month, thousands of dollars (if you happen to be in a financial position to do so), or even a million-dollar donation by a corporate executive, it's through that funding that we can provide the technology and services that we've been talking about that will help your local law enforcement agencies find justice on behalf of victims and their families.

On our website, www.coldcasefoundation.org, you can see a variety of ways that you can contribute. And it's not just a situation where you give money. But we actively keep you up to date on how that funding is being used and who it has benefitted.

Just looking at the cases in this book, hopefully you have gotten a sense for what these donations have contributed to, including the following:

- providing investigative recommendations on cases that have led to arrests and convictions in the homicide and missing persons cases we featured
- donating funds for advanced DNA testing on evidence that has been stored for decades in some cases
- connecting specialty expertise such as forensic crime scene analysis and arson investigation to investigating agencies that have led to solving years-old cases
- providing guidance and assistance to victims' families in a way that helps them work with local authorities toward solving their loved ones' cases
- getting advanced law enforcement trainings and case reviews that help these dedicated women and men better serve their local communities

These are just a few of the many ways that the generous donations we have received have been utilized to lend assistance to this cause. And, now that we have so much more manpower, there is so much more we can do with that additional funding.

Finally, I want to close by sharing the thoughts and feelings of my heart—and the hearts of so many others involved in this cause—that have been the building blocks for this labor of love.

You probably noticed that the Cold Case Foundation logo is prominently displayed on the book's cover. There's a very specific and deep-rooted reason behind that.

It took me decades to finally find a tangible way to make the difference I've wanted to make since the day I started my career in law enforcement—and, honestly, probably before that.

The symbolism behind our Cold Case Foundation logo has a deep meaning for me and the purpose for which our organization was founded.

I wanted to conclude this book by sharing its meaning with you. You can also find the details behind the logo on our website, but I thought it fitting to end this way. It's my way of saying thank you for caring enough about your communities, those law enforcement officials who serve, and ultimately, about those individuals and families who have suffered so much among us. May we all find a way to do more to help them find a path to some semblance of peace and, ultimately, justice for their loved ones.

In an effort to give greater clarity and purpose to our organization, Cold Case Foundation embarked on an extensive brand-building journey of discovery. This process was far deeper than just purchasing a nice logo, but rather a process of establishing a foundation for our branding and marketing. Our culminating activity involved enlisting more than twenty-seven designers across seven countries, who provided more than 183 logo designs. Our collective energy focused and refocused the overarching philosophies, methodologies, principles, mission, vision, and values—ultimately arriving at the Cold Case Foundation crest you see today. Below is an insightful look into our organization.

COLD CASE—*The gold lettering light play identifies the lost value of the cold case victims and helps them to come forward into the light once again to be made known, to be justified.*

LARGE WINGS—*The large silver wings represent our foundation's ability to help victims rise above their tragedy, empowering them and giving them a renewed sense of personal protection. The large wings propel us forward to seek justice through the identification, apprehension, and conviction of offenders.*

SMALLER WINGS—*These small wings characterize many of the victims, who may feel hopeless, fearful, and powerless. While they desire to move forward, their ability may be limited.*

FINEM EXITUS BANNER—*The Latin phrase FINEM EXITUS means "Final Exit" or "Case Closed," which is an unfurling banner used as the standard we carry forward at the Cold Case Foundation. We proudly join law enforcement in carrying the banner of the cold case victim and invite others to join us on this crusade.*

SHIELD—*The shield evokes a sense of protection. CCF strives to be a defender of Justice, fearlessly guarding victims' rights. This image is also reminiscent of a law enforcement badge or family crest that symbolizes credentials, identification, identity, legacy, values, strength, character, protection, and history.*

SHIELD TIP—*The pointed tip of the shield is also suggestive of offense, not just defense. The Sun Tzu quote, "Victory goes to the one with superior forces at the point of contact" typifies how we view our role at the Cold Case Foundation. In partnership with law enforcement and victims, the Cold Case Foundation along with our contributors, become the tip of the spear needed for victory.*

SUN RAYS—*The Sun rays embody a sense of hope for the future. Today the sun is rising and illuminating new possibilities. The rays represent the core values CCF stands for.*

MOUNTAIN RANGE—*The top of the crest signifies a mountain silhouette with three peaks, each peak symbolizing our three key partners: • Law Enforcement • Victims and Victim Advocates • Our Contributors. Mountains are tall, providing an elevated vantage point for greater perspective. They are solid and are a natural defensive position for those seeking higher ground.*

GRECO-ROMAN ARCHITECTURE—*This structure is most often associated with principles of antiquity, specifically law and justice. Most courthouses have at least some of these elements. The very structures themselves have lasted more than two thousand years on rock-solid foundations.*

DOME—*The Dome has a form laden with sacred meaning and providential overtones. At its core it features a circle, which is inclusive. Crime is no respecter of persons, and neither is CCF. The shape is well-balanced and so is CCF in regard to its mission, vision, and values.*

COLUMNS—*Perhaps the most recognized piece of architecture, the columns' tall presence denotes strength, power, and protection. These columns represent each of the core values CCF upholds: • Accountability • Character • Prudence • Communication • Effectiveness • Resourcefulness • Cooperation • Efficiency • Reliability • Coordination • Flexibility • Understanding • Commitment • Persistence • Honesty • Legacy • Competence • Result Oriented • Truth • Compassion • Teamwork • Justice • Excellence • Diversity • Wisdom • Transparency • Sensitivity • Integrity • Professionalism.*

PEDIMENT—*The facade on the domed building is accented by a triangular pediment. The triangle is the strongest shape in building construction and exemplifies its solidarity through the even disbursement of a weight load. CCF stands as that triangle connecting Law Enforcement, Victims, and Advocates, as well as Contributors, in the joint task of closing cold cases and supporting victims.*

LIGHTHOUSE EFFECT—*The subtle light play on the marble structure alludes to the figure of a lighthouse with a seven-ray beacon calling out to those in need of help.*

WINDOW— *The small window represents that small glimmer of hope that resides in everyone involved in violent crime. Hope for resolution, hope for closure.*

POWER COLORS—*The colors we have chosen are a deliberate effort to highlight certain characteristics each one represents, as well as recognize the struggle and pain crime causes:*

- *BLUE = knowledge, trustworthy, and peace. Our shield's BLUE represents the law enforcement badge of authority, justice, and the thin blue line. Most police uniforms contain blue, and we respect those in this noble profession. We are proud to be a trusted partner in providing peace to those who need it most.*
- *RED = passion, blood, love. Our passion for justice runs deep and so does our devotion to victims and their advocates. Blood is life but also a tragic symbol of death that we want to display as evidence, so we too are reminded daily of the stain violent crime leaves on those still living.*

- *WHITE = purity, clean, virtue. We cannot return our victims to pure innocence, but we refuse to return them to ignorance. Our objective is to offer a clean path to healing through the power of knowledge. By restoring justice, we hope to offer authentic comfort.*
- *GOLD = valuable, triumphant. The small wings are gold and are the wings of the victims and advocates who must remain. They have infinite worth and must be shown how valuable they are and can be to others. Our journey will be one of triumph, regardless of the final outcome—the Finem Exitus.*
- *SILVER = sophistication, priceless. This color is used for the large wings, belonging to the Cold Case Foundation. Silver is said to be a cleansing aid helpful in the release of emotional, mental, and physical obstacles. Such clarity offers new perspectives and shines forward with hope.*

This labor of love truly speaks to the heart of the hundreds of people who selflessly contribute to the Cold Case Foundation. It's one thing to have all the decorated experience and expertise working with us. But it's having the right heart and right mind that is what truly makes this organization special.

I can say with a high level of confidence that everyone involved with our organization—from former and current law enforcement, military, attorneys, forensic specialists, media experts, victims' assistance specialists, and many others—are all in this for the right reasons. They simply want to help. In all that's been written, we come to the most important people to this effort—and that's you.

You are the people in your community who simply want to make a difference in the lives of those who are suffering, and we hope that, in reading this book, you have found some sense of empowerment for yourself, your loved ones, and for your communities.

Our hope is that you will join with us in this labor of love and contribute in any way you possibly can. By so doing, may we all show the victims of violent crime—along with their families, loved ones, and the law enforcement officials that work on their behalf—that we stand with them and that they are not alone.

ACKNOWLEDGMENTS

Benjamin Franklin offered the following advice for those who are in pursuit of creating a legacy: "If you want to be remembered . . . either *write* something worth reading or *do* something worth writing."

This nugget of advice has been demonstrated throughout this book and by the organization of dedicated professionals who have made this project possible. Both the book and the organization represent the combined forces of individuals who have unselfishly forged their unique talents, abilities, and relationships into a dedicated team of crime-fighting, victim-advocating, and justice-seeking synergy. Additionally, this book and the Cold Case Foundation (CCF) represent a symbiotic relationship that serves as a testament to being able to accomplish great things by a unified force of selfless professionals committed to a high and noble purpose. Neither could have been realized without acknowledging essential individuals. I want to express my profound gratitude to all our team of distinguished experts listed on the CCF website and those cited in this book who volunteer their time, talents, and abilities in support of victims, their families, and law enforcement agencies in pursuit of resolving unsolved cases. I would be remiss, however, if I didn't specifically acknowledge key Executive Team members that I am deeply indebted to, knowing that I could not have undertaken this journey without their support.

Chief among them is John Douglas, my mentor and brotherly friend for over thirty years. From the FBI Investigative Support Unit to the Cold Case Foundation inaugural chairman of the board, John now serves as the current CCF chairman emeritus. When I knocked on the door for opportunities, John graciously swung those doors wide open to me. No one has had a more profound and positive influence in my life, both personally and professionally.

Dean L. Jackson, CCF deputy executive director. For fifteen years my trusted confidant, loyal friend, and "wingman," who has faithfully executed his duties and stood shoulder to shoulder with me on our CCF journey. His contributions, unwavering support, and resolute dedication have been indispensable to the success of the CCF.

Chris McDonough, CCF director of investigations and law enforcement relations. My friend and esteemed colleague for twenty-plus years; homicide investigator, police instructor, and "bridge builder" extraordinaire. Chris has been especially resourceful in promoting CCF and its mission.

Robert E. Taylor Jr., CCF director of training. My steadfast friend and professional colleague for twenty-plus years; Robert accepted the challenge of establishing CCF's Global Academy, which has delivered training to law enforcement, civilians, and for the federally mandated "Operation Lady Justice Presidential Task Force on Missing and Murdered American Indians and Alaska Natives," established in 2019.

A. J. Jackson, CCF creative director. A. J. has the central role of producing, overseeing, and developing content for Cold Case Live and manages media, marketing, the website, and our internet presence.

Tom McHoes, twice my coauthor: *Cold Case Foundation: How a Team of Experts Solve Murders and Missing Persons Cases*, 2024; and *Predators: Who They Are and How to Stop Them*, 2022, 2007. From an aspiring and sometimes annoying investigative reporter who persistently knocked on my chief of police door, to my good friend and coauthor for over seventeen years. Without Tom's writing skills and storytelling talents, our experiences, lessons learned, and case successes would have been forgotten memories.

Inaugural team members: Every successful, legacy-building enterprise requires a durable foundation to build upon. CCF has been favored from the start with some of the best and brightest in the forensic and investigative profession. Included among our cadre of distinguished associates and friends are Dr. Todd Grey, CCF chief medical examiner; Dr. James Claude Upshaw Downs, forensic pathologist; Francine Bardole, CCF director of forensic sciences; Karen Elliot, CCF senior forensic scientist; Nate Sumbot, CCF principal legal advisor; Jon Taylor, legal advisor; Dana Boss, CCF crime analysis supervisor; Kathy Vallas-McKenzie, CCF triage team supervisor; Butch Rabiega, CCF senior crime analyst; Linda R. Wheeler-Holloway, CCF senior investigator; Gary S. Hodson, arson investigator; Bryan Crump, arson investigator; Kacey Robinson, search and recovery; Brett Sayer, search and recovery.

Thanks to our CCF team members, mentors, and friends Dr. Ann Burgess and Dr. Gary Burcato for introducing us to Alice Martell, our authors' representative at the Martell Agency. Also, thanks to Jake Bonar, Nicole Carty, and our team at Prometheus Books who helped make this dream a reality.

Last but not least, thank you to our wives. Chris Cooper: My wife, best friend, and partner who has provided sustaining encouragement from the inception of CCF to the realization of this book. It never would have happened without her. Audra McHoes: Tom's best friend and greatest teammate. Without her support, Tom would not have made it through all the late nights and weekends writing. Thank you for supporting him in taking this incredible journey with me throughout the years.